NO GOOD DEED

NO GOOD DEED

TOM BASINSKI

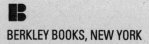
BERKLEY BOOKS, NEW YORK

THE BERKLEY PUBLISHING GROUP
Published by the Penguin Group
Penguin Group (USA) Inc.
375 Hudson Street, New York, New York 10014, USA
Penguin Group (Canada), 90 Eglinton Avenue East, Suite 700, Toronto, Ontario M4P 2Y3, Canada
(a division of Pearson Penguin Canada Inc.)
Penguin Books Ltd., 80 Strand, London WC2R 0RL, England
Penguin Group Ireland, 25 St. Stephen's Green, Dublin 2, Ireland (a division of Penguin Books Ltd.)
Penguin Group (Australia), 250 Camberwell Road, Camberwell, Victoria 3124, Australia
(a division of Pearson Australia Group Pty. Ltd.)
Penguin Books India Pvt. Ltd., 11 Community Centre, Panchsheel Park, New Delhi—110 017, India
Penguin Group (NZ), Cnr. Airborne and Rosedale Roads, Albany, Auckland 1310, New Zealand
(a division of Pearson New Zealand Ltd.)
Penguin Books (South Africa) (Pty.) Ltd., 24 Sturdee Avenue, Rosebank, Johannesburg 2196,
South Africa

Penguin Books Ltd., Registered Offices: 80 Strand, London WC2R 0RL, England

NO GOOD DEED

A Berkley Book / published by arrangement with the author

PRINTING HISTORY
Berkley mass-market edition / May 2006

ISBN: 0-425-20960-1

BERKLEY®
Berkley Books are published by The Berkley Publishing Group,
a division of Penguin Group (USA) Inc.,
375 Hudson Street, New York, New York 10014.
BERKLEY is a registered trademark of Penguin Group (USA) Inc.
The "B" design is a trademark belonging to Penguin Group (USA) Inc.

PRINTED IN THE UNITED STATES OF AMERICA

10 9 8 7 6 5 4 3 2 1

For my parents, Ralph and Mima Basinski, who never laughed at my odd pursuits, and for my late brother, Len Basinski (1956–1992), who always laughed at my odd jokes.

ACKNOWLEDGMENTS

I would like to thank San Diego County District Attorney Bonnie Dumanis for her assistance and encouragement in the preparation of this book.

I would also like to thank San Diego Police Homicide Team III, especially Detectives John Tefft, Joe Cristinziani, J. R. Young, and Sergeant L. D. Martin for their candid comments and recollections of the investigation. In many instances the comments toward them were not favorable, but they did not shy away from telling me what was said about them.

Deputy District Attorney Chandra Carle is to be thanked for her openness and assistance in the preparation of this book. Her theory of the case was right on from the beginning.

Defense attorney Marc Carlos was generous with his time in reciting to me a painful, frightening, and conflicted part of his personal and professional life during his involvement in this case. My thanks also to Judge Frederic L. Link. Although the usually open and candid Judge Link was constrained by the impending retrial of defendant Ny Nourn, Link was as helpful as he could be, given the circumstances. I am indebted to Deputy District Attorney Stephen Robinson for sharing information and his insights regarding the real estate fraud charges brought against defendant Ronald Barker, and Robinson's explanation of how and why the charges were handled as they were.

Investigative reporter John Stevens is to be thanked for his honesty and forthrightness in relating things to me he believed to be true.

A special thanks to fellow writer Bruce Gibney and former detective magazine editor Rose Mandelsberg-Weiss who started me on this journey over twenty years ago.

My agent, Jim Cypher, has been terrific to work with, returning every call promptly, and always keeping my best interest at heart. One cannot ask for anything more from an agent.

Thanks to editor Samantha Mandor who painstakingly pored over this work. Her suggestions were followed because they were the correct things to do.

Finally, thank you to my long-time, long-suffering wife, Judy, for her patience over the years.

AUTHOR'S NOTE

This is a true story. The real names of all the participants are used. This book was written based on a careful examination of official documents, including police reports, transcripts of police interviews, reports from the medical examiner, and memorialized communications between various parties. When information, including direct quotes, was obtained from printed, published articles, proper attribution was given to the author and publication.

Many people were interviewed during the preparation of this book. The people are named. If direct quotes are used, these statements are designated with quotation marks. In some cases comments are paraphrased. No quotation marks are used in the paraphrasing. Quotes from court come directly from official transcripts.

Some opinions of the author are contained in this book. These are easily recognizable as opinions.

CHAPTER 1

Sharp, spiny fingers of yellow-orange flame danced out of the block of fire alongside the street accurately named La Jolla Scenic Drive. Any other night but tonight the view and surrounding area could be called "scenic." Fire illuminated the darkened sky and licked at the leaves on an adjacent tree. San Diego firefighters, roused from sleep at 4:34 A.M., arrived at 4:43 to begin showering water on the source, a fully engulfed car.

The firefighters intended to extinguish the flames as rapidly as possible, hoping to have the fire out before the gas tank exploded. Someone else in the Department would later check for point of origin and the possible presence of an accelerant. Maybe the blaze was a torch job for an insurance scam. In this location, and at this time of night, it was unlikely the cause of the fire was faulty wiring or other accidental means. Somebody wanted this car to burn.

In a few minutes the blaze would be out, and firefighters would find the charred and smoking body in the passenger seat.

As is the case in many a real-life scenario, this one had its moment of mirth—causing temporary panic not appreciated until later. When Fire Engine 9 rolled up, the two firefighters hopped from their perches inside the cab. (Nobody rides on the running board or hanging off the back anymore.) One man held a two-inch red hose ready to pour water until hell wouldn't have it. The only problem was that the hose dribbled a weak stream suitable only for watering flowers.

While the engineer scrambled to correct the problem, the side of the fire truck suddenly became illuminated from a light attached to a video camera. Aided by the bright light, the engineer turned a single valve and water gushed onto the car. The mystery cameraman quickly moved to where the firefighters were working.

The hose men stood on either side, starting from the rear, moving toward the front. In a matter of seconds, the fire was out, steam and smoke rising into the night. Based on the exposed roof frame, they knew the car was a convertible, and the top had been up when the fire started. Broken, exploded glass on the pavement led them to believe the windows had also been up. The windshield had melted into a mass of goo on the floor and front seats. The floor gearshift in the forward PARK position indicated the vehicle had not stopped suddenly or had been involved in an accident and come to a skidding halt. Someone had put the vehicle in PARK before exiting the vehicle, leaving the unlucky passenger.

Two police officers stood across the street watching. They came over when one firefighter waved to them, pointing to the body, which didn't really look like a body, only a hunk of something that had sort of a torso and a head.

One officer looked while the other led the photographer off to the side.

"How did you happen to be here, and who are you?" asked the beat cop.

He was Ed Baier whose company, All Mobile Videos, covered the city and county of San Diego waiting for breaking events. "I'm a freelance videographer. I was in the area listening to my scanner when I heard the call come out." Baier had already placed calls to local television stations and would sell copies of his tape to them before he left the scene.

The officers took Baier's identifying information before releasing him, telling him the homicide detectives would be contacting him shortly. When they did later that day, he checked out as the real thing. Millions would see his tape before the case was over.

The calls started going out to the "up" homicide team. This week it was "Team III." The San Diego Police Department designates its homicide teams with Roman numerals, just like Super Bowls.

Sergeant L. D. Martin, veteran cop in the twilight of his career, headed up Team III. Martin was a former star softball player, slowed of late by a ruptured Achilles tendon but now back on his feet. At six-foot-four, Martin looked like a fitting leader as he towered over his team, notebook in hand. Maybe he couldn't play ball, but he still could lead a group of homicide detectives.

Sergeant Bob Lopez was the acting lieutenant for the Homicide division while the San Diego Police Department struggled with some manpower issues. Although Lopez was the same rank as Martin, he was filling in the lieutenant's slot on a temporary basis. The lieutenant routinely approved the actions and strategies of the teams. Often, like this morning, he would make a short appearance on camera for the local news agencies covering the story and field phone calls later in the investigation when reporters called seeking updates.

Detectives John Tefft, Joe Cristinziani, Terry Torgersen, and Dee Warrick made up the rest of the unit. Torgersen, a twenty-year-plus, wide-shouldered veteran with a bald top and short, straight hair on the sides, would be in charge of the crime scene. Torgerson's teammates would chase leads as they uncovered them. This squad had been together for years solving many gruesome slayings. They had been together so long they often anticipated each other's moves, communicating silently, like couples married for eons.

It was December 23, 1998. Torgersen's report would sound like Joe Friday's lead-in to a *Dragnet* episode of the 1950s. "It was 45 and clear in San Diego, with a slight breeze from the west." This tiny speck of information about clear skies would become important years later, when a defense attorney would ask Torgersen on the witness stand if he had checked with the weather bureau to guarantee that lightning had not caused the vehicle fire. Lightning had not caused anything, but if Torgersen had not included the information, the attorney could have done fifteen minutes of entertaining monologue in front of a jury about what a haphazard investigation the team had done.

As patrol sergeant Patrick Vinson briefed the detectives across the street, they took notes and sneaked glances over his shoulder at the smoky shell of a car bearing what used to be a person, but now was, sadly enough, a piece of evidence in a criminal case.

Successful homicide cops need brains, creativity, and patience. A necessary quality often overlooked is that of being organized. In the initial stages of a homicide, the actions of the cops more resemble painting by number. Certain things are done in a prescribed order on every single case without exception. The actions are checked off when completed. Nothing creative or brilliant is involved.

The 1995 Chrysler Le Baron bore Kansas license plates. A check with dispatch revealed the car was registered to David Stevens in La Jolla, only miles from where they were now standing. Due to their knowledge of the city, the officers knew the address on the registration was a nationally known private mailbox company that sold office supplies and packing equipment. Detective Tefft would go to the mailbox business after it opened in two hours and get the identifying information and home address David Stevens had presented when renting the box.

Fire captain Javier Mainar and fire investigator Michael Merriken arrived, along with police forensic specialist Mike Callison. Any crime scene is a puzzle. One contaminated with smoke and water is worse. Evidence not destroyed by flame is often washed away by water. What remains is not much of anything except charred, wet material and smelly, muddy ash.

The dispatcher notified the medical examiner, writing the time on the callout sheet. Investigator Mark Malamatos arrived within the hour. From years of experience, Malamatos knew it would be a while before police relinquished the crime scene to him to take custody of the body. Dr. Brian Blackbourne, the medical examiner, responded, along with Dr. Rob Whitmore, another forensic pathologist. Although Blackbourne was the administrator in charge of the entire M.E.'s staff, he often came out to interesting crime scenes or scenes where he thought his organization might come under scrutiny at a later date. (Blackbourne's office would fare okay in the future on this case, but the same could not be said about the homicide team, based on complaints the victim's family would lodge.)

Mike Callison, the police photographer, took pictures from all four points of the compass, gradually moving in until he was at the interior of the vehicle. The body, which looked like it was on its stomach, lay on the passenger side; the seat back was lowered to the "recline" position.

A long December 23rd lay ahead for Team III. One hoped they already had their Christmas shopping done.

CHAPTER 2

Forget about television, movies, and the latest cop mystery thrillers from James Patterson, Tami Hoag, or T. Jefferson Parker: Homicide investigations don't progress with the thrill-a-minute pace depicted in these books. Real cops investigating real homicides must immerse themselves in the most mundane, painstaking duties in order to ensure a thorough investigation.

Each member of the department at the scene knew what duties had to be done. Detective Torgersen had the responsibility to direct them, but he seldom told anyone what to do. Evidence technicians collected samples of the vehicle upholstery to test later for the presence of a fire accelerant. Callison checked around the exterior of the vehicle. He found and collected an empty Pacifico brand long-necked beer bottle. One never knew what peripheral objects were important at a homicide scene; therefore, they took everything.

Dr. Blackbourne ordered the corpse put into a plastic body bag. Before the assistants ("body snatchers," as they

are called by the cops) put the body in, Dr. Blackbourne
looked closely at the head. The veteran pathologist noted
all the hair had been burned off, along with the eyes being
totally burned and gone. Since the skull was brittle and
crumbling, Blackbourne ordered the assistants to put an
additional bag over the head. Once the body was removed
to the medical examiner's office at 9:35 A.M., some five
hours after discovery, the detectives looked at their list of
things to do:

1. Attend autopsy that afternoon.

2. Check area gas stations to see if anyone purchased
   gasoline in a can.

3. Call area hospitals to request information on burn
   victims. There was a good chance that whoever set
   the Chrysler on fire received a backflash.

4. Go to postal store listed on vehicle registration to
   get home address for David Stevens.

5. Alert Dr. Skip Sperber to attend autopsy to make
   dental X rays and impressions of the deceased.
   (Sperber is the forensic odontologist who does bite-
   mark identification in some crimes of violence and
   also identifies "John Doe" bodies by means of dental work.)

6. Check with taxicab companies to see if any made a
   pickup in the immediate area. Maybe the killer
   worked alone and had not planned out the escape
   until the fire started. It was unlikely, but this task
   had to be done. Imagine the embarrassment if that
   simple check had not been performed and the killer
   had left in a taxi.

History has shown that if the smallest of details is overlooked in a case, countless hours of investigation could be wasted. For example, the detectives might find a gas station attendant who remembered a customer purchasing a gallon of gas in a red can the night of a deadly fire. Perhaps the station had surveillance cameras that captured the patron's picture when he paid for the gas. The picture could be put out to the media. Someone like a neighbor, ex-girlfriend, or parole officer might recognize the patron, and the case would be well on its way to being solved. If the detectives failed to do that, they might work for months when the key to the case was right in front of them all along.

Detective John Tefft was standing out front when the mailbox store employee unlocked the doors at 8:00 A.M. Tefft, a twenty-three-year veteran, was a medium-built blond with a ready smile and patient demeanor. His soft voice and deferential manner came in handy during interviews. With three years in Homicide, Tefft was smart and never forgot a fact, a trait he capitalized on when someone was trying to lie to him and get out of a jam. Tefft showed his identification to the employee and asked to see the subscriber information for the box number depicted on the vehicle's registration. Sometimes postal store employees, especially if they are new, are reluctant to supply subscriber information, mainly out of ignorance of what constitutes "privacy." Business and Professions Code 22780 in the State of California mandates that private mailbox information be given to a police agency for the purpose of an official investigation. No such problem existed today for Tefft, although it had in the past.

David Stevens had listed a home address in Olathe, Kansas, but he had written a local work phone number on his mailbox application. Since it now was business hours, Tefft called the work number from his cell phone. The number had been changed. Nobody answered the new number, but a recording informed him the company dealt in nutritional supplements and produced a magazine designed for triathletes. Tefft phoned Sergeant L. D. Martin to relay this information. Tefft hooked up with Detective Dee Warrick, and the two headed for the nutritional supplement company in the hope the doors opened at 9:00 A.M.

The business in La Jolla was Southern California Sports Supplements and *Pump Magazine* in the 500 block of Pearl in La Jolla, a "high-dollar" business area. The manager, Jason Mathas, told the detectives David Stevens had left the company in the summer of 1998, and now worked for a telemarketing dating service called Perfect Match.

Jeff Brady, a former co-worker of David's when Stevens was with Southern California Sports Supplements, told Tefft and Warrick he had last spoken with David about two weeks ago. They talked about University of Nebraska football, a favorite topic of Stevens's. Brady told the detectives David dated a lot of girls, including girls he met in clubs in Tijuana, Mexico, a few miles to the south. Brady also told them David's car was his baby. He would not lend it to anyone.

Tefft and Warrick went to Perfect Match in an area of San Diego known as the "Golden Triangle," an area in the northern part of the county so named because Interstate Highways 5 and 805 come together to form a "Y." Many of San Diego's high-tech businesses are located within the triangle of the "Y." Radio and television traffic reporters even called it the "Golden Triangle" when telling San Diegans where the heavy pockets of slow travel were.

The on-duty manager of Perfect Match checked the employee time cards. He told the detectives David Stevens had worked the night before, getting off at 9:00 P.M. They phoned David Stevens's apartment from the business but received no answer. The employees from Perfect Match talking to Tefft exchanged anxious glances. Why were two Homicide detectives here looking for their friend, and why couldn't they find him? One of the workers had seen the burning car on the morning news and was putting things together in his head. He didn't like what he was coming up with. He told the officers David would never lend his car to anyone. David's Chrysler convertible was the love of his life.

Stevens had only his mailbox address listed in his personnel file at Perfect Match. One friend at the business had been to Stevens's place before, but couldn't remember the exact address. However, he described in detail where Stevens's apartment was located.

Detectives Warrick and Tefft knocked on the door of Michael Antonopoulos, the apartment manager at 840 Turquoise in Pacific Beach later that morning. Antonopoulos let them in David Stevens's apartment for a quick check to see if anyone was inside. If Stevens was the dead man, maybe there was another body in the apartment? Tefft and Warrick had seen many bizarre things over the years, and they had to proceed with caution and thoroughness.

There was nobody, and no body, in the one-bedroom apartment. They did not conduct a search, but couldn't help notice a briefcase just inside the door, an unmade bed, two drinking glasses on the nightstand, and a tube of lubricant next to the glasses.

Antonopoulos said Stevens had moved in just over a year ago, on December 15, 1997. He was a good tenant who kept to himself, rarely had visitors, parked where he was supposed to, and paid his rent punctually.

Antonopoulos told the detectives David Stevens's boss, Carl Withrow, lived in the apartment just below Stevens. Withrow became agitated when the officers began questioning him. Withrow cried and fell to the floor while the puzzled detectives looked at him, then at each other. Withrow shook and clutched at his arms, pulling them in toward himself, all the while shrieking, "No. It can't be! It can't be him. Not David. No! No!" Withrow was in such a state the detectives had concerns about whether they should leave him alone or call someone to be with him. Withrow eventually calmed down, but not a lot. While it is usual to express grief over the potential death of a co-worker, they noted his over-the-top reaction and went about the business of trying to find out more about David. They knocked on neighbors' doors and asked about him. Someone had seen David yesterday afternoon. No one had seen him in the evening.

That afternoon at almost the same time, two things happened simultaneously. At 1:50 P.M., Doctors Christopher Swalwell and Christina Stanley witnessed while Dr. Blackbourne began the autopsy on the charred corpse. Present in the examining room were Detective Terry Torgersen, police evidence technician Mike Callison, fire captain Javier Mainar, and Fabian King, the forensic autopsy assistant. Also at 1:50 the detectives were talking to Stevens's neighbors.

The body was x-rayed while still inside the plastic body bag in order to preserve trace evidence. The X rays showed no metal objects, like bullets.

A cursory examination of the body revealed it was a male. The left hand was missing, the right hand only a stump of charred flesh. The right foot had also been burned off. The left stump of foot dangled, but remained attached. No fingers were available to get prints.

When Dr. Blackbourne surgically opened up the torso, Fabian King took samples of blood, urine, and liver bile as per forensic protocol. Blackbourne detected no stab wounds anywhere. Blackbourne removed the windpipe and throat. There was no sign of strangulation or compression. Neither did Blackbourne see black discoloration in the mouth or throat, indicating ingestion of smoke, soot, or flames.

The forensic pathologist examined the lungs and found them pink, indicating no ingested smoke. The pink color meant the person was already dead during the fire. There were no bullet holes or stab wounds in the chest. Detective Torgersen, if he were a betting man, would have bet they would find bullet holes in the head, even though the X ray showed no bullet.

Dr. Blackbourne removed the skull top to examine the brain. Sure enough, two holes were at the right temple, proceeding through the brain. "Here's your cause of death," he said to Detective Torgersen. Callison moved in with his camera to record the trauma. The left side of the skull was so damaged and fragmented by the fire Blackbourne concluded the bullets had exited through there although there were no holes. The first portion of the autopsy was concluded for the day at 4:30 P.M. Blackbourne wasn't through, but he had a commitment to be somewhere else. He knew a thorough job was demanded in this case. The doctors would be back at it the following day, Christmas Eve, and work on this body from 9:30 A.M. until noon.

When the complete report was finished several weeks later, it would show that the blood had no alcohol or drugs present. Further analysis of the blood revealed caffeine and a slight amount of pseudoephedrine, an ingredient of cold medicine. There was no carbon monoxide in the blood, which meant the person was already dead when the fire had started. There was no soot in the mouth, larynx, or trachea, further underscoring the absence of life when the flames began.

Dr. Blackbourne carefully measured the bullet hole paths. The size was consistent with a "medium-caliber bullet," similar to a .9-millimeter, .38-, .357-, or .380-caliber. The pathologist was fairly certain the holes didn't come from something as small as a .22, or as large as a .45. In a thirty-plus-year-career, Blackbourne had seen his share of gunshot wound paths through a body. Blackbourne knew his stuff and was confident when he told Torgersen the bullets were "medium-caliber."

At 1:44 P.M. on December 23rd, while Torgersen watched the autopsy, Detectives Tefft, Warrick, Cristinziani, and Sergeant L. D. Martin returned to David Stevens's apartment in Pacific Beach. Police photographer Tom Washington accompanied them. Once again, landlord Michael Antonopoulos let them in. If David Stevens had a roommate, the police would have had to get a search warrant for the apartment. Since he lived alone, it was not necessary.

Along with evidence, the detectives hoped to find phone numbers and addresses of family and friends of David Stevens. Tom Washington first photographed the exterior of the upscale four-story building. Then he photographed the entire one-bedroom apartment. Nobody touched anything until he was done because they knew they might have to testify at a trial someday that the photos depicted the apartment *exactly* as it was when they entered. If so much as a book had been moved, a skilled defense attorney could proclaim that the cops had *staged* the homicide scene, if it was eventually proved the crime had been committed there. The attorney would ask the jury to consider *what else* the police had manipulated and moved, in order to bolster their weak case against his client. It would be much easier for the lead detective to sit in the witness box with a bored look on his or her face and say, "We didn't touch anything until the photographer had recorded everything in the apartment the way it was when we walked in."

The defense attorney would glance at the jury and ask incredulously, "You mean you didn't touch *anything*?"

The detective would say, "That's right. We didn't touch anything." There was nothing more even the most skilled attorney could do with that, unless he had proof.

The detectives found an address book with a phone number for David Stevens's parents in Randolph, Nebraska.

They played his answering machine and heard friends frantically asking him that morning to call them. Some had seen his burning car on television. Others from Perfect Match and the vitamin company had called other friends, and the information was out on the streets that David Stevens might be in serious trouble.

One call was especially troubling to the police officials. "Dave, it's Mom. Just give us a call when you get a chance . . ." Even for people who work with the worst aspects of life, and death, this call was unsettling.

Based on their experience, the detectives knew they were on solid ground assuming that David Stevens was, in fact, the person at the medical examiner's office. Even though confirmation was probably a few days away, they were sure they were searching the apartment of a dead man.

From examining the contents of the briefcase just inside the front door, the detectives knew it was Perfect Match material belonging to David Stevens. He had come home from work the night of December 22nd. The $64,000 question was, what had happened after he came home?

In the small bedroom, next to the unmade bed sat a pair of eyeglasses on the nightstand. Two drinking glasses stood next to the eyeglasses. Washington carefully photographed them. A close examination revealed something that looked like lipstick on one of the glasses. Washington collected a sample of whatever it was. He also collected a tube of Johnson & Johnson K-Y Jelly Personal Lubricant lying between the drinking glasses. Some hairs lay on the green bed sheets. Washington bundled up all of the bedding, including the pillowcases. In separate bags, he collected everything on the nightstand.

The bathroom light was on. Did that have any meaning? Who knew? It might. Everything must be recorded. The cops weren't fortune-tellers. Small facts might prove to be nothing, or they might be something that could impact the case tremendously. Strands of long, dark hair were located on the bathroom vanity and in the sink. Photographs of Stevens showed him to have close-cropped hair.

The bed had a large V-shaped mirror taking up most of the headboard. Washington lifted two sets of complete handprints, palms and fingers, from the mirror, a near-perfect surface from which to lift prints. One set was quite small, and the fingertips were pointing toward the ceiling. The two small handprints were bracketed by two larger handprints. The larger set had the fingertips pointing downward. When Callison pointed out this curious display, Sergeant Martin said something quite direct, but not necessarily politically correct. "It looks like someone was getting laid. The guy, or the one with the bigger hands, was on the bottom and put his hands on the headboard, fingers down. The girl was on top of him and leaning into the headboard, fingers up."

Before he was done, Callison would lift eleven cards of latent fingerprints from the headboard, nine from the closet doors, and two from the bathroom vanity.

By the time the detectives phoned the father, Gerald Stevens, in Nebraska, he had already heard of the possibility that harm had come to his son. He gave the detectives the phone number of David's dentist, Dr. Fred Underhill in Lincoln, Nebraska. Underhill would mail the dental X rays to the medical examiner's office. It was with a heavy heart and anxious churning of the stomach that Gerald Stevens concluded the conversation with the San Diego homicide detectives. It was not the last time he would speak with them. The conversations would not always be pleasant, either.

That afternoon Tefft and Cristinziani went back to Perfect Match, the telemarketing dating service where Stevens worked. Their purpose was to find out who Stevens's friends were and what he did when he wasn't working. The obvious investigative technique is to find out whom the victim was last with, where they were, and what they were doing.

Carl Withrow, the manager, was there and was now more composed than he had been that morning. He told them David Stevens was a nice guy with no enemies. "A helluva nice guy," said Withrow. "Everyone here liked him. He was a supervisor. Really knew his stuff. He was, uh, *is* a nice guy," Withrow said, trying to keep David Stevens in the present tense. Withrow had trouble keeping his composure when talking to the officers about Stevens, but he was better than he had been that morning.

When asked what David Stevens did in his private life, Withrow told them David often went to strip bars. The one he frequented most often was the Dancer's Club on Miramar Road, just down the street from Perfect Match. David didn't have a steady girlfriend, and referred to himself as a "California virgin."

The detectives knew they would be at the Dancer's Club in a few hours. They theorized David may have taken one of the strippers home with him, and those were her fingerprints on his headboard. They had more to learn about David Stevens.

Stevens was five-foot-eight and weighed about 215 pounds. Back at the apartment, they had seen photos of Stevens when he was a bodybuilder. He was cut and ripped, with a six-pack stomach and prominent pecs. Recent photos revealed a softer, more "well-marbled" version of the former athlete.

Documents and photos at the apartment depicted Stevens as a Nebraska high school wrestling champion some twenty years before. Anyone familiar with athletics knows that wrestlers are the toughest guys on campus. Football players may be bigger. Basketball players may be taller. But, pound for pound, you don't mess with the wrestlers. They are in tremendous physical shape and can endure pain, along with knowing how to administer it. Wrestlers are fast, savvy, and always alert. The detectives wondered how someone could have persuaded David Stevens to let them put a gun to his head and pull the trigger. Wrestlers never give up. Wrestlers keep fighting and fighting until they have nothing more to give, or the tide turns in their favor. Wrestlers don't go quietly into the night. What had happened to David Stevens?

Late that evening, on December 23rd, John Tefft and Joe Cristinziani went to Dancer's Club in northern San Diego County, just down the street from Perfect Match. The bar is located in a strip mall on the north side of Miramar Road. Nondescript and low-key in appearance, the business has a small sign with little to call attention to the place from the road.

Inside, the bar had an octagonal stage raised about one foot in the middle of the floor. Purple, green, and gold neon lights adorned the borders of the stage. The obligatory gold pole stood in the center of the stage so the dancers could grasp on it and slide seductively to the floor to perform their sultry moves.

A quick appraisal of the girl dancing let Tefft know this place was not exactly "high dollar." The girl was young and, by being kind, could be called voluptuous. However, despite her tender age, in a few years, she would be called

"fat." The other girls, who were serving drinks while waiting for their two-song set to come up, were not high-
caliber strippers.

The detectives carried a picture of David Stevens.
After low-key introductions to the manager, the detectives
spoke with two dancers. "Sierra" held a towel in front of
her barely covered breasts as she looked at the photo. "He
was just in here. He left about a half hour ago. I did a sofa
dance for him. He gave me five dollars."

"Sassy," the next dancer, told the officers, "He was
here tonight. He gave me a pretty good tip."

As Cristinziani and Tefft scratched their heads while
watching the dancers walk away, the bartender came over.
He had heard what the girls said. "I know this guy. I don't
know what the hell those two are talking about. He wasn't
in here. He hasn't been here in about two weeks. He
comes in and sits at the end of the bar. He doesn't drink
much; just takes up real estate, as I call it. He doesn't
cause any trouble, though. He's quiet. He hasn't been in
here today. Who knows what the hell they [the dancers]
are thinking?"

Fortunately, the bartender provided some sanity for
that encounter. Unless it hadn't been David Stevens in the
car . . .

On Christmas Eve just after 5:00 P.M., sixty-one-year-old
Gerald Stevens, and Dan Stevens, David's brother, would
land at San Diego's International Airport, Lindbergh
Field. A cousin, Mark Stevens, a Las Vegas police officer
who was also an attorney, would accompany them.
Sergeant Martin would meet them, even though he had
other commitments. Martin had given the rest of his crew
the night off to be with their families. As he waited in his
office just before going to the airport, Martin mused at
how deserted police headquarters was on this night;
everyone gone home, even the janitors, to make holiday

preparations. It was quiet. But for Martin and his crew, there was a killer out there who needed to be caught. His team would be back at it on December 26th.

Airports anywhere on Christmas Eve have certain energies, not necessarily in total confluence with one another. Baggage handlers and clerks are looking at their watches, waiting to go home. Pilots, flight attendants, and passengers on outgoing flights know their Christmases will be postponed until they arrive home. Often single workers, and those with no family, will volunteer to work that night to give their co-workers a break. Expectant arriving travelers, eager to see loved ones, scurry to get their bags and be on their way.

Christmas trees, with the usual array of red and green lights, decorate the airport. Christmas carols play softly in the background interrupted by the occasional, "Mr. John Grady. Please meet your party at the Baggage Claim, Terminal Two." And so it goes.

Sergeant Martin stood with his hands thrust in the pockets of his overcoat. Even though it was San Diego, it was night, and it was December. No matter what the Chamber of Commerce said about San Diego weather, it was cold at night in the winter.

After meeting the Stevens family in the baggage claim area, Sergeant Martin answered their questions the best he could, telling them everything allowable about the crime scene. He withheld telling them the number of bullet holes found in the corpse's head. If some kook came forward at a later date claiming to have killed a man in La Jolla by shooting him in the head and burning the vehicle, the number of shots would be an important fact that someone confessing would have to know. Stranger things than a phony confession had happened.

Sergeant Martin drove them to La Jolla and showed them the area where the vehicle had burned. Gerald

Stevens was a successful farmer in his home state. He was comfortable there, and well-known in the community. Now, Mr. Stevens stood along the side of the road on a cold, damp night before Christmas visiting the very scene where his son most likely had been executed and his remains degraded. Sergeant Martin thought a man could undergo no greater torture than what Mr. Stevens was experiencing. His heart ached for the Stevens family. Mr. Stevens was polite and thoughtful during that encounter on Christmas Eve. Sergeant Martin would later long for the polite man he met on Christmas Eve. Certain things would change that relationship.

Just after Christmas, Detectives J. R. Young and Joe Cristinziani began checking on the hospitals to see if any burn victims were treated on December 23 or 24. In all, they called sixteen emergency rooms. One supervisor at Scripps Hospital in La Jolla told them a woman came in suffering from a burn on December 24. Patient confidentiality laws dictated no additional information could be released to the police without a search warrant.

Cristinziani, a twenty-year veteran, three of those in Homicide, is a handsome man with a full head of black hair and a neatly trimmed black mustache. He is slight of build and stands about five-foot-ten, sporting stylish clothing a cut above what the average homicide detective wears. Cristinziani wrote an affidavit for a search warrant and took it to Superior Court Judge Frank Brown for his signature. Brown read the affidavit in his chambers and shook his head while reading. Brown had been a San Diego police officer himself many years ago while working his way through law school. Brown later became a deputy district attorney prosecuting a variety of crimes, including homicides, before getting elected to the bench. He knew a vehicle fire intentionally started by means of an accelerant could easily produce a flash eruption that would burn the person striking the match. Brown signed the warrant and issued his usual closing remark: "Good luck."

The luck wasn't that good, however. The hospital released the name and address of the burn victim. The barely legible notes from the treating emergency physician said the woman had dropped a turkey and was splashed by the hot liquid. Her injuries were consistent with that version. Nonetheless, the detectives paid her a visit. She was a domestic worker, preparing dinner for the family who employed her. The story checked out. Her spatter burns did not come from a burning car. It was back to square one for the detectives, another disappointment in a long line of future disappointments.

CHAPTER 3

Mr. Stevens and his son returned home with a few personal belongings the police released to them. Each detective knew Stevens's family back in Randolph, Nebraska, must have been feeling anguish. A decorated tree stood in a living room, surrounded by gifts that would have no meaning this year. Friends would drop by, not to exchange Christmas cheer, but to offer condolences. It was as if everyone knew David Stevens was dead.

The detectives had knocked on doors up and down La Jolla Scenic Drive and on Moonridge Way, the immediate area where the car burned. One resident reported hearing some gunshots followed by squealing tires. He did not hear a crash. This observation gave credence to the fact that someone in a following vehicle had provided an escape for the driver of the Chrysler.

Eric Groeger, an accident investigator from the SDPD Traffic Bureau, performed an extensive examination of Stevens's vehicle to determine if it had been in a crash. In spite of the peeling, blistered paint and melted hoses under the hood, it was easy for Groeger to determine the car had suffered no collision.

A check of the taxicab companies proved to be negative. Any pickup of a fare in this semi-remote area would be remembered. Cabs flourished in the downtown area of La Jolla, some two miles away. When the bars and nightclubs closed, the taxis were busy. The area where the vehicle had burned was secluded, with large hedges protecting the property owners. These were not tract homes; the average lot was a half-acre or more. Most of the houses had gates activated by pushing a numeric code. Limousine pickups were more commonplace than taxicabs, but certainly not at 4:30 in the morning.

The detectives knew it was imperative to "get to know" David Stevens, even though he was probably the homicide victim and could not speak to them. Homicide detectives learn about the dead by interviewing their friends and, sometimes, their enemies. The reports from different people might conflict. This practice makes for a confusing, but often interesting, investigation. People who knew David were consistent when talking about him. Friends indicated Stevens had no girlfriend. Perfect Match hired David when he signed up as a customer, ostensibly looking for a girlfriend. One friend of David's said David jokingly referred to himself as a "California virgin" meaning he had not been intimate with anyone in the year he had been in California. It wasn't the first time the police heard someone remember Stevens call himself a "California virgin."

Homicide investigators routinely start with the "inner circle" of a victim's life and then move outward. Statistics show that most homicide victims are killed by someone known to them, someone in the "inner circle." In this case, it did not look like Stevens had been robbed or abducted by a stranger. A good start for the detectives was Carl Withrow, David's boss. He lived in the apartment directly below David and often socialized with David. During several subsequent interviews, Carl Withrow told the detectives David was still a "country boy," meaning that David was not a real "street guy." When asked to clarify, Withrow said Stevens, although not exactly gullible, was just a nice guy who looked for the good in everyone. Even though David Stevens lived in California, his values and outlook on life were still in Nebraska.

Withrow repeated that Stevens went to topless bars, often accompanied by Withrow, or sometimes alone. The bar most often frequented by them was the Dancer's Club in nearby Mira Mesa, down the road from Perfect Match. Detectives Tefft and Cristinziani exchanged glances. They had already been there once, with confusing results. The initial idea of going to a strip club for interviews might captivate some new detective. It might seem romantic and flashy and cool to travel in the world of flesh and get to know strippers. These two veterans knew it would be a grind and a pain, and the strippers would be difficult. The managers of the bar would grudgingly cooperate, but only to the extent that they didn't want the vice squad breathing down their necks later if they didn't cooperate.

In California, total nudity is not allowed in an establishment that serves alcohol. The Dancer's Club served booze, which meant the girls could only be topless. In many topless establishments around the country, girls perform "lap dances" for the patrons. The city of San Diego has an ordinance, however, prohibiting the dancers from coming within six feet of a patron. The girls performed sofa dances where they got as close as they could. The dancers might also look around the bar and try to figure out if any of the customers were vice cops. If their instincts said no cops were present, some dancers might take their chances earning a bigger tip.

What would David Stevens do at the Dancer's Club? Withrow told them David would stay a couple of hours, usually nursing one beer. He wasn't a big tipper, either. After a girl would do a set on the stage, she would come by to get her tips. A patron would usually leave a dollar bill on the bar for the dancer. Sometimes David would leave a buck, and sometimes he wouldn't. This description was consistent with what the bartender had told them during their first brief stop at Dancer's.

Team III sat down together, as was their custom, to examine all the information they had. The purpose of this round-robin discussion was to make sure everyone knew what everyone else knew. So far, at least one thing did not add up. It was obvious from examining David Stevens's bedroom that he had lost his "California virginity" that night. There were two drinking glasses on the nightstand, one glass bearing lipstick prints. There was the tube of K-Y Jelly, a lubricant commonly used for sexual purposes. Considering its placement on the nightstand, one could construe why it was there. There were long hair strands in the bedding and in the bathroom. These things added up to a possible sexual encounter. They needed to get David's fingerprints from someplace. While they were confident the prints on the mirrored headboard were his, they needed proof.

Then, there was the crime scene with the burning car and the corpse with two bullet holes in it. This was not a street robbery. The crime scene had "rage" written all over it. If Stevens picked up a street hooker who had an accomplice as part of a robbery team, it is unlikely they would have gone to his apartment for a completed sexual encounter. Most street heists by hookers involve someone lurking in the shadows of an inner-city alley. The "john" picks up the scantily-clad girl on the main boulevard. After getting in the car, she directs him down the street to an alley. Then she tells him to pull over. The accomplice jumps out, sticks a gun in the john's face, and usually does a robbery or carjacking. Girls never go to a guy's apartment, give him sex, and *then* take his car. Also, robbers would have left his body in the apartment. And the crooks would have ransacked the apartment, taking everything they could. A street-robbery scenario did not fit these facts. Nor would robbers go to the trouble to carjack Stevens's car then burn it.

Smart homicide detectives know enough not to jump to conclusions and not to box themselves into a theory too quickly. At the same time, they could not ignore the obvious. In this case, the obvious seemed that David Stevens had sex with someone who probably had a relationship with another person. They thought they knew the "why" in the killing. They just needed to know the "who." The only problem was that there were others who would dispute this theory and would burden the homicide detectives with other theories. The media would become involved, putting pressure on Team III to respond, diverting time and energy that could have been better spent working on the case.

CHAPTER 4

Since most of David Stevens's friends were from work, the detectives went out to Perfect Match again to interview everyone who worked there. Workplace romances are common. Good homicide detectives don't start out with exotic theories of espionage and intrigue. They start out with who knew the victim, and who might want him dead, and why.

What they got was a dead end. Nobody had a bad word to say about David Stevens. He was polite to the women, like a country guy from Nebraska would be. He was a "guy's guy" with the men. Among his passions was Nebraska football and his vehicle.

Initially, Team III was skeptical when they saw photos of the cut and ripped muscular David Stevens in his competition trunks posing for a bodybuilding meet. Cynical cops immediately wondered if Stevens might go for men. It's okay to lift weights for strength, but they wondered about someone who devoted hours a day to his body then put on a thong and a light coat of oil, while practicing posing in front of a mirror or a camera. They subtly explored the possibility of potential homosexuality while conducting interviews. The answer was always a resounding "no."

They bluntly asked Carl Withrow. "If he was gay, he never indicated it to me," said Withrow. "He might have gone out with one of the strippers from the Dancer's Club. I'm not sure [if he dated a stripper] because David was very secretive about his private life. He used his post office box to receive bills. He didn't want anyone to know anything about him. David used to be a private eye back in Kansas or Nebraska, and he knew how easy it was to trace someone. But gay? I don't think so. In fact, I'd be the most surprised guy in the world if he was."

Stevens's co-workers at Perfect Match couldn't tell the detectives much more than the police already knew when they walked in. Other than going to some strip bars in San Diego and clubs in Tijuana, Stevens didn't have much of a social life. Formerly a workout fanatic, Stevens only dabbled in weightlifting now. He had a membership at the Powerhouse Gym on Mission Boulevard in the beach area, but rarely used it. They did learn of some other strip clubs where David frequented. Those places were put on the list of establishments to visit.

David Stevens's apartment was neat. Withrow called Stevens an "order freak." He had to have everything in its place. When they told Withrow about the placement of the body in the passenger seat, Withrow expressed even more curiosity, if not puzzlement. "David had some kind of chronic motion sickness," said Withrow. "He had to drive everyplace. If he rode in the passenger seat, he'd become ill. And, if he was in his own car, I know damn well he'd be driving. He would take Dramamine if he had to ride as a passenger. A passenger in his own car? I don't think so. Not willingly, anyway."

Since Stevens had not worked at Perfect Match for too long, the detectives decided to check back at So-Cal

Sports where he worked before Perfect Match. John Cribbs was Stevens's former boss, and often went out with him socially when they worked together. Cribbs said David started working for him in late 1997 and stayed until the summer of 1998. He was a hard worker who put in a lot of hours.

Cribbs did say something that caused a reaction in the detectives. Apparently Stevens had been warned for sexual harassment of some of the female employees. It was not blatant or aggressive. Stevens saw himself as a warm, caring person. He had a habit of touching the women, rubbing their backs or shoulders when he would come up behind them. He did not accompany the rubbing with sexual comments. It was just that some of the women took exception to being touched and let the management know. Stevens was warned, and the offending conduct ceased.

Cribbs could explain Stevens's demeanor. "David was very naïve. I don't think he was trying to do anything wrong. I just don't think he understood the way that his touching was being perceived. I did pull David in and told him I had complaints about that activity. He agreed it was inappropriate, or at least he said he did. I had no more problems or complaints after that."

Cribbs did remember going to a strip bar with David. The place was De Ja Vu, a well-known spot in San Diego. David gave his phone number to a dancer named Raven. Cribbs couldn't remember if she ever called him. He suspected she didn't call because David would probably have told Cribbs. Without prompting, Cribbs also mentioned that David referred to himself as a "California virgin," a familiar refrain. The detectives kept quiet, but exchanged glances. David's "inner circle" of friends was not being much help, not that they weren't trying.

At De Ja Vu, Tefft and Cristinziani flashed their badges so they wouldn't have to pay the cover charge. "We're not going to be here long," they explained to the bouncer.

They asked about the dancer named Raven. She wasn't there, but they received her real name and home phone number.

The detectives went back to the Licensing Division of the police department and pulled her file. Each dancer in San Diego must register as an "adult performer." From her file, they obtained her home address and fingerprint card. A good place to start was to have her prints compared with those on the drinking glass and mirrored headboard.

When they interviewed Raven the next day, she couldn't remember Stevens until they produced a photo of him. She did remember going out to breakfast one night after a shift. They had gone to a Denny's and had omelets. She went home by herself. She said she thought Stevens wanted to have a relationship with her, but she had strict rules against that. She subtly indicated to the officers that she really didn't care for men who went to topless bars, but she did like their money.

The trail led them back to the Dancer's Club. One of David's friends said David had been attracted to a black girl at Dancer's. After asking around, they spoke with a girl whose stage name was "Fabray." When they showed her a picture of Stevens, she said, "I know him. His name is David. He was one of my customers. Yes, I guess you could say he liked me. He kept asking me to go out on a date, and I kept refusing him. I have a personal policy that I don't date my customers. When he came in, he would have a beer and nurse it for an hour or two. He never tipped very much. If he tipped at all, he would sit at the stage and tip a dollar. After my dance, I would walk around, and he always wanted to talk to me. He never bought a dance from me, never tipped me, or bought me a drink.

"He would sit at a table in the back, finish his beer, and move up to the bar. When he was at the bar, he drank water. He was a nice guy, but he never really talked about himself. I knew he worked at some dating service that was down the street, and I knew he wasn't from California. I don't remember where he said he was from; somewhere in the Midwest. I'm not sure. I never went out on a date with him. I never went out with him at all. I haven't seen him in here for a couple of weeks now. He usually comes in with another guy; snappy dresser; likes to spend money. I worked on the twenty-second, and he wasn't in here. If he was here, he would've talked to me. That's all I can tell you. I know him from here, but I never went out with him." Fabray's weren't the prints on David's headboard.

The list of strippers interviewed grew. Yet the quotes were mostly the same when the girls described David Stevens and his actions at the bar: He was friendly and appeared to want to get more than friendly. None of the girls were attracted to him. They liked Stevens better than many of the lecherous dregs who frequented those places. But they didn't like him enough to go out with him.

The only good thing about Stevens being involved with strippers is that the detectives had fingerprints on all of them. After each interview Tefft would go to Licensing and pull their fingerprint card. One of San Diego's team of forensic examiners would compare the prints with those on the mystery drinking glass and headboard. In each instance, the response was "negative."

As long as Joe Cristinziani was on a search warrant roll, so to speak, he wrote affidavits for Stevens's bank records. He used the basic fact situation he did when writing the affidavit for the hospital records. Cristinziani "cut and pasted" the parts about why he needed to see the account activity. If there had been any withdrawals after the twenty-third, it would mean someone had access to Stevens's accounts. Cristinziani was fairly certain there would be no activity. Yet, in the "paint-by-number" technique previously mentioned, the detectives did certain things even though they were confident nothing would come of it. These things just had to be done. Superior Court Judge Lillian Lim signed the warrants.

When the records were mailed to him several weeks later, Cristinziani's instincts were validated. There had been no bank account activity.

CHAPTER 5

When the dental X rays arrived from Nebraska, the medical examiner's office phoned Doctor Norman "Skip" Sperber to compare them against the chart and X rays Sperber had made on the corpse at the medical examiner's office.

Skip Sperber is probably the most recognizable civilian in the San Diego law enforcement community. In his late sixties, Sperber is a diminutive, tanned, fit, cheerful man. His ready smile and friendly manner belie the gruesome work he often performs. For example, in 1978, 144 people were killed in a mid-air crash of a private airplane and a Pacific Southwest Airlines jet over San Diego's North Park community. Most of the victims were passengers and crew, but some of the fatalities were residents of the neighborhood.

Sperber's task in this historic tragedy was to identify the dead by means of dental work. Sperber labored in a makeshift morgue in a nearby community center until exhausted, then worked some more. Many victims simply disintegrated on impact. In the end, families and insurance companies were grateful for the work Sperber did.

In many violent sex crimes or child abuse cases, either the perpetrator or the victim might bite the other. Sperber is a nationally known expert in matching up, or excluding, someone as the biter. He has been consulted in cases all over the West Coast up to the Canadian border, and as far east as Florida.

Not a shill for the police, Sperber has also cleared many people under suspicion. "I go where the facts and evidence lead me," he has said. Regarding bite marks, Sperber has four classifications: "excluded," "possible," "probable," and "to a reasonable medical, dental certainty."

Sperber has been present during exhumations of corpses to make an on-the-spot comparison of dental work for identification purposes. He has also examined bodies submerged in water for extended periods of time, a very unpleasant task to the senses.

Through it all, Sperber has time to give thousands of hours of instruction to professionals in law enforcement and social work, increasing their awareness to recognize bite marks when they see them. Despite his avocation in the law enforcement community, Sperber maintains a thriving dental practice near the beach area of San Diego. His staff has explicit instructions that when a police officer walks into his office, he is to be notified immediately, no matter what he is doing. Dr. Sperber has a "no-waiting" policy for the police. Somehow, with his winning personality, Sperber makes it right with his patients who have to sit there while he deals with the police about a case.

On December 29, Dr. Sperber examined and compared the dental work of the burned corpse and announced it was, in fact, David Stevens. With their fears realized, the police could now go forward.

• • •

Workers and managers at Perfect Match suggested the detectives talk to a receptionist at the business named Karina Quirk. On January 5, 1999, Dee Warrick and Terry Torgersen interviewed her at police headquarters. Quirk had started at Perfect Match a few months before Stevens. She had just moved to San Diego from Arizona. Quirk said David was polite and friendly. She learned from others that David liked her. Stevens offered to take her sightseeing or to a movie. She told them she and David didn't talk much on the job because she worked the reception area and was very busy.

Quirk and Stevens had four dates. They went to the movies or to eat. He came to her apartment one time. She was never at his place. David told her he wanted to save money, get married, and have kids. He was thinking of going back to Nebraska for Christmas to be with his family.

Detective Warrick asked Quirk if she had ever been intimate with Stevens. Quirk denied it. Since Quirk was not a stripper, the detectives did not have her fingerprints. Ms. Quirk let them roll her prints. She also gave them a hair sample. Subsequent examination revealed neither the prints nor the hair found in Stevens's place were hers. The dead ends were piling up in the case.

Carl Withrow told the police that Stevens used to work for a private investigation firm. Sergeant Martin thought the company might have David's fingerprints on file. They wanted to compare his prints with those found in the apartment for purposes of elimination.

Sergeant Martin learned David worked for a John Stevens (no relation) in Portland, Oregon, several years before. On December 29, Martin phoned the private eye Stevens. He learned David last worked for John Stevens in 1988. Private eye Stevens agreed to mail David's prints to the San Diego police. Stevens asked a lot of questions and seemed eager to be in on inside information. The prints arrived on January 7, 1999. Most of the lifts in the apartment were Stevens's. The larger of the prints on the headboard were David's, no surprise to anyone. Before the case was over, Sergeant Martin wished he had never heard of John Stevens, the supplying of David's fingerprint card notwithstanding.

The detectives went through David's personal telephone book. They contacted each and every person listed. Some of the numbers had been disconnected. The people in David's book could offer nothing to help the officers. If someone they interviewed sounded tentative, or reacted inappropriately, the detectives would pay him or her a personal visit. All of the people in the book were subsequently removed from the shadow of suspicion.

On January 11, Sergeant Martin's heart began to beat more rapidly. Sitting at his desk, going over the list of property taken from Stevens's apartment, he received a phone call from someone who called himself "Jamie Stewart." Stewart readily gave his name, but refused to give a callback number, always a red flag to a thorough, if not cynical, cop. This mysterious caller told Martin they should be looking at "Scott" and a subject called "Renegade," who frequented a bar called The Shack on La Jolla Boulevard. Furthermore, Renegade owned a recreational vehicle he kept parked at Campland, a commercial campground in Mission Bay, an area not far from Pacific Beach where David Stevens lived. Scott drove a white van.

On January 22, Detectives John Tefft and J. R. Young went to The Shack. Young was assigned to the "Cold-Case" team. But a swap of personnel was coming. Terry Torgersen was going to Cold Case, and Young was coming to Team III. The swap hadn't been completed, but Young was filling in while Torgersen took some time off.

The detectives showed the bartender a photo of David Stevens. She did not recognize him. When asked about "Scott" and "Renegade," she said Renegade had not been in the bar since last summer. Scott, if it was the Scott she was thinking of, came in once in a while. She took Young's business card and told them she would have Scott or Renegade call Detective Young if one of them came in.

Renegade called six days later. Confusingly enough, his given name was also Scott. His friend was named Scott, too. Detective Young concealed his temporary confusion and made an appointment to interview Renegade at police headquarters. Renegade did not recognize a photo of David Stevens and said he did not know anyone by that name. He could not remember where he was on December 22 or 23. He said he probably was home because he was on workers' compensation and didn't have money to do anything or go anyplace. He said he has known the other Scott for several years and could not believe he would be involved in a murder. He was upset that someone would make a phone call implicating him and his friend.

Detective Young allowed Renegade to read the report Sergeant Martin had written that implicated him and Scott. Renegade agreed the reporting person was someone who knew something about him. He did own a recreational vehicle he parked at Campland, and Scott had driven a white van but had gotten rid of it a year ago.

Renegade gave a correct spelling of Scott's last name and supplied his phone number for Detective Young.

Young met with Scott the next day, after Scott finished work. Scott was cooperative, but upset that someone was out there throwing his name around as being involved in a murder. He listened to a tape recording of the mysterious caller's call to Sergeant Martin. He didn't recognize the voice, but agreed the caller knew him and knew things about him, but the information regarding the vehicles was dated. The information had been correct at one time. Scott was cooperative. Detective Young believed neither Scott nor Renegade was involved in the murder. He had just wasted two days. Such is the life of a homicide detective.

CHAPTER 6

The Homicide Division is located on the fourth floor of police headquarters at 1401 Broadway. The station itself is curiously situated in an area of flux. The brand-new Padres' baseball stadium, Petco Park, under construction, sits only blocks away to the southwest. Older tenement buildings and fading businesses are being continually torn down to make room for upscale lofts and trendy shops, hoping to cash in on the baseball stadium's draw. The seven-story police building is an attractive gray edifice with blue horizontal columns along each story. It doesn't look like the standard, government-issue, scrimp-on-the-money police station. The building is a landmark visible from the Interstate 5 freeway, which passes by two blocks to the east.

The new police headquarters opened in the late '80s and, like most municipal buildings, was overcrowded a few weeks after it opened, despite the modern plans of the architects.

The property room in the basement bulged with evidence. Parking for citizens and visitors remained available in the main lot for only about two years. Due to the large and still growing numbers of official police vehicles, citizens were required to find a meter somewhere around the neighborhood and park on the street. Parking enforcement officers patrolled the area on their little utility vehicles, keeping a vigilant watch on the quarter-devouring meters. Many a citizen returned to his or her vehicle after clearing a police matter inside the station only to find municipal greetings in the form of a $25 parking ticket.

Someday, a police administrator, or city official somewhere, will demand that the next police station will have half-again as much space as they think will be needed. Then, it will only take five years for the building to be filled to capacity instead of five weeks, as is the case in most police stations around the country.

The San Diego Police Department has four homicide teams. A captain oversees both the Homicide and Robbery divisions. Two lieutenants govern the four Homicide teams. Each team is made up of a sergeant, four detectives, and one civilian evidence technician.

The "up," or "on-call," period for the primary team is from 8:30 A.M. Tuesday until 8:30 A.M. the next Tuesday. One team is the "primary" team to get a call when a homicide happens or a body is found under suspicious circumstances. That doesn't mean the other three teams go down to the park and shoot baskets, however. Even though one team is the primary team when called on, another team is in the "next-up" rotation, standing ready when the primary rolls on a case.

A third team is in the "emergency-up" mode, ready to take over if all hell breaks loose, as it has on occasion. The fourth team is the only one that is fairly certain it will not be pressed into action. This last group can devote full time to exploring the leads already developed on cases under investigation. If they need to schedule a trip out of town to interview someone, the team in the fourth position will do it during that week. Of course, all the teams, no matter what their on-call status, spend all their time tracking down information on their cases. A team will stop investigating a case only when a new one comes in, and will resume work later on old cases as time permits.

Team III occupied their time during the month of January 1999 by interviewing strippers, co-workers, neighbors, and anyone who had even remotely been in contact with David Stevens. Sadly enough, in each instance, they came up with nothing. They could find no one who had been intimate with David Stevens, making his claim of being a "California virgin" ring true, except for the owner of the long black hair found in the bed and bathroom and the full set of small handprints on the mirrored headboard.

Stevens's family in Randolph, Nebraska, was getting restless. David's father, Gerald, called Sergeant L. D. Martin on a regular basis. If he was not in, Martin returned each call promptly. Martin had filled Stevens's family in on every detail, except for some few facts that had to remain only with the Homicide team.

Martin thought David's family had confidence in the work they were doing. But soon, Mr. Stevens tried to contact the media in San Diego about publicizing the case. He was also questioning the methods and results of the officers. The *San Diego Union-Tribune*, San Diego's main daily newspaper, showed only mild interest in Mr. Stevens's inquiries. The editors and police-beat reporters deal with the Homicide unit all the time. San Diego Police Department's closure rate on homicides is nationally impressive. The reporters have sat through many complicated homicide trials and rarely uncovered even a minor slip-up among the SDPD personnel, from responding beat officers to the most technical aspects of forensics. In short, the San Diego Police Department is among the best when it comes to solving homicides. So, when Gerald Stevens clamored for the newspaper to turn up the heat on the case, the newspaper didn't bite.

The Reader, a free weekly alternative San Diego newspaper, could afford to be more cavalier when it came to stories. While the *Union-Tribune* was steeped in politics and run by a governing board of directors wearing tailored suits, conducting meetings at long, mahogany tables, *The Reader* was more of a "dirty-faced" boy wearing blue jeans with a slingshot hanging out of his back pocket, much like the cartoon character Dennis the Menace.

The Reader didn't care who it took on. Especially vulnerable were San Diego politicians who appeared to be protected by the "big" paper. It wasn't unheard of for the *Union-Tribune* to bury a story about an influential San Diegan doing something wrong or embarrassing in the middle of the paper, only after *The Reader* had given the story front-page coverage a week earlier. *The Reader* was a thorn in the side of the *Union-Tribune*. Objective outsiders viewed the David-Goliath rivalry as healthy. "*The Reader* keeps the *Union-Tribune* honest," said one observer. In spite of their "alternative" status, *The Reader* stories were researched thoroughly and had a high accuracy rate. Many newspapers in the "alternative" vein were sensationalistic. Not so with *The Reader*.

Since Gerald Stevens couldn't generate any press interest from the *Union-Tribune*, he called *The Reader* and hooked up with reporter Bill Manson. The January 28, 1999, edition ran a story that started out: "Raymond Chandler never had it so good. His town, La Jolla, is becoming notorious for bizarre murders that don't get solved . . ." Well, maybe *The Reader* was a *little* sensational. Manson went on to tell, very briefly, about an Asian scientist and his thirteen-year-old daughter killed in

1996 in La Jolla in a case that remains open to this day. After establishing there was more than one open murder in La Jolla, Manson dove into the David Stevens case.

Ever the good reporter, Manson called Sergeant L. D. Martin for a quote. He got one. "We're stumped," said Martin, a minimalist when it came to the press and publicity.

Then, Manson was off to the races. He contacted Carl Withrow who said, "I don't want this thing to die till his killer's found." The detectives read that story and commented that Carl Withrow had been open and honest, but hadn't been a whole hell of a lot of help in clearing anything up.

David's younger brother, Dan, seemed more agitated. "The police haven't told us anything," he said. "I think they're trying to decide if we're the type of family who just wants it to all go away or [if] we actually want to know more . . . We want to know more."

Homicide detectives were angry when they read that. They chided Sergeant Martin and told him that the nicer and more empathetic he was to the Stevens family, the more they derided the police to the press. In fact, Martin had given the Stevens family more information than he usually released because they lived so far away. "No good deed goes unpunished," mused John Tefft.

Also in the story, Sergeant Martin truthfully told the reporter, "Every time we open a door, there's a blank wall behind." The Stevens family was hinting Team III wasn't opening any doors. Nothing could have been further from the truth.

The Stevens family told the press about the long black hairs found in the bed and bathroom. They told the press about the glass with lipstick. Carl Withrow allegedly told the Stevens family when he was in Nebraska that the police should be looking at the strippers from Dancer's. He didn't know it, but the cops were all over that establishment, interviewing everyone from the doorman to the girls to the guy who cleaned up at closing.

According to Stevens's brother, Withrow told the Stevens family David liked a dancer with long dark hair, and the police should have tried to talk to her. When Bill Manson tried to confirm Withrow's alleged statements to the Stevens family, Withrow wasn't quite so adamant. "What I said to them," Withrow told Manson, "was David and I had been to Dancer's, and there was a young lady over there that David liked." Withrow had warned David about that girl. "I just didn't want him going over there and blowing his money. Those girls are pros at that [getting money]. And David was very naïve. I just didn't want to see them take advantage of him."

Bill Manson interviewed John Stevens, the private investigator and former employer, who had supplied David Stevens's fingerprints. Stevens was about to go on a roll with the press.

He said David began working for him twelve years before. John Stevens was expansive, telling Manson David had approached him and said he wanted to make a life change. John said David went into training, interning under him. John said, "We worked day and night together, getting him in shape to be an investigator. We traveled the country and did some pretty good cases together. I tell you what: I wouldn't want Dave on my tail if he thought I'd done something."

Stevens said David worked everything from kidnapping to narcotics to intelligence gathering. "Sure, we accumulated enemies," he said. "Our enemy list would run from Oregon to San Diego and probably back. People get even, now, more than they did before. . . . To me, his death smells of assassination and cover-up."

The homicide detectives were incensed. "Who the hell is this guy?" they asked. They thought Stevens had delusions of grandeur. In real life, private eyes snoop around, do computer work at courthouses, follow a suspected wayward husband or wife, and conduct interviews. The majority of criminal work they do is for the defense. Private eyes don't solve cases, especially major cases like kidnap and murder. That is the stuff of television and the movies: the single private eye in a messy, walk-up office with a bottle of bourbon in his desk drawer. It makes for good stories but isn't factually true. The detectives had never met John Stevens, but based on his comments to reporter Bill Manson, they already had formed an impression of him.

Investigator John Stevens was doing more than talking to the press. He came to San Diego and began interviewing people associated with the case. The cops wondered if he was getting paid. They hoped Gerald Stevens wasn't throwing his money away.

Information came in that David Stevens's death might be related to a pending lawsuit. Detective Terry Torgersen reinterviewed John Cribbs, David's former boss at So-Cal Sports, the business dealing in nutritional supplements. Cribbs admitted his company did have some lawsuits pending, but that David didn't have any part in them. Torgersen received a tip that So-Cal Sports had a life insurance policy on David. Cribbs denied it. Torgersen checked the insurance industry's database and learned the company did not have a policy on Stevens. As bogus information trickled in, it had to be dealt with. Tracking down every tip took time.

Cribbs said the private investigator had interviewed him. John Stevens brought in pictures of David on a flier and posted them around. Cribbs thought that was odd because almost none of his current employees worked there when Stevens did, and no one would know David Stevens. Cribbs confided that he thought John Stevens was trying to get a sensational deal for a movie or television script based on some exotic theory about David's death, possibly relating to the lawsuit. Cribbs thought the lawsuit theory was outlandish because David had virtually no involvement in the company's turmoil.

The detectives contacted Jeff Stout, a good friend of David's, and a former co-worker. Terry Torgersen called him in early January at Stout's home in Omaha, Nebraska. Stout held a Ph.D. in exercise physiology from the University of Nebraska in Lincoln. "Whatever the hell that is," offered one cynical, unnamed detective. Stout had a BA from Concordia University in Seward, Nebraska, and a master's of physical education in exercise science also from the University of Nebraska. Stout's credentials are impressive in that he is a Fellow of the American College of Sports Medicine. Stout was currently on the faculty of Creighton University in Nebraska.

Stout explained he had known David Stevens for over ten years. Stout formerly worked at So-Cal Sports Supplements as a consultant. When So-Cal needed a marketing manager, Stout recommended David. So-Cal hired David, and Stout felt responsible for David's moving to California.

Stout explained that the sports supplement business is highly competitive and cutthroat. He wondered if maybe David's involvement with So-Cal might have had something to do with his death. Torgersen was puzzled. David Stevens had quit the sports supplement company, had been gone from there for several months, and was working outside of that industry. What could the sports supplement industry have to do with a death? Responding to Torgersen's question, Stout didn't know. He just had a bad feeling. Torgersen tried to remember the last time he was able to put a "bad feeling" before a jury. The answer: Never.

David had also told Stout he was a "California virgin," a theme that remained constant.

What remained constant for Team III were leads that started out as promising, but turned out to be nothing.

January turned into February. One of the detectives from Team III thought about getting the story on *America's Most Wanted*, the nationally televised program. San Diego had a good relationship with John Walsh because they had given him some juicy cases where the program had helped bring fugitives to justice. San Diego police and John Walsh had a mutual admiration society based on the way they helped each other.

The only problem was there was no identifiable person who was wanted. The show shied away from that kind of situation. But Sergeant Martin told one of the producers they had the film of the burning car taken by Ed Baier, the freelance videographer. As it turned out, someone high up in the *America's Most Wanted* hierarchy loves stuff that burns. They agreed to do a segment in March 1999, so long as they could use the footage of the flaming car. Against that fiery backdrop, the announcer could lead with a terse, sobering, dramatic account that would send chills up the spines of devoted watchers. The cops were only too happy to comply.

The segment aired March 13, 1999. The narrator showed footage of the burning car, followed by a still picture of a smiling, goateed David Stevens wearing a sport coat and looking like the son any mother would want. The program interviewed friends of David. Detective Joe Cristinziani was in-studio ready to take calls personally. Then, the circus started. Quotes from private investigator John Stevens took over the program. "He may appear naïve," said Stevens, "but David had an earthy side to him." Stevens was identified as the investigator who showed David the ropes of sleuthing in the late '80s.

John Stevens told the program he worked closely with

David, training with him in hand-to-hand combat, learning the legal system, and traveling across the country gathering intelligence.

Stevens speculated David may have been doing a bit of freelance investigation and might have gotten into something bigger than he could handle. When they saw the interview, the SDPD homicide detectives didn't know whether to laugh or get angry. "That guy's speculations are coming right out of thin air," said one detective. "There's not one spec of evidence, or even information, that David was doing P.I. work. We're getting a lot of bogus leads, but this is ridiculous."

"It's something he saw, smelled, or touched in that San Diego area," John Stevens confidently said. "That's what got him." Stevens repeated what he had said to *The Reader* reporter, Bill Manson, who was only too happy to have a follow-up story; that David worked on some tough cases dealing with everything from kidnapping to narcotics.

David's brother, Dan, proposed another theory to the program. He thought the death was related to David's frequenting of topless bars. When told the cops had interviewed and checked the fingerprints of every stripper who knew David, Dan wasn't satisfied. "My guess is it's connected to that," said Dan Stevens in a story written by Kimberly Halkett, a news anchor and reporter living in Washington, D.C. Information for that story was researched by Bambi Dmitra Denmark, then a student at Virginia Wesleyan College and an intern at *America's Most Wanted*. The cops had difficulty getting angry or annoyed at Stevens's family. They had lost a good son, one who never caused them any trouble.

Team III had handled enough cases where the deceased was an ex-convict and a major problem to the surviving family and society in general. Some of their homicide victims were people arrested every week for any kind of crime imaginable. Team III worked those cases as hard as they worked the David Stevens case. Sometimes the police feel even sorrier for a grieving family when the family themselves are relieved, in part, that their troublemaker son finally wouldn't be making trouble for them anymore. That was not the case with David Stevens's family. Sergeant L. D. Martin showed the most compassion.

The television program mentioned David might have had a woman in his apartment just before his death. Sergeant Martin said, "If there was a woman there, I'd like to find out who that was. We're hoping that woman will come forward." The detectives weren't optimistic that woman would come forward, because they thought she was involved in the murder.

The television show generated twenty-two tips. The majority of them were not really tips, but merely suggestions about what happened. Only three of the calls provided specific information that could be followed up on to assist in the investigation.

One caller, a "Hector" from Utah, said he thought he had seen Stevens in Dancer's on December 27. That was wrong because David Stevens was long dead and already autopsied at that time, a fact revealed on the program, but not absorbed by Hector.

Another "tip" gave vague information, but supplied a callback number. When the number was dialed, it was obvious the call had been nothing but a prank, and the information was nothing more than a fictionalized expansion of information released on the program.

A psychic "saw" two males and a female. "The female is short and has a small scar by her right eye. The female is a customer of the dating agency and started talking to David there." In truth, David was a supervisor and didn't deal with clients. On to the next tip.

Another caller speculated David brought a girl from

Dancer's home with him. Her boyfriend followed and ultimately killed David. Maybe, but it had been established that David had not been at Dancer's that night, or even for a week before the murder. Besides, they had worked the hell out of the stripper/Dancer's theory.

Another caller from San Diego claimed to have seen David on December 27 standing in front of the Naval Base at 32nd Street holding hands with two girls. A detailed description of the girls followed. The exhausted cops flippantly said to one another, "It couldn't have been David holding hands with two girls on December 27. First, he was dead by then. Second, one of his hands was burned off." The detectives were getting punchy with fatigue and frustration. Their private, dark humor is common in the business.

Another caller told *America's Most Wanted* the officers should check on the bodybuilder with whom David competed. That was easy. David no longer competed, and rarely trained.

Other callers said David was bisexual. Still others said he was homosexual. The police were told to look for gay clubs near the strip places David frequented. Callers said gays and bisexuals are able to "find" others of the same ilk by their mannerisms. And on and on it went.

Another caller told the *America's Most Wanted* phone operator a female impersonator killed Stevens. When asked why, the caller said it was obvious because of the K-Y Jelly found in the bedroom. The detectives had investigated all manner of sexual murders over the years and had never seen a connection between lubricant and female impersonators. Another caller told the detectives to check the gay bars in the area. "Not me," groaned one detective jokingly. "I'm sticking to the strip bars."

Another lady from Canada called to say she was currently reading a book called *Flash Point*, published in 1996. In that book, a victim is shot and stabbed, and the car is set on fire. The cops wondered what the hell that had to do with anything. They thumbed through the tips and scratched their heads.

"Carla" from El Cajon, a suburb of San Diego, called in to name "Melody" (not her real name) as being involved in, or knowing about, the killing. Melody was allegedly a former stripper at Dancer's. Carla said Melody would come to her house to see Carla's son. Melody would do drugs and rant and rave and say she knew a bodybuilder who was killed by another stripper from Dancer's.

Carla described Melody as being almost six feet tall with dark brown eyes. She had a tattoo of a dagger across her shoulder blade. Along with pierced nipples, she had another tattoo on one of her buttocks.

Since this tip had information the detectives could follow up on, Young and Cristinziani contacted Carla on March 18, 1999, at her residence. Carla said Melody used to dance at Dancer's. Carla said she used to be a dancer herself, and girls like Melody tended to confide in her. Melody was dating Carla's son. Her son told Carla Melody did drugs, mostly methamphetamines.

Young and Cristinziani came prepared with a photograph of Melody they had obtained from the Adult Entertainment file of the police department's Licensing Division. They showed Carla the photo. "That's her," said Carla.

Carla revealed Melody had told her back in November that Melody knew a girl who, along with her boyfriend, had killed a guy, then burned him in his car. Melody came to Carla's house shortly after hearing this, visibly shaken. Melody told Carla she knew the girl and her boyfriend were going to rob the guy, but had no idea they would kill him. Melody said she didn't know who else to tell so she told Carla. Carla didn't know the name of the girl who participated in the killing, only that she, too, was a dancer.

Melody told Carla the dead guy had a "beautiful body" and drove a convertible.

As the detectives gently bore in with more specific questions, Carla was unable to give more specific answers. Of particular interest to them was that Carla said it happened in November. They revisited that part of her statement. Carla said she was quite sure it was just before Thanksgiving. When J. R. Young told her the murder happened just before Christmas, Carla said, "Well, maybe then it was just before Christmas."

Detective Young asked Carla if she was certain Melody worked at Dancer's. She was. The police had already confirmed Melody never worked there, although she had worked at other topless and totally nude establishments. It was obvious to the officers that Carla had an intense dislike for Melody. When they asked her if the dislike was the reason she was telling them Melody was involved, she denied it. Carla said she was not making anything up, that it was the truth. If they had been betting men, both Young and Cristinziani would have bet Carla was not correct. Nonetheless, their next stop was to interview Melody.

They found her at her newest place of employment, a topless dive on University Avenue in a depressed area of San Diego. After introductions, the detectives got down to business, detailing why they were there. Melody seemed nonchalant. She listed the five places where she had been employed as a nude dancer before her current place. It was a long list for a girl not yet twenty-one years old. She denied ever working at Dancer's.

They showed her a picture of David Stevens. She shook her head negatively. "I've never seen this guy before. If he came to any of the places I worked, I don't remember him." Melody denied telling anyone about anyone getting killed.

Finally, the detectives told her where they received their information. "Oh, Christ," said Melody. "Carla's nuts. She hated me after I broke up with her son. I broke up with him because of her. I never told Carla anything about being involved in this murder. She's lying and making the whole thing up. It doesn't surprise me it came from her, but it's pissing me off. We've never had a conversation like the one you're telling me about. Carla liked me a lot and thought I was the best girl [her son] ever dated. She told me she would kick both our asses if we ever broke up."

Melody agreed to take a polygraph test. Her finger-prints checked negative when compared against the ones collected at David's apartment. She took, and subsequently passed, a polygraph exam. The detectives concluded Carla fabricated the information about Melody—another "tip" resulted in several wasted days for the weary cops.

Homicide Team III had done just about everything they thought possible in checking David Stevens's "inner circle." They had even ventured outside, contacting people such as Dr. Jeff Stout in Nebraska and the ever-annoying investigator, John Stevens, in Oregon. They thought it was time to get back to the closer acquaintances in San Diego and give every bit of information in their possession another good going-over.

The *America's Most Wanted* venture was a bust, but one they were glad they had tried. There is nothing like national exposure to help the cause. It just didn't work this time.

David's dad, Gerald, had contacted Team III and sent back an item from David's apartment they had released to him. It was a caller ID box. At first, the Stevens family did not know what it was. The box was small and had been attached to the wall about six feet from the telephone. Neither crime scene detective Terry Torgersen nor the crime scene specialist had known what it was. There was no marking depicting its purpose. None of the other detectives on Team III knew what it was. When Stevens's family saw what it was, they sent it back to San Diego. The detectives examined all of the numbers captured by the box and made sure they contacted those who had called David Stevens. Most were from work.

One of the callers was a girl named Ny Nourn. She had worked at Perfect Match for only a short time. When the detectives contacted her over the phone about her call to David Stevens on December 22, the day before he was killed, she said she could not remember why she called him. It must have had something to do with her work schedule. She had not worked on December 22. She worked at Perfect Match only a short time after David was killed.

Another number generated great interest with the police. The outside intercom phone at the front door of the apartment complex dialed David's number at 3:05 A.M. on December 23, just an hour and a half before his burning car, and body, were found. Someone had come to David's apartment and called him from outside. There was no way of knowing who called, and that was what rankled the police. Maybe the killer had come to his apartment at that time. The call represented great interest to the police. Unfortunately, the existence of that phone call did nothing to solve the murder.

Meanwhile, shortly after the discovery of David Stevens's body on December 23, 1998, San Diego Police generated a statewide teletype inquiry asking assistance from other jurisdictions with similar cases. They received a few replies, mostly from other agencies with unsolved cases. "I'd sure like to hear from someone who has *solved* one of these," said John Tefft. "We need a closed case, not another mystery." Team III looked at each of these cases with predictable results—nothing. And each examination took valuable time.

The informal axiom in homicide investigation is, if you don't solve the homicide within twenty-four hours, the job becomes increasingly difficult. It was well into March 1999. They had managed to go through the San Diego Police Homicide "on-call" rotation and even solve a case the next month. The David Stevens case remained a mystery.

CHAPTER 7

On the outside chance that strippers might still be the key to the case, Team III went back to square one and decided to look at the boyfriends of the various strippers at Dancer's. The romantic view of the stripper being either a struggling girl earning her master's degree in linguistics or astrophysics is a myth. Many of them have kids, are single mothers, and are just trying to make it. Theirs is not a romantic lot. No Richard Geres are out there waiting to forge a lasting relationship with any of them and whisk them away to eternal bliss with never another worry about money.

Mostly, the dancers have disdain for the losers who frequent their establishments, closely guarding their single dollar bills stacked on the bar in front of them like some kind of cherished booty. The guys have the money. The girls want the money. It's as simple as that. They might talk to a guy to pass the time, or to ply him into giving more money, but that's it. No lasting relationships are generated from someone sitting alone in a darkened bar while a bored woman slowly disrobes and seductively licks her lips while batting her eyes at a patron. Like the myth of private eyes solving complicated homicides, the myth of the loving and intelligent stripper flourishes. It is largely that: a myth.

The strategy of looking for the killer through the boyfriends of the strippers sounded good when Team III batted it around in one of their meetings. In practice, this idea fell flat. Many of the girls didn't have boyfriends. Some had girlfriends. Of the ones who had boyfriends, the guys often didn't care what the girls did, as long as they brought home the money. These boyfriends know what goes on in strip clubs. They get immune to jealousy, mostly after listening to their girlfriends disparage the men who go to the clubs.

Nonetheless, the detectives questioned the girls and their significant others, all to no avail. Sergeant Martin knew the key to the case was finding the owner of the small set of handprints on the mirrored headboard. Since none of the strippers belonged to those handprints, the police were stymied.

The fingerprints were sent to the "CAL-ID" section of the California Department of Justice. This organization has a database of fingerprints on file. If the person who left the prints on the mirrored headboard had ever been arrested in California, or officially fingerprinted, there would be a "CAL-ID" hit. There was no hit.

Toward the end of March, Gerald Stevens showed up in San Diego accompanied by the colorful, if not abrasive John Stevens. By this time, the police had heard enough from John Stevens. They had read about him in *The Reader*. They thought he had ulterior motives that would lead to fame for him. They were not mistaken.

Stevens had a pipeline to newspaper reporter Lori Pilger from the *Norfolk Daily News*. John Stevens reported back that the police would not respond to his and Mr. Stevens's list of questions. The truth is that Team III became tired of seeing their answers printed in the newspaper. Homicide investigations are supposed to be confidential, unless the police want information disseminated for some reason.

A meeting with Team III ended badly. Both Gerald and John Stevens told the police they were going to look into the case themselves. Detective John Tefft knew this was coming from the first moment he ever read a quote from investigator John Stevens. "I knew that guy wanted his fingers in the pie," Tefft later said. "He just had to be involved. I don't know why, but he did."

At the close of the heated meeting, when the Stevens duo told Team III they were going to work on the case themselves, Team III told the Stevens men to do whatever they believed they had to do. Perhaps Gerald and John hoped Team III would be intimidated or somehow threatened by the knowledge that a private investigator would be following up on what the homicide team did. Once again, this goes back to the myth of private investigators who solve homicides. It simply doesn't happen. Humphrey Bogart and Sam Spade are long dead. Mike Hammer and Phillip Marlowe are retired. Spenser is busy in Boston on whatever case Robert B. Parker has him chasing. The only private eyes in San Diego who work on criminal cases do defense work, usually trying to discredit victims of domestic abuse. For the most part, these P.I.s aren't too successful. So it is not known exactly what Team III told Gerald Stevens and John Stevens, but it was akin to, "Knock yourselves out." Things had definitely gone downhill from when Sergeant L. D. Martin gave up his Christmas Eve to meet members of the Stevens family at the San Diego airport and show them empathy and support. *A long way downhill.*

CHAPTER 8

When all leads on the homicide case had been checked with no results, the homicide detectives started over and rechecked the leads again. Witnesses received follow-up telephone calls where the detectives would say, "I know I spoke with you several months ago, and you told me everything you knew at the time. Since then, has anything come up that changed, or added to anything you told me?" Or "It's been a long time since we spoke. Have you remembered anything you forgot to tell me?" And on it went. The detectives touched bases with everyone involved. They received a new name or two of some strippers who might have known David. Each girl was contacted and interviewed. The results were always the same: nothing.

On March 24, 1999, Detective J. R. Young interviewed a stripper from Dancer's named Kitabakel Jones. She was a tall, attractive, light-skinned black woman. Jones, who danced under the name "India," differed from the other strippers in that she had actually gone out with

David Stevens. Her phone number was in David's day-book, but not on his November or December phone bills. She said she met David in October 1998 while dancing. Jones categorized their relationship as "sort of" going out.

Jones said she was just breaking up with her boyfriend, and she and David would talk at the bar when she wasn't dancing or serving drinks. They would talk about non-sex-related things. Jones knew David worked for a dating service, and she was interested in possibly subscribing. They exchanged phone numbers the first night they met.

She could tell David was interested in her romantically, but the feeling wasn't mutual. She liked him as a friend only. They did go to dinner or a movie now and then, but nothing more. She knew David wanted more out of the relationship, but Jones wasn't willing. She kept making excuses until they finally stopped calling each other. November had been the last time they spoke.

Jones temporarily stopped dancing in December because she came down with Bell's palsy, where half of her face became paralyzed. Eventually, the condition subsided, and she went back to work in January.

Jones currently danced in Las Vegas on the weekends and spent the week in San Diego. She explained she could make more money commuting than by working full-time in San Diego. Police compared Jones's on-file fingerprints to those found in the apartment. There was no match.

Months went by, and nothing happened. In April, private investigator John Stevens came to San Diego again, presumably to resume his investigation. Naturally, he didn't do any of the work without the appropriate fanfare. Stevens grabbed Bill Manson from *The Reader* and took him out to see what a good job of investigating the P.I. was doing.

Their first stop was the site of the burning car. Stevens

pointed out the tree-lined area and told Manson, "It's the perfect spot for a murder. I've been out here real early in the morning. It's dark and isolated. Someone could easily have been waiting in the trees. For this upscale neighborhood, it's a perfect area. Somebody knew what they were doing, picking this spot." There was no evidence Stevens had been lured to the death site and ambushed. It sounded good, though. John Stevens spoke with convincing authority.

Stevens confided to Manson that after being a P.I. for twenty years, he was now a freelance investigative reporter for television stations in Oregon. Once he arrived in San Diego, Stevens began doing basic police work on the case, such as interviews and looking around. To his surprise, Stevens told Manson he was often the first person to contact potential witnesses, meaning the police had not yet spoken to them. He found one woman who heard noises and popping around 4:00 or 4:30 A.M. Stevens told Manson the police never contacted her. Stevens did acknowledge the police contacted many people in the neighborhood, but not the woman who heard the noises.

Stevens drove Manson to the apartment where David lived. Across the street was a gas station with surveillance cameras on the business. One camera focuses on the outside and takes in the intersection of Mission Boulevard and Turquoise. Stevens criticized the police for not commandeering the tape from the business.

Across the street from the gas station is a Union Bank with an outdoor automated teller machine, also equipped with a camera. Stevens said when he interviewed the bank manager, San Diego police had not contacted him to view the tape.

Stevens was, once again, on a roll. In the article, he chided police for their lack of aggressiveness. "How many crimes are really getting solved based on good old shoe leather?" he asked. "I bet if you do a statistical trace on it, the majority of crimes are being solved by 'tipsters.' Somebody calls and says, 'The guy you're looking for is in room 32, Motel 6, on La Mesa Boulevard.' And that's why the police are so interested in working with shows like *America's Most Wanted,* because it looks like they're really doing something, but really, they're just waiting for someone to call. I don't know what you call that. I guess it's the way they gotta do their business. Me, I'd want to get out and do something."

John Stevens made a big deal out of the caller ID box the police had overlooked. He chided the police for not knowing what it was. "To have had that information up front, and not two months down the line, could have been crucial." Stevens was steamed at the incompetence of the San Diego police detectives.

He took Manson down to the parking area of the complex. "When David's family was here on Christmas Eve, the family found a red gas can down right next to where David parked his car. The one-gallon can was in a brown bag. The family doesn't know what happened to that can."

Stevens's biggest gripe with the police was that they didn't communicate with the family. "They don't call Gerald. Period. This is a big thing missing from San Diego Homicide. Call it the 'bedside manner.' I think you can do wonders with a little PR. Just be nice, even if you don't want to. I don't want to tell you anything, so I just have a junior detective call you up and say, 'Everything's going okay, don't worry . . .' A little of the public relations stuff makes us all feel good. And that gets back to why I'm so damned angry wherever I go with law enforcement—and I know it gets me in trouble—they don't have to be nice if they don't want to. Who's going to do anything? Everyone's always apprehensive about speaking against the police; about doing anything because 'Oh my God, we might be obstructing justice, or interfering with an investigation.' So they've got you every way you go! And guess what? Nothing gets done."

John Stevens was also irate because the police would not let them look at David Stevens's vehicle. "Gerald spoke with Sergeant Martin about taking a look at the burned-out car. We wanted to see it so we could photograph it . . . Just look it over. Gerald was told in no uncertain terms. 'No. You can't see it.' "

In an effort to be balanced, Bill Manson contacted Sergeant Martin. Manson asked Martin about Martin's failure to share information with the Stevens family. "Here is the problem that we have with Mr. [Gerald] Stevens," said Martin. "I shared information with him and asked him not to share it with the press, and then he did share it with the press. He and John Stevens went on a San Diego talk radio talk show (Rick Roberts, then with KOGO-AM 600, now with KFMB 760) and said that I hadn't told them anything, which wasn't true. I pretty much kept him up to date on everything. And then he wanted to know every little detail, and I told him I wasn't going to tell every little detail. I said that because it would compromise the investigation. Because every time he gets a little bit of information, he puts it out to the public. And, that's going to impact our ability to—if and when we get a suspect—complete the investigation and go forward with a prosecution.

"However, let me share with you that Mr. [Gerald] Stevens was probably calling me three times a week. He's a concerned parent who wants his son's murder solved, and I understand that because we deal with that all the time. You understand relatives and their grief and their despair, and you want to help them get closure on it. However, after all the things that I told him and asked him not to share with anybody, and after he did, I told him I'm not sharing anything with him anymore until we make an arrest. So he's unhappy about that."

Regarding private investigator John Stevens, Martin wasn't so conciliatory when talking with reporter Bill Manson. "I feel no obligation to deal with John Stevens," Martin said. "He's a private investigator, and we don't share information with private investigators." Martin told Manson that Gerald and John Stevens came into the office the Thursday or Friday before *America's Most Wanted* with a long list of questions. Martin said they had already asked most of the questions, and he had answered them. Martin said he told them whatever they wanted to know, except they wanted to look through their murder notebook and view David's car.

Martin said, "We don't let anybody look through the murder book. That's the book that documents the investigation of the case. It's a large three-ring binder, and everything we do generates a report, to document the actions we've taken, and the follow-ups we've made, the people we've interviewed, the evidence . . . And there's no reason for them to look at the car. It's evidence. And we don't allow anybody to look at the evidence. For fear of contamination."

Martin said this was the first time since he came into the unit at the end of 1992 that he ever had a private investigator try to investigate a homicide. Martin said private eyes don't have the resources or the skills to solve homicides.

When asked about Team III's handling of the red gasoline can found one space away from David Stevens's parking place, Martin only shook his head. Detective Joe Cristinziani found the can the very morning they first visited David's apartment. The can was chained to the wall. It was covered with cobwebs and dirt. It had obviously not been touched recently. While John Stevens was correct in saying the police had done nothing about the red gas can, he was very selective in not saying anything about the condition of the can. Anyone, even a layman, could have seen the can had not been used, or moved, in a long time. It is inconceivable that the killers could have doused the car in the garage with that can, and then driven to La Jolla Scenic Drive with a car full of fumes. The gas had been poured at the fire scene and had not come from that particular can. It was even more absurd to think the can had been taken to the crime scene, emptied into Stevens's car, then returned to the garage and rechained to the wall with someone reconnecting the cobwebs.

Reporter Bill Manson directly asked L. D. Martin how near they were to an arrest. It took guts for Martin to answer as honestly as he did. "Barring somebody coming forward and saying, 'I have information about this,' which we're still hopeful of, right now we don't have any real viable leads. We're hopeful that somewhere along the line somebody will say, 'Hey, look, I feel bad about this. I gave this person a ride, or I came and picked him up here, and maybe you should talk to them.' But there's nothing real hot right now."

Private investigator John Stevens loved Sergeant Martin's comments. "Like I said," he beamed, "they wait for tips."

CHAPTER 9

Real professionals, like Team III, on one level, can ignore the biting comments and second-guessing of someone like John Stevens. They had no fear of being embarrassed by him. They would gladly have accepted a suspect if Stevens had uncovered one. Justice was more important than their egos. They knew he wouldn't produce a suspect because he was going down the wrong road. Although his comments were irritating, they ignored him. It was as if Team III was an all-star outfielder playing major league baseball and John Stevens was a leather-lunged fan sitting in the bleachers heckling them. When the outfielder went home at night, he was still an all-star, good enough to be playing in the majors. When the heckling fan went home at night, he still didn't possess the skills or the resources to be a professional baseball player. All he could do was make noise.

The months rolled by. On May 16, 1999, Gerald Stevens wrote to Senator Chuck Hagel in Lincoln, Nebraska. Stevens told Senator Hagel he had been a crop and dairy farmer for forty years in Nebraska. Stevens said although he was proud to be an American and a Nebraskan, his pride and confidence in America had been tested.

Stevens summarized his son's murder. He said the San Diego police investigation had caused him much grief and made the situation even more difficult to handle. Stevens told the senator he had been working with private investigator John Stevens and the two of them had come up with "several possible leads." Yet the San Diego police continued to stonewall what Gerald and John had done and refused to work with them.

Mr. Stevens sent Senator Hagel the articles written by Bill Manson from *The Reader*. Mr. Stevens asked the senator to help get some cooperation from the police, or from some federal investigative agency. At the minimum, Stevens asked Hagel to contact one of the senators from California and try to get some intervention or assistance.

In another follow-up letter, Mr. Stevens wrote Senator Hagel his investigation had come to some conclusions:

"1. There exists known sources who were made known to Sgt. Martin and his Team III that have plainly described what only could lead to the conclusion that **my son had found himself in the middle of a group of individuals engaged in serious, continuing criminal enterprises centered around the La Jolla area, and extending across state lines.** I believe that this matter should not only have sparked interest with the local police, but would be extremely important to the federal authorities whose job it is to combat racketeering and organized crime.

"2. The investigation into my son's death as early as January 22, 1999, had been relegated to publishing a "tip-line" and hoping that someone would come forward and help them solve the crime. Although I recognize that this technique can be useful, I have spoken to Sgt. Martin of Homicide Team III, and his explanations in short have been both inadequate at times, and proven false on other occasions."

When the working detectives on Team III saw a copy of the letter, they chided Sergeant Martin for being such a good guy in the first place. They reminded him he had given up Christmas Eve so he could help Mr. Stevens and his son begin to come to grips with what had happened to David. As John Tefft said early on, "No good deed goes unpunished."

The letter (which strangely enough, sounded like private investigator John Stevens's style and words more than Gerald Stevens's) went on to trumpet the "blatant police incompetence." The writer wrote, ". . . many witnesses who have provided deep background, have either been overlooked, or have kept information close to their vest for fear of police mishandling of it, which could put their lives at risk." (The term *deep background* reeked of the vocabulary of the private eye.)

The paragraph that sent the detectives into orbit read, "Of deep concern was the sharing with potential persons of interest, not to mention the world, hypersensitive information relevant to the case. SDPD's work can only be described as at minimum, grossly incompetent and, at worst, possibly corrupt." The detectives knew words like *blatant, hypersensitive, grossly*, and *corrupt* didn't come from Gerald Stevens. He was a ruddy-faced man of the soil. Those words sounded like they came from, oh say, a private investigator who might be living in Portland, Oregon.

The detectives howled when the letter chided them for sharing information with the wrong people. The detectives weren't the ones who went on Rick Roberts's KOGO

radio program and mentioned everything Sergeant Martin
had said.

In conclusion, Mr. Stevens (or whoever had written
the letter) asked Senator Hagel to try to get the federal
government involved because the federal government
". . . would competently get to the bottom of my son's
murder. If that is not possible, we would request that you
join other members of our Nebraskan elected federal and
state officials in voicing our displeasure with their California counterparts." It was signed, "Sincerely, Gerald
Stevens," followed by his address and phone number.

The sergeant and four homicide detectives had well
over thirty-five years collective experience investigating
homicides. Over the years, they had made mistakes, as
any homicide detectives had. Yet their cumulative knowledge was immense. Their pride in their work and their
dedication to professionalism were unmatched. Even
though the news articles and letters hurt, the police were
secure in the fact that they had done everything they
should have in the investigation. Even when John Stevens
said they had done nothing, they knew he was babbling.

Someone gave the detectives a one-page memo on "International News Service" letterhead called "Talking
Points," signed by John Stevens. The memo detailed how
John Stevens, at the request of David Stevens's family,
had reviewed San Diego PD's investigation of David
Stevens's murder and uncovered "gross incompetence as
well as indifference by the Homicide Division."

He ridiculed the police for their honesty in saying they
"were stumped." He said his investigative team turned up
evidence that strongly suggested a probable motive and
persons of interest who were overlooked or ignored by the
police.

Stevens's memo said his preliminary research suggested that David may have been conducting some sort of
directed intelligence operation within the world of body-

building—he may have found himself in the middle of a group of individuals engaged in serious, continuing criminal enterprises centered in and around the San Diego/La Jolla area, and extending across state and national borders. Those were the same words used by Gerald Stevens in his letter to Senator Hagel.

Stevens reminded the recipient of his memo, whoever it was, that "Internationally-known Tijuana (Mexico) drug cartels smuggle everything from cocaine, heroin, and marijuana, to steroids and other banned consumer products."

Stevens vaguely, but with mysterious confidence, wrote, "Many bodybuilding insiders have provided sufficient documentation suggesting that Dave's murder may open the door to the whole bodybuilding industry, including the dark and seedy side." He added in parentheses, ("Many key players within this industry, academia included, are working exclusively with I.N.S.") Of course, I.N.S. is Stevens's investigative agency.

No one knows exactly who was the intended recipient of this memo, but it is believed that one or more of the investigative prime-time network news programs were the intended targets. Stevens closed by writing, "This story has many potential angles. It could be packaged as one large, in-depth story or fractioned out as many substories." Was John Stevens trying to solve a murder or pitch a story?

Ever the promoter, John Stevens interviewed a man named TC Luoma, a columnist from *Testosterone Magazine*, a publication that features articles on muscle building and advertises vitamin supplements. Luoma claimed to live in La Jolla at least part of the year. He also wrote he lives close to where David Stevens's body was found. In October of 1999, Luoma printed an account of his encounter with John Stevens. Luoma injected himself into the story by suggesting that his conversation with John Stevens now put Luoma's life in jeopardy. Luoma compared himself to Robert Redford in the 1975 movie *Three Days of the Condor*.

Stevens told Luoma that because Luoma agreed to speak with Stevens, he (Luoma) might now be a target. Luoma shared the story of his brave interview with his readers so that the killers might now be afraid to kill him. Luoma's logic surmised that since the readers now knew Luoma might be killed for writing about the case, the killers would be wary of killing him.

Luoma wrote that David Stevens had been shot in the head "gangland style." ("Gangland style" usually means the hands and feet are bound and the victim is shot in the back of the head.) Luoma said David Stevens had moved to southern California on the recommendations of one of *Testosterone Magazine's* contributors. Luoma cagily refused to mention who that contributor was.

Luoma echoed what John Stevens had already written, especially the stuff about the police doing a hack job on the investigation. Luoma bluntly and dramatically wrote that nobody in the supplement company would talk to Stevens because, "they're afraid of dying." Here Luoma went out on a very thin limb when he wrote that David was probably killed because he may have supplied customer mailing lists to competitors.

The mailing list theory was pulled out of thin air. Luoma tried to salvage his credibility when he closed by backpedaling and saying he wasn't making any accusations, but when millions of dollars are at stake, anything could happen. He published L. D. Martin's phone number, then the number for John Stevens, asking anyone with information to call.

It seemed to the cops like Luoma wanted to be a player and get somehow connected to the case, maybe to impress his friends, or just to have something to write about in *Testosterone Magazine*.

The months passed with no productive events happening on the case. Team III worked new cases, and solved them. They never forgot David Stevens and his burning car on La Jolla Scenic Drive. Their motivation didn't require the prodding of John Stevens to spur them on. They worked all their cases the same: with dogged diligence and dedicated determination.

What many people don't realize, and it's not just the poetic, flowery rhetoric of some pro-cop enthusiast, is that homicide detectives see themselves as the last representative of the victim. The victim can no longer speak. No one can look out for the victim. He or she is dead. The detectives take seriously their duty of bringing killers to justice. It doesn't matter if the deceased is a street hooker, a stockbroker, or a noted surgeon. The players may change, but the determination of the cops who work the cases remains the same. Maybe police administrators might dedicate additional resources if the victim is a small child and the media is flocking around the command post, clamoring for breaks in the case. Even if the media is everywhere and police command officers are looking their best for the cameras, the men and women who actually do the work do it the same way.

Sometimes street hookers or crack dealers have no one who cares if their killer is caught. The police always care. Just because a victim isn't much of a contributor to society doesn't mean a killer should walk around free.

America's Most Wanted repeated the David Stevens segment on September 19, 1999. More callers responded. As with the first airing, most of them had only opinions and theories. No callers provided tips that would result in follow-up information. Things were looking bleak.

CHAPTER 10

The detectives held fast to the theory the facts and evidence gave them the first day they started the investigation: David Stevens had sex with someone in his apartment. Someone objected to the sexual encounter, either the partner, or a friend of the partner. The officers also believed David Stevens was lured from his apartment, or kidnapped from it, taken somewhere in his car, and shot. They believed his dead body was transported in his car to La Jolla, where it was incinerated. They believed they were looking for two people—one who drove Stevens's car, and the other who drove the car that took the killers from the fiery crime scene.

The evidence supported this theory. Robbery was not a motive. Nothing was missing, yet a killer could have taken anything he or she wanted from Stevens's apartment. From every indicator they could uncover, *Testosterone Magazine* notwithstanding, there was nothing in the sports supplements or bodybuilding industries that lent itself to David's death. While the police were surprised at the cutthroat nature of the businesses and the competitiveness of the various enterprises, there simply was no connection to David Stevens's involvement in the conflict except that he formerly worked for one of the companies. The lawsuits and wrangling going on now never had anything to do with David Stevens when he worked in the business.

Neither was there ever any evidence that David Stevens was conducting an investigation into bodybuilding or sports supplements, or investigating anything else for that matter. Certainly David had nothing to do with the investigation of the legal or illegal sale of steroids either. Stevens may have used them sporadically when competing. Those days were long past. A search of Stevens's apartment at the time of his death revealed no dossier on any case he might have been working. His private investigation days were as long over as were his bodybuilding days. David was trying to make a living and find a decent woman (or maybe an occasional indecent woman), according to every fact they uncovered.

The detectives didn't discount that a stripper or her boyfriend might be involved. After all, they thought the murder was somehow related to the sexual encounter in his bedroom just hours before his body was found. Every stripper they interviewed checked negative through fingerprints. None of them, except Kitabakel Jones, even saw David outside of Dancer's. All of the boyfriends of the girls checked out, too. It was frustrating.

1999 ended, and the new millennium arrived amid much fanfare, with fear of computer crashes and mass pandemonium when the stroke of midnight hit. Nothing of the sort happened. The survivalists were left with their solar-powered refrigerators, emergency water jugs, and their unused multiple-ammunition clips for their extensive arsenal of weapons. It was life as usual in the world, and life as usual in the Homicide division.

Gerald Stevens in Randolph, Nebraska, hired the legal firm of Monson, Behm, and Carlson to look into the case. Attorney Lance Carlson decided to sidestep Sergeant L. D. Martin and even leapfrog Martin's boss, the lieutenant, in favor of going higher and speaking with Captain Ron Newman, himself a former homicide detective. Managers are managers are managers. It helps if a manager of a homicide division was once a homicide detective himself, putting up with the call-outs, the irregular hours, attending autopsies, and sometimes interviewing unsavory members of society. Newman had walked in those shoes. The detectives hoped he hadn't forgotten what their lot was like.

Mr. Stevens did not hire the law firm to *solve* the murder. He wanted their assistance in dealing with the higher echelon of the San Diego Police Department. Carlson's was a civil law firm. Often celebrities or families of victims in high-profile cases hire attorneys. These attorneys usually don't do much of anything but accept a fee. Sometimes they broker book or movie deals for the family. In this case, Mr. Stevens presumably wanted someone experienced in legal matters to communicate for him.

Lance Carlson wrote to Captain Newman on January 12, 2000. The letter was a follow-up to a phone conversation the two previously had. In the letter, Carlson thanked Newman for speaking with him about the case. Newman apparently had told Carlson the police department would gladly open up lines of communication with the Stevens family. Previous to this, Sergeant L. D. Martin had spoken extensively with Captain Newman, bringing him up to date on all of the turmoil the police had experienced in dealing with Mr. Stevens and the private investigator Stevens. Martin also briefed Newman on the facts of the case.

Attorney Carlson wrote back, based on his conversation with Newman, that it didn't look like a meeting with the family, just to have a meeting, would be productive. When Carlson relayed to his client that the police thought communication was certainly a problem, Gerald Stevens told Carlson the bigger problem was the way the family had been treated by the police and the way the investigation had been conducted.

Mr. Stevens told the attorney he had information to share with the police, but would share it only if there was a commitment to follow up on the information that he and the private investigator Stevens had uncovered.

Carlson continued, writing that Mr. Stevens would welcome the type of treatment that Newman had promised. That is, Stevens wanted better service.

Carlson's January 12 letter was followed up with another on January 21, where Carlson expressed disappointment that Newman hadn't followed up on Carlson's previous letter. Newman hadn't followed up because the police had no intention of sharing any more information with them. Nor did they want to listen to any of John Stevens's theories. They had had their fill of his half-baked ideas of national intrigue and cloak-and-dagger espionage. It was rubbish, the police believed. The motive for David Stevens's death was sex and anger, and, to this date, nothing contrary to that idea had surfaced.

The next step for the Stevens family was for Senator Chuck Hagel to contact the San Diego District Attorney's office and get a new team assigned to investigate the homicide of David Stevens. Hagel's office wrote to the Chief of the Superior Court Division that Mr. Stevens had information the San Diego police refused to follow up on. Hagel wanted the District Attorney's office to do the investigation.

Jim Pippin, the Superior Court Division Chief, called Ron Newman, a man he had known for years, asking what was going on. Pippin and Newman had put on homicide cases when Newman was a working cop and Pippin was a working prosecutor. Pippin remembered what it was like dealing with the families of victims. He also remembered how difficult it is to investigate a homicide. Newman filled Pippin in on what was going on with the case.

Pippin wrote Mr. Stevens he had heard from Senator Hagel's office regarding the case, including the statement that Mr. Stevens had information not yet considered by the San Diego Police Department.

Pippin continued that the San Diego police would welcome any information Stevens might have. Pippin added, "The San Diego Police Department is the appropriate agency to conduct the investigation and you are encouraged to send whatever information you may have directly to them." One could only surmise the reaction Mr. Stevens had when he read that. Pippin was effectively telling Mr. Stevens that the San Diego District Attorney's office didn't meddle in what the San Diego police was investigating.

Mr. Stevens turned Pippin's letter over to his attorney, Lance Carlson. Carlson, in turn, wrote to Pippin on May 15, 2000. Carlson wrote Pippin that, although Captain Newman was cordial and polite, Newman did not indicate he would welcome any information Mr. Stevens might have. Newman also wrote Carlson to say he would not meet with attorney Carlson or private investigator John Stevens.

Carlson, in turn, wrote Pippin he did not believe Newman was interested in listening to Mr. Stevens. Carlson informed Pippin that Newman believed nothing was wrong with the way the investigation had been conducted. Furthermore, Carlson believed Newman was not interested in listening with an open mind to what Mr.

Stevens believed was strong evidence of serious over-
sights on the part of the investigative team.

Carlson's last paragraph read:

"Mr. Stevens's request is not unreasonable. All he is
asking for is for an opportunity to meet with someone
in a supervisory position at the San Diego Police Department and be given sufficient opportunity to set
forth the results of his yearlong investigation into this
matter. His hope is to have this matter reassigned or a
special task force appointed to investigate this crime.
Any assistance you could provide in facilitating such a
meeting would be appreciated."

What was Pippin to do? He respected the San Diego
police. Mr. Stevens was asking Pippin to override the
operational procedures already in place. It seemed as if
Stevens wanted the D.A.'s office to step in and take the
case from the police and either work it themselves, or
turn it over to a federal agency. Either action was unacceptable. Cops investigated crimes, and district attorneys
prosecuted them. True, the district attorney had a large
staff of investigators and investigative support personnel. Their roles were confined to getting the cases "fine
tuned" and ready for court. Outside of the gang and
fraud units, the D.A. investigators rarely solved crimes.
Cases were presented to the D.A. that already had been
solved.

Team III read the various correspondences with typical shaking of heads and mutterings. All of the investigators in Homicide had been police officers for several
years. They knew the ins and outs of police work, including the political ramifications of what police administrators do. They hoped the administration would back
them.

Team III was unhappy when they learned the case was

transferred to the Homicide Evidence Assessment Team (HEAT) unit. These are the cold-case people. Fortunately, Terry Torgersen, who was with Team III when David Stevens was killed was now with HEAT. It was unusual for a homicide to be transferred to the cold-case unit after such a short time. Usually, the cold cases are cold a long time before HEAT examines them.

The detectives believed Newman capitulated to pressure from Stevens's family when he allowed HEAT access to the case. Sergeant L. D. Martin had laid everything out to Newman about what his team had done on the case. Newman appeared to be in agreement with Martin. After all, Newman had walked in those shoes before. He believed Martin and his team had worked hard and thoroughly. And their theory on the case was sound. The team had pursued the leads of steroids and supplements that John Stevens presented. They came up with nothing. As for David Stevens doing freelance investigating that got him in trouble, there was never any evidence of that.

Investigators found nothing indicating David Stevens was investigating anything other than how to find a girlfriend.

A kind of tacit understanding was reached that *both* Team III and the cold-case unit would work the case. This was an unprecedented compromise that did not sit well with Team III. They accepted the decision because they had to.

Detectives who have worked cold cases say those cases are sometimes easier to work. On one level, this statement might seem confusing. It is well settled that if a case isn't solved in twenty-four hours, the chances of it ever getting solved decrease proportionally to the time involved. However, cold cases have some positive attractions. Often, suspects in cold murders are in prison for other reasons. Over the passage of time, witnesses might no longer be afraid of killers who are already in jail.

Friends of the suspect who might exact retribution may also be in jail, too. For these reasons, detectives often find witnesses in stale cases more agreeable to help. A cold-case detective might have a report in his hand where a witness who lived across the street from a murder might have given a statement saying he didn't see anything the night of the killing. When the detective goes back five years later to go over the witness's statement, the detective might be in for a surprise. The witness might say, "Yeah, I saw a guy about six-foot-five wearing a white jacket shoot that guy." In fact, the police, that very night, might have questioned and released a guy who was around six-foot-five and wearing a white jacket.

The detective would ask the witness why he didn't tell that to the first officer. The witness would say, "Man, that guy is dangerous. He's always jackin' people around down at the liquor store. Everyone's afraid of him. We ain't so afraid now because he's in jail for a robbery, and so are most of his damn friends." And so it goes, with many cases being resolved in that same fashion.

True, a defense attorney might try to discredit the witness for lying initially. A good prosecutor can convince a jury that the witness gave an incorrect statement for a good reason: to save his life.

Nonetheless, the wheels of politics were turning. Captain Ron Newman made arrangements with Jim Pippin to have a deputy district attorney assigned to the case. This is somewhat unusual because the D.A.'s office usually doesn't get involved until a suspect has been identified.

In May of 2000, Terry Torgersen and Sergeant Jorge Duran from HEAT met with Jim Pippin, who mentioned the correspondence from David's family in Nebraska.

Pippin said he was inclined to assign a deputy district attorney to look into the matter for review and evaluation.

The police met with Chandra Carle on June 13, 2000. They explained the case to her. When the investigators were done, Carle examined the photographs and discussed the physical evidence at Stevens's apartment.

Carle, a prosecutor with twelve years' experience trying cases, always had an enthusiasm for cases involving fire. Some prosecutors bring specialized interests with them to the office. Some D.A.s love cases involving computers, while others love cases with medical ramifications. Some love financial crimes with sophisticated paper trails of money, complicated deposits, pyramid schemes, and foreign bank accounts. Carle's unofficial forte was cases with flames. She had prosecuted several arsonists. She knew the officers from Metro Arson Strike Team (MAST). Carle had a good reputation among the police as being a strong advocate of their cases. Yet she knew she was the one going into court to put the case on, and she did not ever want to be embarrassed by a loss because of weak evidence.

A few weeks later, after going through the file, Chandra Carle got back to Sergeant Duran. She said she agreed with the original police assessment that this case involved sex and rage. She said the case was a love triangle, and they needed the other two points of the triangle, David Stevens being the first. She didn't see any connection with steroids. Carle knew a woman was at the heart of this case.

Carle evaluated the physical evidence: the lubricant at the bedside; the glass with lipstick next to the bed; the long hair in the bed; the two sets of handprints on the mirrored headboard. Someone was having sex with David Stevens, and someone else took exception to it. She told the officers to keep digging and call her back when they had a suspect in custody or needed someone to approve a search or arrest warrant. Now Captain Newman could tell the Stevens family that the district attorney was looking at the case.

Chandra Carle was asked if she gave any credence to the various theories espoused by private investigator John Stevens. "His theory of steroids and espionage was okay, but it wasn't based on any evidence. It might make for a good movie plot. The reality was poor David Stevens played no part in the lawsuit between the feuding vitamin people. I couldn't take a movie plot and ask a jury for a conviction. I had to have evidence.

"The detectives from Team III and the HEAT guys are pros. They investigate homicides for a living. They know what they're doing. Nothing against John Stevens. He was just pulling things out of the air and, in my opinion, was further victimizing David's family. I don't know what they were paying him, but . . ." Carle's voice trailed off, reluctant to finish her sentence. She shook her head slowly, leaving the interviewer to form his own conclusions.

The case of David Stevens presented a first in the handling of a homicide within the San Diego Police Department. The case was officially given to the HEAT unit, but long before a case is traditionally given to that team. The case unofficially remained with Team III. Both teams worked it. If Gerald Stevens wanted to raise a stink, Captain Newman could placate him by saying the case had been assigned to another team. Stevens hated Team III so much the change in personnel might make him feel better. Furthermore, the police could say that not only had they given the case to another team for a fresh look, they also gave it to the district attorney for an even fresher, dispassionate, and professional assessment and evaluation. No matter what the truth was, it sounded good. And the truth wasn't that bad, anyway.

CHAPTER 11

Unfortunately, nothing happened for the rest of 2000. If some tip or bit of information came in, Team III would look into it. The only problem was that nothing was coming in.

Team III talked about the case numerous times at their meetings. Chandra Carle read the case over and over. She looked at the pictures of the burning car. She looked at the pictures of David Stevens's apartment. She read about the location of the two sets of handprints on the mirrored headboard. She believed, on the night David Stevens lost his "California virginity," he also lost his life. When she spoke about the case, she referred to the love triangle with two of the corners representing the killers of David Stevens.

The police department sent the smaller of the handprints to the Federal Bureau of Investigation's national database to be checked. Previously, the prints had been compared against those people in California who have had their prints taken. This time, the search for a match was expanded to include those within the entire United States. A few months later, the disappointing message came back: negative.

Spring became summer, then autumn. Football season was nearly done when one of the detectives thought it might be productive to put the David Stevens case on a segment of *Crime Stoppers*. This is a crime scene re-enactment played in short spots on local television. In this case, the detectives envisioned showing David Stevens's burning car followed up by the narrator giving some slight details of the crime. They would also show a photograph of David Stevens. Then, the telephone number for *Crime Stoppers* would flash across the screen with directions to call if anyone could offer information.

The decision was made to run the clip the last week of January 2001. The first airing was to come at the conclusion of the Super Bowl. During the rest of the week, several spots would be aired. It might not help. But, as one detective said, "It can't hurt."

On January 29, 2001, the day after the Super Bowl, someone called *Crime Stoppers* at 12:45 P.M. The caller said he had been watching the game in a motel with a woman named Kathie Newkirk. Newkirk casually commented that her former girlfriend and the girlfriend's boyfriend were responsible for the murder depicted in the crime segment. The caller said Newkirk was still at the motel, was active duty military, and would be going out to sea the next day. There was one other bit of information: Newkirk's former girlfriend was a stripper named Kitabakel Jones.

Crime Stoppers called Detective John Tefft immediately. Tefft notified Sergeant Martin and Detective J. R. Young. As Tefft and Young were driving to Newkirk's motel, Young consulted his notebook. He had interviewed Kitabakel Jones on March 24, 1999. Jones seemed to check out okay at the time. The prints on the headboard next to Stevens's were not hers. Her phone number was in Stevens's address book. She knew David from Dancer's, but never had much to do with him outside the club, according to Young's notes.

Newkirk admitted the detectives to her motel room. They never asked the question: "Why the hell didn't you tell someone two years ago?" They thought it, though. They were in the information-gathering mode and didn't want to make her angry; especially someone who might be giving them information that would solve a case.

Newkirk established her credibility initially when she said Jones used to work at Dancer's. She indicated she was not only Kitabakel Jones's roommate; she was also her former lover. She said Jones had a couple of boyfriends. It was obvious Jones and Newkirk were no longer an item because Newkirk spoke disparagingly of her, saying Jones only used men for money. When the man's money was gone, Jones was also gone. Newkirk's credibility was so important because people purporting to help had previously burned the detectives on this case by fabricating information. So far, Newkirk seemed to know what she was talking about.

Newkirk said at the time of the murder, Jones was dating a male professional kickboxer who used to live in Nevada, but now lived in San Diego. She said Jones was also going out with David Stevens. Upon being shown a picture of Stevens, Newkirk said that was the David she knew. She said he was a bodybuilder who was nice, soft-spoken, and polite.

Newkirk said Jones would do private after-hours parties away from Dancer's. She said Jones had been to David's place several times and had done some private shows for him. Newkirk said Jones told her David Stevens had run out of money.

Here, Newkirk laid a bomb on the detectives. She had

a good recall of a phone message David left for Kitabakel. It was romantic and flowery, and the kickboxer named Jason overheard it. In his rage, Jason tore up the apartment Kita and Newkirk shared. Several of Newkirk's figurines were broken during the outburst.

While the detectives were writing feverishly, Newkirk casually informed them Jason, Kitabakel, and she all practiced the Santerian religion. It is a form of voodoo, she explained to the wide-eyed detectives. She said she used candles, incense, and earthy things, while Jones and Jason dealt more in witchcraft and spells. On December 24, 1998, Kitabakel Jones told Newkirk she had to "get ghost," which Newkirk explained meant she had to leave the area.

Newkirk said she and Jones no longer were romantically involved. She said she was shipping out for Singapore on February 8. Showing them her military ID, she confirmed she was in the navy. The detectives obtained her Social Security number, which guaranteed they would always be able to locate her if she stayed in the military. They told her they would be in touch after they checked on some details.

Tefft and Young hotfooted it back to headquarters to let Team III in on the latest information. Experienced detectives know enough not to get too excited too soon about a possible break in a case, but they couldn't help themselves this time. This case had been a thorn in their sides for over two years. They'd had to endure second-guessing from the press, the police department administration, and the victim's family. Maybe they were finally going to get the break they needed, and, based on the amount of work performed, the break they believed they deserved.

Sergeant Martin and the previously quiet Dee Warrick frowned slightly when Young spoke about the Santerian religion and voodoo. Tefft was more restrained, yet believed they might possibly be onto something. Sergeant

Martin wasn't as excited about the apparent new break in the case, but believed the information had to be checked out. "Go for it," he said. "What do we have to lose?"

Young and Tefft met with Newkirk again on February 6. Young asked Newkirk if she knew he had interviewed Kitabakel Jones in 1999. Newkirk said Jones had told her she had spoken with "some cop." Newkirk said Jones wanted her to be present when Young interviewed her, possibly to be an alibi for her. Avoiding Jones's request, Newkirk made arrangements to be elsewhere when Young arrived.

Newkirk said Jones was nervous about some credit card receipts. Newkirk thought the receipts were from David Stevens's card. However, Tefft had already gone over Stevens's bank and credit card records, and everything had checked out. He would take a second look. Tefft had gone over each entry in detail. Stevens's credit card account had yielded no mysteries. But he would look again. Newkirk said Kitabakel Jones always had guys pay for things for her. Guys would make her car payment and sometimes pay portions of her rent. She thought the credit card from David Stevens might have been used for that. Tefft was still skeptical but made a mental note to look again at Stevens's account. Newkirk said her ship-out date had been changed to the end of February.

Later, Tefft confirmed that Stevens's credit card had no connection with Kitabakel Jones. Where was this leading?

About two weeks after the February 6 interview, Newkirk phoned the Homicide office. Her military assignment had been changed, and she was staying in San Diego. She said she had not been completely honest in the two previous interviews and wanted to talk again.

Sergeant Martin shook his head. "She waits two years to talk to us, and then doesn't really volunteer to come forward. Some guy rats her out while they're watching

the Super Bowl. Then, she isn't honest for two interviews and wants to come clean now. Something stinks."
Tefft clenched his jaw in anger and shook his head in
agreement.

Their next interview with Newkirk, on February 23,
was audio and video recorded in an interview room in the
Homicide office. Newkirk said she lived off and on with
Kita Jones from 1995 until 1998. During this time, Jones
had a few boyfriends. She said Kita danced under several
names over the years. Kita was known as "December,"
"Katriana," and finally, "India," the name she was using
when she danced at Dancer's.

According to Newkirk, Kita was having problems with
one of her boyfriends named John. She asked Kathie
Newkirk to put a spell on him. Not only that, Kita wanted
spells put on several people. According to Newkirk, who
said she herself was trying to get higher in the Santerian
religion, it is not correct to put too many spells on too
many people. Putting numerous spells is akin to "spread-
ing yourself too thin." It just isn't done.

At first, Kita wanted a spell to get John back. Then, she
wanted a spell to kill John. Newkirk had to tell Kita it (the
Santerian religion) didn't work like that. Newkirk was
talking faster than the detectives could take notes, even
though the interview was being recorded. She said a
Polero (a form of Santerian high priest) named Vladimir
had cleansed Kita after David's murder. Vladimir is from
Cuba and was very high in Santeria. Newkirk said she,
too, was a Polero and was trying to elevate herself in Santeria. She couldn't help Kita because she was emotionally
involved with Kita, and Santeria didn't allow that kind of
activity. Newkirk said Santeria was about control of the
mind and that is what Kitabakel wanted to do. To say the
detectives were confused at this overload of information
would be an understatement.

Nonetheless, Newkirk kept going at rapid-fire speed,

her low voice often not being picked up by the tape recorder. The detectives learned the "Jason" previously referred to by Newkirk was Jason Van Dusen. Newkirk identified a picture of Van Dusen as being the correct Jason.

She said Jason used to have a shaved head. He claimed to be a champion kickboxer. He told Newkirk he once was dead for three days. Jason loved Kita, but Kita didn't love him. Newkirk said Kita merely used Van Dusen for money.

So far, the interview had not exactly been enlightening. The detectives wondered when they were going to get to the part about someone killing David Stevens. Newkirk said she received a call from Kita's brother on Christmas Eve. He was furious, saying Kita was in big trouble. He asked Newkirk if she put Kita up to killing the guy and burning his car. Newkirk told the brother she didn't know what he was talking about. The brother then asked Newkirk if she knew who put Kita up to killing the guy. The brother asked Newkirk if she had taught Kita how to do the voodoo stuff. Newkirk said that although Santeria was similar to voodoo, it was actually different. The brother then asked Newkirk, "Did you tell my sister in order for her to right things that she had to burn a body up?" Newkirk denied it. The brother said Jason was in on it, then terminated the phone call.

The detectives hung on these words because they were finally getting to the topic of murder. Newkirk then went into an explanation of parts of Santeria. She explained that while her own spirit (Orisha) is water, Kita's Orisha is fire. In order for Kita to get rid of her problems, she would have to burn them. When Newkirk and Kita were discussing problems, Newkirk said she unwittingly told Kita that if somebody had wronged her, she would have to kill the person, then burn the body to rid the person's spirit from her. If someone wronged Newkirk, whose Orisha was water, she would have to cleanse herself by means of water. She would have to put the body in a lake or a large body of water.

Newkirk said she paged Kita just after Kita's brother hung up on her. When Kita called, she told Newkirk to call her only from pay phones in the future. When Newkirk asked Kita what was going on, Kita merely said, "He's dead." Kita told Newkirk she wanted Newkirk to accompany Jason back to David's apartment to look for a receipt for something that cost $1,600. Newkirk didn't know specifically what the item was, only that it was a receipt.

Newkirk said, "You want me to go to a dead man's house? Are you crazy?" Newkirk did not go. She said she had never been to David Stevens's apartment. Kita wanted Newkirk to stand guard while Jason climbed in David's window to look for the receipt. Kita told Newkirk she couldn't be seen at David's.

Newkirk said she pressed Kita for details, but received few. Kita told Newkirk, "[things] just got out of hand." Newkirk asked Kita why she burned the guy up. Kita said, "Didn't you tell me to?" Newkirk said she had only explained to Kita the crux of the Santerian spirit that Kita's Orisha was fire. Newkirk now claimed she didn't tell Kita to burn anyone. Kita didn't go into details, only saying that David, "Got shot and burned the fuck up."

The detectives said they would have to speak with Kita's brother, who had called her. "You can't," Newkirk said. "He got killed, too."

With their heads spinning, the detectives confirmed the brother had been shot and killed on May 19, 1999, six months after David's death. The case, being handled by another team, was open. Yet an arrest was imminent. It had no connection to Santeria or anything exotic.

CHAPTER 12

Newkirk transferred to the East Coast shortly after David's murder. She was only too happy to be away from the turmoil of the murder and the soap opera of Kitabakel Jones's love life.

Newkirk told the detectives she and Jones stayed in contact only sporadically since then. Jones told her about her original interview with the detectives. Jones apparently tried to tell Newkirk details about the murder on two different occasions, but Newkirk did not want to hear about it. She did not want to be involved. Newkirk finally said she was "kind of" ashamed she hadn't said anything until now. She rationalized by saying she wasn't there (at the murder) and couldn't tell the police things she didn't know about firsthand. Tefft silently mused that she could have told them things she had heard, and not limited her information to things she saw.

Newkirk said David Stevens and Jason Van Dusen knew each other. "Something was going on with steroids," she said. She indicated the two possibly supplied steroids for others. Newkirk supplied the first name of a girl from Dancer's who was a bodybuilder and supposedly obtained her steroids from Jason. Newkirk surmised that David was getting the steroids, and Kita and/or Jason was selling them. Newkirk said she thought David either stole the steroids or ordered them on his credit card. She said she saw Jason with a brown carton of steroids and that he had obtained them from David.

The detectives mused that perhaps private investigator John Stevens or Jeff Stout may have been correct about some aspect of the steroid theory. They didn't care. They wanted to solve a homicide. They would apologize to Stevens and Stout later.

Newkirk said she was present at Kita's place when Jason had a heated phone conversation with Stevens. Newkirk surmised Jason and David were arguing over the cost of the steroids. After Jason hung up, he told Newkirk he had no intention of paying David for the steroids. "In other words, they were going to rip David off," she said.

When Newkirk asked Jason where he was taking the steroids, Jason said he was going to sell them at Dancer's. "If you're going to get paid by someone from Dancer's, what is the problem with you paying David?"

"Fuck him," said Jason.

The detectives asked Newkirk to give her theory on what happened. "I don't really know what happened," she said. "I don't know if they tried to rob David or if David tried to rob them. I know something went wrong, and it got out of hand. I mean, David was into steroids. He wasn't all that clean. You should probably talk to that girl from Dancer's about the steroids, the bodybuilder."

Once again, the focus was back on steroids. Could it be possible John Stevens was right?

Cops get into trouble when they latch onto a theory and won't let go. They might form an opinion on a case and close themselves off to other theories. The detectives believed they had not locked themselves in on this case. They had been open-minded. They went where the facts took them. Aside from the sensational proclamations of John Stevens about the death being steroid-related, this was the first time they had heard about steroids from someone else.

Detective Joe Cristinziani was less than enthusiastic while listening to Newkirk's ramblings about Santeria, voodoo, cleansing burning, purifying water, kickboxing champions, and steroids. All this was too much to process in one sitting. And she had not come forward on her own. Some clown watching a football game with her had snitched her off. Without that vigilant fan, she would never have spoken with the police. Newkirk was active duty in the United States Navy, for God's sake.

The meeting with Team III became unusually contentious. Sometimes even old, married couples had to clear the air. Where to go next? It didn't matter. They had to go wherever any lead took them. Team III regrouped and decided to explore the bodybuilder-stripper from Dancer's who supposedly bought steroids from Jason and Kita.

It took several days to track her down, including another trip to the Dancer's Club. Tefft had hoped he had seen the last of that place. The dancer they wanted worked as a receptionist for an insurance agency during the day. "Dawn" was an attractive, if not unusual looking, woman. She had some masculine characteristics, but real beauty, too. If you saw her out shopping, you would undoubtedly stare at her for a while.

She shook hands with John Tefft and J. R. Young with a firm grip and sinewy forearm. Tefft waited for her to say, "Wanna arm wrestle?"

Dawn was surprisingly pleasant and at ease, in spite of being interviewed by two serious homicide detectives.

She said she had used steroids a few times when an important bodybuilding competition was approaching. In order to get her skin stretched, she would lift weights feverishly and drink only a few ounces of water each day, accompanied by a diet of baked, skinless chicken breasts. It was at that moment Tefft realized why he decided not to be a bodybuilder. Near dehydration and bland chicken breasts were not his idea of fun.

Dawn remembered David from Dancer's. For Dawn, being a stripper was not her main occupation, nor her goal in life. She did it for the money. Being a bodybuilder, exhibiting her body in a bar was not that much different from posing on a competitive stage. In bodybuilding, the judges did not tip you. Of course, you could keep your bikini top on when competing. She did not have the jaded opinion of men that many of the other strippers had. Dawn was at Dancer's to do a job, show her stuff, and get paid. She did not dance for private parties after hours.

She explained that the girls actually had to pay a small fee to work at Dancer's. Then, they had to split their tips. In spite of this, she made a pretty good supplemental income. She enjoyed competing in bodybuilding events, and she enjoyed her job at the insurance agency. Dawn was the smartest stripper they had encountered so far.

Dawn never bought steroids from David. She recognized a picture of Jason; she didn't like him. He often stayed in the back area of Dancer's, shooting pool. She did speak with David many times. They spoke about bodybuilding competitions. They even spoke about steroids. She said David told her he had used them when he competed years ago. Dawn's trained eye told her David's slightly soft appearance meant he no longer competed or trained.

When the detectives told Dawn what Kathie Newkirk told them about the shipment of steroids around the time of David's death, Dawn shrugged her shoulders and said

she didn't know what the police were talking about. She
said she obtained the few doses of steroids at the health
club where she trained. Dancer's club had no connection
with steroids, as far as she knew. She knew Kitabakel
Jones, but never had a conversation with her about
steroids. As far as David's having a relationship with
Kitabakel, Dawn didn't think so. She said David was at
Dancer's a lot and spoke with a lot of the girls. But he
didn't date any of them, as far as she knew. She cautioned
that she was only at Dancer's part time. But when she was
there, there was no talk or activity relative to steroids that
she knew about.

The detectives left Dawn's place of employment even
more puzzled than when they arrived. It was time to delve
into Santeria.

CHAPTER 13

The biggest enemy of a homicide detective, besides laziness, is a closed mind. Any supervisor should be able to deal with a lazy homicide detective. The lazy detective would be driving a patrol car on graveyard shift in a matter of weeks. Having a closed mind is worse than being lazy. Cops have to go where the facts lead them in a homicide case. They can't have preconceived ideas and knock a square-pegged theory into a round-holed-fact situation just to make it fit.

Prior to meeting Kathie Newkirk, the steroid theory was that square peg, and it just didn't fit. Doctor Jeff Stout and private investigator John Stevens, and even more lately, TC Luoma, the eccentric columnist from *Testosterone Magazine*, were the only people who claimed steroids were at the heart of this case.

Now, on her own, Kathie Newkirk supplied information relative to steroids. But Newkirk's information didn't have to do with the sale of steroids within the sports supplement business. Nor did her statements have to do with competition within the industry or the sale of customer lists. The latest theory from Kathie Newkirk had to do with a ripoff of drugs among users and the death of someone who wanted to be paid for the drugs he had supplied. To add to this, Newkirk had injected a love interest between David Stevens and Kitabakel Jones that Jason Van Dusen objected to. The new twist supplied by Newkirk added confusion. The detectives knew what they had to do: check everything out.

J. R. Young bought a book about Santeria. He devoured the contents, reporting back with information extensive enough to write a college term paper. He familiarized himself with the terminology. He explored the customs and rituals. In spite of his research, he found nothing in the Orisha of fire that talked about killing anyone, or burning a body. The fire referred to in Santeria was burning candles or incense. The Orisha of water consisted of sprinkling holy water. It didn't have anything to do with drowning someone. Like the square peg, this Santeria theory didn't fit. Yet it couldn't be discounted, at least not yet.

They even put a wire (tape recorder) on Kathie Newkirk and sent her into a session with Vladimir, the Santerian Polero. Newkirk would try to see if Vladimir would say he had counseled Kita either before or after the killing, about the subject of killing. In spite of their checking out the equipment before Newkirk went in, the transmission was a garbled mess. Monitoring detectives couldn't hear either of them well enough to discern what they were saying. Newkirk told them Vladimir didn't say anything of value. Another wasted day.

The detectives attempted to contact Kita Jones. She didn't return their calls. Then, she moved away from San Diego. Her mother wouldn't supply her new location, saying she didn't know it.

Since Team III was having no luck locating Kita, they tried to get Kathie Newkirk to help. She couldn't, or wouldn't, do it. Her excuses were numerous, and in the detectives' eyes, weak. Was it possible Newkirk didn't want them to talk to Kita? They knew they had to sit Kita down and get information from her. They would confront her on the statements Newkirk made, either confirming or eliminating them. Some of the detectives thought Newkirk was either being untruthful or being creative with facts—creative to the point of turning the so-called facts into fiction. If one could ever say being a homicide detective was "fun," this wasn't one of those times.

Since finding and speaking with Kita was proving to be difficult, the team decided to focus on Jason Van Dusen. In an investigation, you always try to find, and exploit, the weak link. If Jason was the weak link, they could get information from him to build on. If he was the killer, they could tie Kita into the murder, if she was indeed involved. If Kita was the killer, Jason might somehow implicate her, if he had the knowledge.

J. R. Young called Jason Van Dusen on September 11, 2001, one of the most turbulent days in the history of the country. In the generation of the homicide detectives, it was certainly the most important day since November 22, 1963. None of them had been around for December 7, 1941, although they accused L. D. Martin of having enlisted shortly after Pearl Harbor.

Arrangements were made for Van Dusen to come to headquarters for an interview on September 13.

From the get-go, Van Dusen was a strange character. Just as "turbulent" doesn't do justice to September 11, 2001, "strange" falls short of describing Jason Van Dusen. John Tefft took the lead, and J. R. Young sat in on the interview. Van Dusen tried to control the meeting. He told them he had a lot of information and it was so much they should tape record and not bother to take notes. Tefft ignored him initially until Van Dusen brought up the subject again when he saw Tefft writing. Tefft, in his polite and understated manner, thanked Van Dusen, but told him he had been doing interviews a long time, and this is the way he did them. The interview was being recorded anyway.

Van Dusen said he had met a girl named Angelica in downtown San Diego at a nightspot in 1998, although Van Dusen said he wasn't good with dates and times. Angelica told Jason she worked at Dancer's, a place he had never heard of. She invited him to drop by. Jason showed up one night. Even though Angelica was not there, Kitabakel Jones was dancing when Van Dusen walked in. That night, Jason and Kita talked a lot, even though Kita was working. They exchanged phone numbers. Tefft noted that almost all of the strippers he had spoken with so far would never give their number to a customer. Yet Kita's number had been found in David Stevens's book, and she had given it to Jason Van Dusen the first night they met. Kita was not the usual kind of stripper.

Van Dusen said Kita called him three days later, telling him she was in love with him. Van Dusen spoke in earthy terms to the detectives. His profanity-laced recitation implied that he never had a woman come on to him this aggressively in the past. He was overwhelmed, but flattered. Van Dusen provided explicit details of unverified sex acts with Kita that sounded more like bragging than anything else. The cops didn't ask for graphic details but Van Dusen rattled them off anyway. They never learned, and never tried to learn, whether Van Dusen was telling the truth about the sex.

Van Dusen told of several gifts he bought for Kita. He also bought groceries for her. This was in keeping with what Kathie Newkirk said Kita had men do for her. Van Dusen went on and on about Kita and about her murdered brother. Van Dusen had been her brother's friend. Van

Dusen had vowed to Kita's mother that he wouldn't rest until the killer of her son was brought to justice.

Tefft and Young decided it was time to bring up the subject of David Stevens. They hadn't told Van Dusen why they were interviewing him. He didn't seem to care. Van Dusen was happy to be talking nonstop about his sexual prowess with Kita and about her life, and rattling on about vengeance for her dead brother.

They showed him a smiling picture of Stevens. He said he did not know the man. He asked if it was one of Kita's boyfriends, saying she liked white guys. Then, he asked if Stevens was a bouncer at Dancer's. Like the lightbulb in the cartoons coming on, Jason Van Dusen's facial expression changed as he seemed to remember that Tefft and Young were homicide detectives. He asked them if the guy in the picture was alive. When Young told him the guy was dead, Van Dusen became excited. "I never saw him at the bar where India worked."

Detective Young then decided to use a shock tactic. He showed Van Dusen a picture of the charred corpse of David Stevens. Young asked Van Dusen if he had ever seen David Stevens like this.

Van Dusen's response sent them temporarily reeling. "That's him?" asked Jason. "You know what? You know what's kind of weird? I'm kind of psychic. I felt something once where my body was going to be set on fire, that my body was going to be burned up down at the beach. I'm just too lunatic for someone to come up and grab me. I mean if somebody came at me with a knife or a gun, I'm *whoa*!" Van Dusen put his hands up in the classic "surrender" position. "But I had a feeling that I was going to be burned like that."

Van Dusen, interested mainly in talking about himself, went on to tell the detectives that sometimes he believed he was possessed by voodoo African magic, whatever that meant. He said he sometimes heard voodoo chants inside his head, explaining black people did that to him. Young and Tefft looked at each other, possibly waiting for the theme from *Twilight Zone* to start playing in their own heads. It didn't.

Van Dusen then made a leap in logic back onto the track where the detectives were. "So the guy in the picture knew Kita, eh? Did that guy get killed because of Kita?"

Without saying anything Young nodded his head affirmatively.

"What did the guy do to deserve this? I got to tell you, I think this is devil worshipping. I think this is human sacrifice. I think this is pure evil. I think it is Satanic."

Young showed Van Dusen a photo of Stevens's burned car. "I've never seen this car before. I don't want to look at these anymore."

The detectives shifted gears slightly in the interview. Young asked him if, back in 1998, if he were so twisted and so blind with love for Kita that he might have done things for her. Would he have helped her out of a difficult situation with someone? Van Dusen interrupted before Young could finish.

"Yeah, I would have helped her. But, with the law, I wouldn't have done anything that would have brought harm to anyone. I would have done it correctly. I wouldn't have done anything that would have caused a loss of life. I am not capable of killing anyone. I will live my life without taking another person's life. I know the consequences of murder."

Van Dusen pointed at the picture of the murdered David Stevens. "Don't say I did this. That really pisses me off. I'm not involved in any murders. The only murder I was involved in is trying to find out who killed Kita's brother."

Young asked Van Dusen if it was possible Kita may have called him and asked for his help, perhaps *after* Stevens had already been killed. Young gave Van Dusen a way to ease into the situation without saying he had killed Stevens. Young suggested maybe Kita needed some assistance and, out of love and devotion, maybe it was possible he was pulled into that situation [disposing of the body].

Van Dusen denied having any part in doing anything relating to the death, burning, or abandoning of the body of David Stevens.

They asked Van Dusen if he would be willing to give fingerprints and a DNA sample. Van Dusen said he needed to have a cigarette and think about it. The detectives accompanied him outside. After all, this was California, and smoking was not allowed in any public building anywhere. Even if you had a murderer who was on the verge of confessing, you couldn't let him smoke in the police station. You had to break the continuity of the interview and take him outside to smoke. The old days when a detective would pull a deck of Lucky Strikes out of his pocket and shake one out to the crook were over.

Once back inside, Van Dusen announced he would not provide fingerprints and a DNA sample. But he would consent to a polygraph test.

At 12:08 P.M., Jason Van Dusen took a polygraph exam at police headquarters. He failed.

CHAPTER 14

Van Dusen was livid when informed he had failed. He said he was done with the San Diego Police Department Homicide Unit. He said the killer of Kita's brother was going to jail when the killer was caught and that was all Van Dusen cared about. He vehemently denied knowing David Stevens. He said he failed the test because the detectives showed him the pictures of the dead David Stevens, and the graphic nature of the photos upset him. Van Dusen continued to rant, saying he knew nothing about steroids or bodybuilding.

"If I was a murderer, I wouldn't have come down here. I don't fit the psychological profile of somebody who would kill somebody and burn them."

Van Dusen said he would do anything in his power to keep Kita out of prison. He knew she was not a killer nor a murderer.

"Well, that is all I have to say. Goodbye."

Jason Van Dusen left the police station at 2:08 P.M. He was still on the list of suspects, as was Kitabakel Jones.

• • •

At the next meeting of Team III, Young and Tefft told the others about the interview and polygraph of Jason Van Dusen. One detective said Van Dusen was "looney tunes." On top of that, Van Dusen started phoning Tefft and Young, leaving voice messages. Sometimes, during the night, Van Dusen would leave over twenty messages. The repeated calls became so bad they started to tape the messages to keep for the future, thinking the messages might be important. Detective Tefft thought the only use the tapes would have would be in providing an insanity defense if Van Dusen were ever arrested and charged.

Even though Van Dusen had refused to provide fingerprints voluntarily, the detectives weren't dismayed. They already had his prints from a previous arrest. The prints checked negative.

It was now imperative for them to locate and talk to Kitabakel Jones. Because of their interviews, Jones looked like the best suspect so far. Van Dusen was right up there with Jones because of the failed polygraph and his volatile, often irrational, conduct. If anyone was capable of snapping and doing immediate violence to someone, it was Jason Van Dusen.

They took the case to Deputy District Attorney Chandra Carle to keep her up to date. The tall, attractive Carle stroked her light brown hair as she listened to J. R. Young. She adjusted herself in her chair when he was done. Without saying anything at first, she just shook her head. "It isn't there," said Carle, her eyes widening, in sad disappointment. "You don't have evidence of a murder, or a burning. You have a stripper who vanished. You have a nut case who flunked a polygraph. Maybe they're the ones who did it. But we can't prove it to anyone right now with what you have."

They asked Carle to put what they had in front of the grand jury. In California, grand juries are made up of private citizens. They will listen to what witnesses have to say. At the conclusion of the prosecution's case, they vote to indict or not indict. In nearly all of the cases before them, grand juries issue indictments.

The good part, for the prosecution, is that there are no defense attorneys in the confidential setting of the grand jury. There is no cross-examination of witnesses. The grand jury only gets to hear one side of the case. It has been said cynically that a good prosecutor could indict a grapefruit for murder if given a chance.

Also, a grand jury indictment can take the place of a preliminary hearing and send the accused directly to trial. In a preliminary hearing, the prosecution must prove two things: There is probable cause to believe a crime was committed, and probable cause to believe the accused committed the crime.

Chandra Carle told them she wasn't taking those facts before a grand jury. She knew, even if she could get an indictment, she couldn't get a conviction. "You have the wrong people," Carle said. "Van Dusen and Newkirk are unbalanced and attention seekers. They might be murderers, but they aren't murderers in this case, at least not with the evidence we have."

The detectives wanted the case before the grand jury. It was, they believed, their last hope. They also realized that Chandra Carle would be the one facing the heat if the end result, after the indictment, was an acquittal. The detectives were frustrated. They had done everything they knew possible. They wanted to "air it out" and see what happened to their case in the light of day, examined by a judge and jury. They were upset by Carle's response. But in the end, they knew she was correct. It was back to work.

Unfortunately, Team III's "up" duty came at a most inopportune time, and they were out of service for a few weeks. When they could get back to the David Stevens case, they developed a plan. As with any plan worth its weight, this one took money and manpower, two things the San Diego Police Department was lacking.

Team I had investigated the murder of Kita's brother. Although it took them a long time to solve it, they identified a suspect and obtained a warrant for him. The suspected killer, Marvin Locke, was still on the loose, however. The detectives on Team I had developed a cordial relationship with Kita's mother.

On October 10, 2001, at the request of Team III, Detective Joe Howie from Team I called Kita's mother. The call was a ruse to find Kita. Howie asked Kita's mother if Kita was in San Diego. Mom appeared suspicious, asking Howie why he needed to speak with Kita. He said he was trying to find Marvin Locke, the man for whom they had the murder warrant.

Kita's mother informed Howie that Kita would not have any idea where Marvin Locke was. It was then Howie told her that Jason Van Dusen said Kita might have information on Locke. Howie needed to speak with Kita to learn that information. Kita's mother said Jason was crazy and had been stalking and harassing Kita for some time. In fact, that was why she had moved away. Howie asked for Kita's phone number and was refused. She said a "Detective Young" once interviewed Kita about a different murder. The detective treated Kita like a suspect, something that did not sit well either with Kita or her mother.

Kita's mother said, "My daughter is an exotic dancer, and she used to dance at a club in San Diego where she met a man who got murdered. Detective Young spoke to my daughter and treated her like she killed the guy. I know she didn't have anything to do with his death because my baby was home with me that entire night. I have to protect my baby."

Later that afternoon, Detective Howie received a pre-arranged conference call between Kitabakel Jones, her mother, and Howie. Kita said she did not know the where-abouts of Marvin Locke. Kita told Howie that Jason Van Dusen had mental problems. His actions in the past caused her to move from San Diego to Las Vegas, where she currently lived. She would not provide her phone number or address. At least they now knew where Kita lived.

It was now time to implement the "plan" the detectives hoped might solve the murder of David Stevens.

Phase one involved finding out where Kitabakel Jones lived and worked. She told detective Howie she lived in Las Vegas. The Las Vegas Metro Police Department has one of the best vice units in the United States. It has to be the best, because there is so much opportunity for vice vi-olations.

Every strip club in Vegas must keep accurate records on their dancers. The comings and goings of the girls is well documented. Stripping is such a transitory profession that a girl might work in one club one week, then move down the street to another one the next week, or even work at more than one club at a time.

Kitabakel Jones worked at a place called The Library. The elaborate plan called for several officers to stay in Vegas for a few days. Normally, checking out strip clubs in Las Vegas would be considered good duty. However, this plan was going to be very involved and would de-mand constant attention and effort on the part of the offi-cers. In other words, more work than play. The veteran detectives didn't miss the irony in the name of the club where Kita worked. Cristinziani said, "It's perfect. The wife asks the husband where he's going. He says, 'To the Library.' I like it. She probably wonders why he always takes a handful of dollar bills, though."

The plan was for an undercover officer to go to Kita's

strip club and pose as a customer. The detective would already have a hotel room rented near the club. The room would be set up with electronic surveillance equipment, both audio and video.

Then, the officer would go to the strip club and become a "customer" of Kitabakel Jones. Here is where the plan would get tricky. Las Vegas Metro Police told John Tefft that the strip business was in business to fleece the male customers. The fleecing was legal, but it was fleecing nonetheless. At a club of the type Kita Jones worked, a stripper would dance her set on the stage, usually two or three songs. Then, she would saunter seductively around the bar and tables, picking up her tips. If a guy really liked her, the customer and stripper would retire to the back portion of the club where she could perform a "couch" dance for him. This usually cost $100 for four songs.

During the couch dance, the floor man would walk back and forth nearby, keeping a watchful eye on things.

If the couch dance went well, the dancer might suggest a more "private" dance in one of the back rooms. When she said "private," she might wink at the customer. This dance usually cost $500 for about an hour "show." The back room encounter involved a bottle of champagne and who knows what else.

Somehow, the undercover officer had to get Kita to skip the private show in the back room at the club and accompany him to his hotel room, previously equipped with audio and video recording gear, in order for "THE PLAN" to begin.

The undercover officer slated to do this job was a rather rough-looking gentleman from the Narcotics unit. He appeared muscular and dangerous. Hopefully, he could convince Kita to go to his room at the nearby hotel for a more intimate show. Once in his room, he would tell her he really didn't want a private show. He would tell Kita he really was a parolee who had spent time in a halfway house with Jason Van Dusen. He would tell Kita that Jason told him about the David Stevens murder and how both Jason and Kita were involved. Since a reward existed for information on the murder, the parolee was interested in the money. However, because of his prior experience with the police, he didn't want to deal with them.

The undercover officer/parolee would tell Kita she needed to pay him money to keep quiet and not go to the police, although he would go to the police as a last resort if she refused to pay. After all, money was money.

This part of "THE PLAN" involved Kita's hopefully making some incriminating statements about herself or Van Dusen if she really was involved in the murder of David Stevens. She might say something like, "We killed him, but you can't prove it." In the absence of a type of admission of guilt, she might actually offer to pay money for the parolee's silence. Either act would be admissible toward the guilt of Kitabakel Jones. They would not arrest Jones, but would use this encounter and her reaction to build their case.

John Tefft wrote up the operational plan. Included in the memo was an estimate of what it would cost, both in man hours, and in money. A meeting was set up with Tefft and Captain Ron Newman. Newman was less than enthusiastic. He was skeptical. The Bible refers to "weeping and gnashing of teeth" in some encounters. There wasn't any weeping in this meeting, but there was a hell of a lot of gnashing of teeth.

Newman wanted Tefft to guarantee the plan would work. Newman pointed out too much money was involved to have the result be a "maybe." Tefft was livid with Newman's mention of a guarantee. Even though he was merely a detective and Newman was a captain, Tefft spoke his mind forcefully. "We can't guarantee anything, damnit," Tefft fumed at his superior. "We gotta go over there, do our job, and hope for the best. Nothing's for sure. We gotta do this to get some kind of resolution for this damned thing. We've been messing with it for years. You know that. You've been on the hot seat on this case yourself. We don't know what the hell's going to happen over there. But we gotta at least try. This is the first decent lead we've had in a long time. We gotta look at it." Tefft's face and eyes, normally placid, burned with emotion, barely controlled.

Perhaps because Newman had been involved with the disgruntled Stevens family and the annoying private investigator John Stevens, and had to answer pointed questions from the press, Newman reluctantly agreed to let them do it for a three-day, two-night stint.

Deputy District Attorney Dave Lattuca, the liaison to the San Diego Police Department reviewed the operational plan, along with Bill Holman, a deputy district attorney in the appellate division of the D.A.'s office. The attorneys were looking for possible entrapment issues, but found none. With the blessing of the D.A.'s office, and the reluctant, qualified blessing of the San Diego Police Department, Team III and one scroungy, tough-looking undercover cop set out for "Sin City."

Amid the flashy neon lights of Vegas, the headaches began. Kitabakel Jones no longer worked at The Library. She now worked at the Spearmint Rhino, whatever the hell that meant. They found out where Kita lived. They also learned she was living with a male county jail corrections officer.

When the police tried to learn Jones's work schedule, they were met with another glitch. There is no schedule for a Las Vegas stripper. The girls work when they feel like it. As was the case in San Diego, the girls have to pay the club a certain amount per shift in order to work. The tips must be split with the house, too.

The San Diego undercover officer had a picture of

Kita. He went to the Spearmint Rhino and nursed a couple of beers for a few hours. No Kita. John Tefft and Joe Cristinziani paid the cover charge and also nursed their beers, closely guarding their dollar bills stacked in front of them. The hours went by. No Kita.

Two officers had been watching the apartment where Kita and the corrections officer lived. They weren't even sure if Kita and her man were home. One of the officers knocked on Kita's door to see if someone was there. The male answered. A weak reason was given for the intrusion, with the police officer trying to look past the man to see if Kita was inside. Nothing productive came of that.

The police repeated that routine the next day. Unfortunately, the results were the same: no Kita. Lots of strippers. Some beer. A glum Team III headed back to San Diego. Although the undercover officer felt bad he didn't get to play his role, he didn't have the same emotional stake as Team III. No one felt worse than John Tefft. He had to report to Newman that the thousand-plus dollars in salary and per diem costs for meals were for naught.

CHAPTER 15

October 2001 came and went. In December, it would be three years Team III had been pursuing this case. Three long, frustrating, disappointment-packed years. Back in Nebraska, and up in Oregon, two guys named Stevens would be shaking their heads and saying, "I told you so," if they knew what had happened in Las Vegas.

A single telephone call would soon change that.

On November 7, 2001, the phone rang in the Homicide office. A word processor operator filling in at the reception desk during the lunch hour took the phone call that would signal a change in the case.

One of the attractions of police work is that a street cop never knows what will happen every day when he or she goes to work. Police administrators and the bean counters who control the department's purse strings seldom venture out on the street except for lunch, so they don't experience the same uncertainty as patrol cops. The days of administrators are predictable: meetings, number crunch-

ing, and policy setting. Not so for people who wear guns
and respond to radio calls.

The story of never knowing what is going to happen was
the same for Team III back on November 7, 2001. It was
another day of tracking down leads, following up on information that had come in on yet another recent case.
While not forgotten, the case of David Stevens was definitely on the back burner. The failed operation in Las
Vegas appeared to be the last hope of the dedicated detectives. The Las Vegas fiasco seemed to be a bitter finale to
an already frustrating case. The David Stevens murder investigation wasn't dead; but it barely had a pulse.

On November 7, 2001, at about 1:15 P.M., word processor operator Rebecca Aguilar was toiling at her desk
within the Homicide Unit. Aguilar answered the phone. A
woman caller said she was at work in San Diego. During
lunch, the woman's friend related she had witnessed a
murder three years ago. The murderer was now threatening the woman who had witnessed the murder.

Aguilar asked to speak with the woman who was the
witness. Upon Aguilar's asking her, the woman said her
name was Ny (pronounced NEE) Nourn. Knowing what
was necessary to get to the bottom of the mysterious call,
Aguilar asked the name of the victim. When Aguilar heard
it was David Stevens, she asked Nourn to stay on the line.
Aguilar transferred the call to J. R. Young, whose heart
soon began a rapid, involuntary pounding.

In response to Young's questions, Nourn gave enough
information to let him know they were talking about
someone who *might* actually have knowledge of the murder. Nourn knew about a shooting, a burning, and the
abandonment of a body inside a convertible in La Jolla.
Anyone could know that. But, since the case was so old,
almost everyone in San Diego had forgotten those details.

Young learned Nourn was now at a mortgage company

where she worked just north of La Jolla. He obtained an exact address of the company, then paged John Tefft. Would Ny Nourn's information lead to another steroid-Santerian-voodoo-gangland style–espionage wild goose chase, or was it the real deal? They would soon find out.

Before starting the fifteen-mile drive to the office building, Detective Young researched Ny Nourn in the case file. She had been an employee of Perfect Match and had been interviewed because her telephone number was on the caller ID box in Stevens's apartment. During the brief telephone interview back in January 1999, Nourn said she had made one phone call to David Stevens's apartment. She told the detective she had called David one time at home to ask about her work schedule. Stevens had been her supervisor. Nourn quit shortly after Stevens's murder. With Nourn actually having worked at Perfect Match, maybe they were onto something at last? When interviewed, none of the people at Perfect Match had mentioned Ny Nourn as being possibly involved in the death of David Stevens. She was a peripheral, part-time employee. Nothing more.

The detectives went into a private office with Ny Nourn. Looking almost like a child, Nourn was just under five feet tall and weighed around one hundred pounds, if that. She appeared Asian. The detectives eventually learned Nourn had been born in Thailand and had come to the United States with her parents as a young girl. Nourn had turned twenty-one the month before. If she had truly witnessed the murder of David Stevens, she was only eighteen at the time. Nourn's co-worker was allowed to sit in on the initial session, in order to help Nourn feel at ease. Nourn was quiet and respectful to the officers. She spoke almost inaudibly, carefully choosing her words in slightly accented English.

In a fifteen-minute monologue, uninterrupted by the

detectives, she told them she had a boyfriend named Ron Barker, whom she had met on the Internet over three years earlier. Despite Barker being married and, at thirty-five, twice her age, the two became lovers, developing an almost everyday relationship. As the years went by, Barker became possessive of Nourn and physically abusive toward her.

Nourn said she started working at Perfect Match in November 1998. David Stevens was her boss. Nourn liked Stevens, finding him attractive. Stevens was attracted to her also, and Stevens quietly asked her out more than once. She always refused, in spite of her attraction to him, because of the jealousy of Ron Barker.

Nourn said December 22 was her day off. Stevens invited her to a movie after he got off work at 9:00 P.M. She agreed to meet David at Perfect Match, and they would leave for the movie from there. Nourn said they were careful not to let anyone at Perfect Match know they were seeing each other. Stevens told her he had a problem with a female employee when he worked somewhere else, and he didn't want anyone to know he was seeing someone who worked for him.

When they started talking in the parking lot of Perfect Match, Nourn became uneasy about going to a movie for fear her boyfriend would find out somehow. They decided to go to David Stevens's apartment instead. She followed Stevens there.

Once at Stevens's apartment, they began watching television in his bedroom. Within a short time, they had sex. In response to Tefft's question, Nourn said her fingerprints probably were on the mirrored headboard. And, her DNA would probably be in the apartment, or on a drinking glass in the bedroom.

Tefft and Young still didn't know what they had, but they knew they had something. This innocent, quiet little girl knew things no one else did. Their investigation had taken them down so many blind alleys that ended up producing nothing. They couldn't believe something might finally be happening.

Nourn said she was at the apartment for about two hours. While they talked, Stevens encouraged her to dump her married boyfriend. Nourn said she was afraid to because he was so possessive. She eventually left the apartment. When she arrived at the home she shared with her parents, Barker was parked outside, waiting for her. Barker angrily confronted her and badgered her about where she had been. Somehow he knew she had had sex. Nourn, trying to minimize her brief affair with Stevens, told Barker Stevens had forced himself upon her. She told Tefft and Young she hoped Barker wouldn't be so mad at her if she said Stevens raped her. Barker's reaction was more than Nourn expected. Barker announced he was going to kill Stevens, and she was going to help him.

CHAPTER 16

Nourn said at first she didn't think Barker would kill Stevens. Barker began to make up a plan on the spot. He told Nourn they would lure Stevens from his apartment on a ruse that she had a flat tire. Nourn went along, thinking and hoping Barker would suddenly announce they weren't going through with it. They stopped by Barker's house, where she believed he obtained a gun, although she didn't see it at the time.

Barker dropped Nourn off at Stevens's apartment very late that night. (Perhaps the 3:05 A.M. call from the outside security telephone?) She told Stevens she had a flat tire and needed him to help her. Stevens drove Nourn in his car while they looked for Nourn's car, which supposedly was parked somewhere. The hastily hatched plan was for Barker to follow them and flash his headlights at them. Nourn had told Stevens her brother was also out looking for Nourn's car.

As they drove along Interstate 52, headlights began flashing behind them. She told David it was her brother

David Stevens was a 215-pound former champion wrestler.
But he was no match for two surprise bullets to the head.
Courtesy of the San Diego Police Department

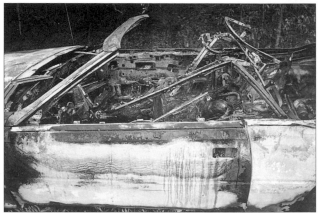

The convertible top was up, the windows were melted, and most of the body was burned beyond recognition in this early-morning car fire . . . a fire that turned out to be a homicide.
Courtesy of the San Diego Police Department

Once firefighters put out the vehicle fire they discovered a charred corpse in the front seat.
Courtesy of the San Diego Police Department

Two sets of handprints on this mirrored headboard were lifted. The larger set belonged to the victim and the smaller set
belonged to the killer. Detectives spent three years trying to
find the owner of the smaller handprints.
Courtesy of the San Diego Police Department

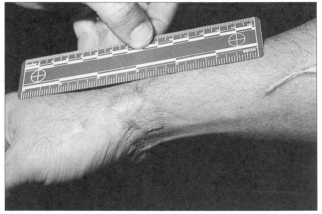

A defense witness said he saw the killer just weeks
after the murder, yet didn't notice the burn marks.
Courtesy of the San Diego Police Department

Ny Nourn was a shy eighteen-year-old alleged
to have a seemingly insatiable sexual appetite.
Courtesy of the San Diego Police Department

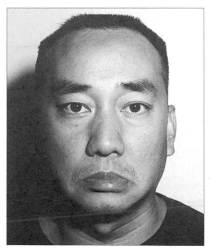

Ronald Barker. Or was it Ron Aragon? Or, was it Brandon?
Courtesy of the San Diego Police Department

San Diego Homicide Team III, past and present. (From left) Terry
Torgersen, John Tefft, Dee Warrick, J. R. Young, and Joe Cristinziani.
Sergeant L. D. Martin (not pictured) has retired.
Courtesy of Tom Basinski

Sergeant L. D. Martin (now retired). His police-leadership skills never wavered, in spite of second-guessing by an investigative news reporter. *Courtesy of Tom Basinski*

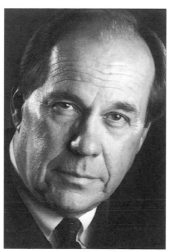

Judge Frederic Link presided over two murder trials involving the brutal murder of David Stevens.
Courtesy of Tom Basinski

Attorney Marc Carlos mounted a spirited defense
of defendant Ny Nourn.
Courtesy of Tom Basinski

Chandra Carle. The prosecution of David Stevens's killers
was a formidable task for the veteran prosecutor.
Courtesy of Tom Basinski

signaling them. She said David seemed puzzled at the co-
incidence of someone knowing what car Nourn was in.
Nonetheless, Stevens took an exit and pulled over. Barker
parked his car and climbed in the back seat of Stevens's
car.

They drove along surface streets, looking for Nourn's
"phantom" car. After directing Stevens to pull over,
Barker put his left arm around Stevens's neck and put a
gun up to his head on the right side. She said Barker said
something like, "How does it feel now to fuck somebody
else's girlfriend?" Then, Barker shot Stevens in the head.

Nourn said she thought she was next on the death list.
Terrified, she complied when Barker told her to get into
the back seat. Barker rolled Stevens over into the passenger seat. Then Barker drove Stevens's car. The three drove
back to Barker's where he obtained a gas can. Nourn followed them in Barker's car while Barker bought gas.

They drove to La Jolla and found a secluded spot just
off Interstate 5. Barker poured gas into the interior of the
vehicle and ignited it. She said the fireball from the car
burned off Barker's eyebrows and burned his arms. She
didn't think he went to the hospital or doctor.

Once away from the burning car, Barker told her she
was as guilty as he was and if he were ever arrested for
what had happened, she would "go down" for it also.
They made a pact never to tell anyone. Nourn felt confident no one at Perfect Match even knew she and Stevens
had been interested in each other.

Tefft and Young sat there, barely breathing, hanging on
every word this little girl from Thailand was saying. By
her appearance, it was unthinkable she could have been
involved in a murder. But one thing soon learned by police officers is that *anyone* is capable of doing *anything*.
She certainly knew a lot of facts about the murder, more
than anyone they had spoken with so far.

Tefft asked her why she was coming forward with this

information now, almost three years after the killing. It appeared they had committed the perfect crime. Nourn sighed, closed her eyes, and said she was just tired of the physical abuse from Barker. It was getting increasingly worse. Barker had beaten her with an aluminum bat two weeks earlier. She had obtained a restraining order against him one week earlier. The restraining order only complicated the situation, she said, because she feared he would kill her if she refused to see him.

Two days before the interview, Barker's wife had confronted her about the affair Nourn and Barker had been having. Barker's wife angrily told Nourn she knew what Nourn and Barker had done three years ago. The wife threatened to go to the police if Nourn would not continue to see Barker.

"Wait a minute," interjected Detective Young. "You're saying she insisted you *continue* to see Barker?"

"Yes," said Nourn. "She said Ron was happier and more easygoing when he was seeing me. When he was happy, it was better for her and the kids. She didn't want to see him unhappy."

Tefft and Young looked at each other. They couldn't wait to meet this piece of work.

Nourn said she couldn't take the beatings any longer. When Barker's wife insisted she continue to see Barker or else get exposed to the murder charges, Nourn decided to tell her co-workers. She was desperate, confused, frustrated, and afraid. If she continued to see Barker, he might kill her during one of the beatings. If she refused to see him, he might kill her because of the rejection. And if he didn't kill her because of that, his wife was going to tell the police she was a killer. All of those possibilities were unacceptable and would end up bringing her down. She knew firsthand Barker was capable of killing. She didn't want to be his next victim.

By now Tefft and Young knew they were on to something. Because of Nourn's specific knowledge, they knew this woman was involved. Now they had to make sure they handled everything correctly, both procedurally and legally. A reader of a murder mystery might say, "Okay, now we know who did it. Wasn't that a good story?" The detectives knew their work had only just begun. Courts demand proof. Handprints on a headboard only meant Ny Nourn probably had sex with David Stevens. They needed a lot more evidence. A gun would be nice. A confession from Barker would also be acceptable.

They asked Nourn if she would be willing to go to San Diego Police Headquarters for a more in-depth interview on tape. She agreed. They told her she was not under arrest and they would take her to her car, or wherever she wanted to go when they were done talking to her. She readily agreed. Tefft later said Nourn appeared to be relieved finally to get the burden of a murder involvement off her shoulders.

Later, when Tefft wrote his report, he specifically detailed how the detectives worded their proposition to Nourn at her place of employment. She rode with Tefft to the police station *without handcuffs*. She rode *in the front seat*. She *was not searched*. She *was treated like a witness*.

While Nourn was gathering her things in preparation for the ride to police headquarters, the detectives phoned prosecutor Chandra Carle at her desk in the Hall of Justice. "This woman knows all the details," they told Carle. Carle knew this person was not like Kathie Newkirk, who speculated, guessed, and possibly fabricated things as she went along. Carle knew the cops had the right person and now her work would really begin. She was happy, excited, exhilarated, and a little fearful, as any good competitor would be at the outset of such a demanding case.

The interview rooms at the police station are of the

"no-frills" style. The walls are bare, removing any chance a suspect might try to divert anyone's attention from what he might be saying. The tabletop is plain, hard, and functional. The chairs are comfortable enough to accommodate suspects for a few hours while they spill their guts, but not comfortable enough to encourage someone to fall asleep.

The video cameras are out of sight in the upper corner of the room. A suspect can tell where the camera is just by where the detective tells him or her to sit. No suspects are ever thinking about cameras when walking into these rooms. They are either planning and plotting their next lie, or preparing to tell the truth.

While it was true the detectives thought they were finally getting information from someone who actually knew something, and they were relieved to get this case wrapped up, their minds were actually preparing for a court battle months or years down the road. Every homicide detective everywhere knows that learning the story and getting the facts are important. Yet they must visualize everything they see and hear within the context of a courtroom. They must be prepared to have their statements scrutinized and dissected by a defense attorney. The thoughts and words they made on the fly will be examined under a microscope by defense attorneys who may take hours to read something a detective had one second to consider before making a decision. And so it goes during a homicide interview.

Detectives Tefft and Young took Ny Nourn to Interview Room #2 on the fourth floor of the police department at 1401 Broadway. The encounter was both audio and video taped. They gave her a glass of water. Young asked her several identifying questions such as date of birth, driver's license number, and Social Security number. Young repeated to her that she was not under arrest and would be going home, or wherever else she wanted, at the conclusion of the interview. He said they only wanted the truth from her, even if it was painful. Young specifically said she could be considered as a witness, or possibly as a coconspirator on a murder charge. The district attorney would evaluate the information and make a determination. She said she understood and would tell the truth, no matter what it meant to her personally.

Nourn said she met Barker in approximately August 1998. She saw his profile on the Internet. They corresponded and eventually met. She said he gave his first name as Brandon. She saw his profile on Digital City San Diego, an Internet chat room. Brandon asked her for her picture, and she sent one. After two or three days, they went to a movie.

When Barker came to pick her up, she had to climb out the back window of her house in order to meet him. Her parents wouldn't let her date at that time since she was only seventeen. Nourn said she was surprised when she first saw Barker. He told her he was twenty-seven. She thought he was in his forties. Later he told her he was thirty-three.

Barker and Nourn saw the movie *Blade* at a multiplex theater near her home. After the movie, they went to a motel and had sex. The detectives asked her if she knew how Barker paid for the room. They were thinking of corroborating information like a credit card receipt, or the hotel's registration files. Nourn stayed in the car and didn't know how the transaction of renting the room played out. The detectives began to wonder about this waiflike young woman. Only seventeen, she meets a man she thinks is in his forties, has one date to a movie with him, and goes directly to a motel for sex. Were they onto another flake, like many of the others they encountered in this case?

She said Barker was rather mysterious. He told her he was a gigolo. He also told her he was in the Mafia. Barker drove a black Lincoln Town Car, which to Nourn looked like a car a Mafioso might drive. Nourn added some confusion when she said she knew him as Brandon, then later she thought his name was Ron Aragon. Lately she learned his real name was Ron Barker.

Tefft asked, "If you told David Stevens that Ron was your brother, how could he believe that? You're Asian, aren't you?"

She said she was born in Thailand and Ron was born in Vietnam.

"With a name like Barker?" asked Young.

Barker had told her his father was white. She didn't believe him because he looked to be full-blooded Asian or Vietnamese. She thought his mother married a man named Barker and he took that name, or the man adopted him as a child. Barker was so mysterious to her, and so deceitful, she never really knew his full story.

The various names used by Barker added confusion to the interview. Barker sometimes used the last name of "Aragon." Nonetheless, things were rolling along. The detectives were collecting information, which, although sometimes puzzling, appeared to be on track. Nourn didn't know what work Barker did, but thought he formerly worked in some kind of automotive repair job.

Initially, Barker told her he was single, lived with his mother, yet had a child by another woman. She later learned that story was a lie, one that Barker stuck to, insisting he was not married. One time she went through his wallet and found a driver's license with the name "Ronald Ely Barker." She also found photo identification for "Ron Aragon." She thought Barker was the correct name.

On the night of the fatal date with David Stevens, Ny Nourn said she was very careful that Ron not find out about Stevens. Barker told her he had killed one girlfriend because she had cheated on him. John Tefft asked a question that would be very important in court at a later date.

Tefft: "Had he ever hurt you up to that point?"

Nourn: "No."

Tefft: "Never hit or abused you?"

Nourn: "He—he hit me that night, the night that happened."

Tefft: "Okay, but prior to that, had he ever hit you before?"

Nourn: "No."

In the absence of physical abuse, Nourn said Barker was verbally abusive. She further described him as "controlling, manipulative, and possessive."

"Despite all that, you decided to chance it and go out with David Stevens that night?" Detective Young asked.

"Right," Nourn said.

When they arrived at David's apartment, she parked her car in the secured lot in the space next to David's, a space reserved for visitors. Stevens cautioned her to be very quiet since he didn't want Carl to know she was there. "Carl" was Carl Withrow from Perfect Match, whom the detectives had interviewed the first day and several times after.

Once inside Stevens's apartment, he offered her a glass of juice. They went into his bedroom and lay across the bed, talking. Nourn was hesitant to get into specifics about their activities once on the bed. Detective Young attempted to put her at ease. "Keep in mind John and I've been cops for over twenty years. We've heard everything. You won't embarrass us. We need you to tell us everything, and it's gotta be in detail. There're reasons why we're gonna ask you certain questions."

After they were on the bed a short time, Stevens asked her if she wanted a massage. Nourn said, "Sure."

The massage progressed rapidly into foreplay. Nourn began performing oral sex on David almost immediately. She said it was dark in the room. They had a conversation about birth control and his use of a condom. Neither had a condom. She told him she just got off birth control, but not to worry. Stevens then fumbled for some lubricant. He never used it on her because she didn't need lubricating. She wasn't sure if he used any on himself or not.

After intercourse, she said David told her he, up until that point, was a "California virgin." Nourn and David laughed about his lost virginity.

In response to their question, Nourn told the detectives she was wearing burgundy lipstick, the same color they had found on the drinking glass. So far, this girl was telling them things that checked out and coincided with what they found at the scene. It was refreshing to hear facts that weren't laced with speculation, fueled by intrigue, or embellished with the stuff of pulp fiction.

When asked later if the detectives felt vindicated that the speculative dramatic theories of private investigator John Stevens were wrong, the detectives said they weren't even thinking about him. They were too busy solving a homicide. The theatrics of John Stevens were the last thing on their minds.

Nourn said she went into the bathroom and brushed her hair. The detectives remembered they had found hair in the bed and in the bathroom. Just as the detectives were about to move on to another topic, Nourn announced they had sex again. A short time later Nourn said she had to leave because her parents delivered newspapers and they left their house around 2:30 A.M. She had to be home by that time. Stevens made sure she knew how to get back to the freeway and safely home.

When she arrived home, Barker was parked in his Town Car on her street. Nourn said she started shaking because she knew she was in trouble. She went up to the driver's side and feebly greeted him, trying to feign joy at seeing him. Barker was quietly menacing, speaking slowly and deliberately. "Where you been?"

Flustered, and unrehearsed, Nourn said, "Wal-Mart."

She knew she wasn't convincing. She wished she could take back her answer. It was too late.

"How could you be at the Wal-Mart for that long?" Barker asked. "Did you buy anything?"

"No, I just looked around."

"Why didn't you respond to my pages?"

She told him she didn't have her pager with her.

"Get in the car." After she got in, he said, "So tell me, where did you really go."

Nourn mumbled that she couldn't lie to him. She said she was with her boss and she slept with him. She said Barker fumed, staring straight ahead at the steering wheel, saying nothing, breathing deeply and slowly.

"Get out," Barker said, a sneer forming on his face.

Then, Nourn began crying and begging him to forgive her. She told him she loved him. She told him to forget about it, that it would never happen again. Just to make Barker think she wasn't completely responsible, she said Stevens had forced himself on her.

"I want to talk to this guy," Barker said slowly, without emotion. "I'm gonna kill him."

Nourn pleaded with him to leave Stevens alone.

"No, you've been violated, you know. You're not pure anymore. You're used goods."

Nourn was desperate. "I'll do anything you want. Please don't hurt David."

They drove in their separate vehicles to Barker's house. Before arriving there, he pulled over on a side street near his house. Ordering her out of her vehicle, he made her get into his back seat where he had sex with Nourn. He called her a slut, telling her she opened her legs for any guy who came near her. He rubbed between her legs and told her he could feel Stevens's sperm. Nourn was sobbing deeply and quietly all the time Barker was penetrating her. He finally told her they were going to go their separate ways. It was over. Nourn begged him to stay with her.

"'Only way you stay with me is if you kill David or I kill David.'"

"Then what?" Tefft asked.

"I do anything you say," Nourn said to Barker.

CHAPTER 17

According to Ny Nourn, they went to Barker's house. Nourn waited outside for only a few minutes. When Barker returned, she said she knew he had a gun, although she didn't see one. Once both were inside the Town Car, Barker laid out the plan.

"You go to pay phone and call David," he told her in his broken English. "Tell him you're stranded with flat tire and you need him to take you to car to help," Nourn said Barker told her.

They tried calling Stevens from a pay phone, but for some reason, Nourn couldn't connect. David's answering machine didn't engage either. They drove in Barker's car to Stevens's apartment. She called his apartment from the intercom phone outside. Nourn told David she was stranded and asked Stevens to take her to her car. Nourn said her brother was also en route to help.

Once in David's car, they headed to the freeway, Interstate 5. Barker had instructed Nourn to have Stevens pull over when he began blinking his headlights. She agreed.

They drove north for a short time on I-5. They turned onto eastbound Route 52 and continued driving. Nourn said she acted as if she were looking for her car. In reality, she was sneaking looks behind her, watching for Ron Barker's headlights.

Shortly, she saw the headlights flashing from behind. She told Stevens to pull over on the freeway, which he did. Stevens stayed in the driver's seat. Nourn walked back to where Barker was. "Just tell him to follow me," Barker said.

Stevens began following Barker. If he seemed puzzled as to how Barker knew which car was his in the blackness of the night, Stevens didn't say anything to Nourn. Stevens did not ask Nourn how she got to his apartment in the first place. Barker took an off ramp to a residential area. Barker parked and walked back to Stevens's car. Barker got into the back seat behind the driver. Nourn gave a hasty introduction. Stevens was going along with the scenario. She said David looked slightly confused, but went along with what Nourn told him to do.

They got back onto the freeway for one exit. Barker instructed him to get off at the Ruffin Road exit from Route 52. Barker told him, "It's coming up pretty soon." They drove a short distance. Barker had Stevens pull over behind a big rig truck that was parked in an open area on Ruffin Road.

Barker grabbed Stevens around the neck with his left forearm. Nourn told the detectives she said, "Oh my god, what are you doing?" Barker ignored her. He told Stevens to put his hands back on the steering wheel. Stevens hesitated initially, probably trying to decide what to do.

"Motherfucker, put your hands on the steering wheel," Barker repeated. Nourn, terrified, glanced over at the men. She saw Barker's gun for the first time.

"How does it feel to fuck someone's girlfriend?"

Barker asked. Stevens was silent. "I asked how it feels to fuck someone's girlfriend?" Barker repeated.

"Man, this is not cool, you know. Don't do this," Stevens said, his survival instincts probably revving into "condition red."

Before David Stevens could think, or react, come up with what to say next, or formulate an escape plan, Barker pulled the trigger. The gun had been at Stevens's right temple, just as Doctor Blackbourne had written in the autopsy report. The only fact that differed was that Nourn said there was only one gunshot. Blackbourne had said there were two. Given Nourn's state of panic, anxiety, and terror at the time, one would bet Blackbourne was correct.

Barker told Nourn to get out of the car. She was in a daze, shaking, staring zombielike. Barker was at the driver's side of the front seat. Within seconds, he told Nourn to get back into the car. Apparently, he had told her to get in the *back* seat. She didn't realize what he had said, probably because she was in a daze. When she opened the front door, a body was in the seat where she had been sitting only seconds before. The body was David Stevens, facedown.

"Get in the *back* seat," Barker ordered. Nourn was shaking and crying. She couldn't move. Barker came around to her side of the car and slapped her in the face to snap her out of her daze. When she took her seat in the back, she could see the hole in Stevens's right temple. Nourn was only a foot away from the bloody, blackened hole. The smell of gunpowder and blood filled the air. She said she had trouble hearing because the loudness of the gunshot had temporarily deafened her. Her ears continued to ring. A man lying on the front seat with a bleeding hole in his head made her think she was having a very bad dream. Nothing like this happened to people. It wasn't even like in the most violent of movies. It could not have been happening. Yet it was.

Nourn asked Barker what they were going to do. She added she didn't think David was dead. "Yeah, he's dead," Barker reassured her.

"Why his blood, his blood come out his mouth?" she asked Barker. "He's making that noise."

"That's a natural reaction when you shoot someone," Barker said.

The "noise" Nourn spoke of is what is commonly referred to as the "death rattle." It happens when someone is struggling to make the last breaths of his lifetime. Experts say that, although someone is technically alive during the death rattle, he is not aware of his struggle. Death follows within seconds. There is no suffering during this time.

They continued to drive. Nourn was confused, not knowing what was coming next. "You tell no one about this," Barker warned, calmly and coldly. "It's just our secret."

Nourn said nothing, still in a daze, trying to believe what she had just seen and heard. She asked Barker what they were going to do.

"We're gonna burn his body so we leave no evidence," he announced. They drove back to Barker's house.

Nourn was visibly upset by this point of the interview, perhaps from reliving the brutal and fatal event again in her mind after keeping the emotional powderkeg contained for so long. She was vague and unclear about how they got the gas can from Barker's house. Nourn struggled to remember details, purposely long blocked out. She and Barker drove to Ron's house, parking around the corner. He left for a short time. He returned with the can. She could see he had changed his clothes. Nourn struggled to remember how they obtained the gasoline to put in the can, shaking her head and closing her eyes. The detectives, confident she was telling the truth but temporarily hung up on details, urged her to go on with the story. They could come back and bore into the details about the gas later.

Somehow, the gas can was full. Somehow, Nourn was driving Barker's car, and she was following Barker driving Stevens's car with Stevens's dead body in the passenger seat. She couldn't remember small things. The torture of reliving the events was evident.

Then, in midsentence, it came back to her. "After he shoot David, we drive back to Ron's car where we left after Ron got in David's car. I drive Ron's car and follow them to Ron's house to get gas can. Yes. That's how it happen."

They left David in his car while Nourn accompanied Barker to a gas station to get some gasoline. She couldn't remember the brand of gas they bought. They returned to David's car. Barker drove David's Chrysler, and Nourn followed them in Barker's Lincoln Town Car.

They drove to La Jolla to a secluded spot just off Ardath Road, where Barker pulled over. He told her to drive down the street, away from them. When she saw the flames, she should pick him up.

Nourn did as instructed, parking about a half block away. Then, there was a big ball of flame. The detectives noted, without saying to her, she could have driven away, perhaps to a police station, or somewhere to notify an authority. Instead, she drove up to where Barker told her. When Barker got in the car, she saw his eyebrows and eyelashes were gone. His arms were burned also.

They drove around for quite a while. Nourn seemed unclear how long. She told the detectives Barker told her, "This is gonna be on the news. If any cops call you, say you don't know anything." Nourn was still numb with disbelief at what had happened.

Barker took Nourn to her house. Before leaving her, he told her to take off her clothes, put them in a bag, and give them to him the next morning. She went inside, crying the entire time. After putting her clothes in the bag as instructed, she showered.

She tried to sleep, but found it difficult. She met Barker around mid-morning. Nourn gave him her bag of clothing. Later that night, he took her to the movies. During the evening, he told her, "You're mine forever, and now that I've did this for you, then you're clean, as in your sin has gone away."

The detectives weren't theological scholars by a long shot. But, they knew Barker's logic was skewed to the hundredth power. Someone commits a sexual indiscretion, but gets the "sin" forgiven by killing and burning the other sexual partner? They shook their heads and kept on writing down what Nourn was saying.

With the main thrust of the crime accounted for, the detectives concentrated on details that would have a bearing on a court trial. Knowing Stevens's car keys were not in the ignition of the burned vehicle, they asked what happened to them. "We drove over Coronado Bridge and threw them in," she said, referring to the mile-long bridge that connects the island of Coronado to downtown San Diego.

Young began asking the necessary, but painful questions. "He tells you he's gonna go to his house and get a gun, okay. He's gonna go kill him. He tells you that. He's gonna go kill him. Yet you go along with this plan. I mean . . . how do you account for that? I mean, what do you say?"

"I was scared he was gonna kill me."

They asked Nourn if Barker had ever been violent before. He had not, she said. The first time he hit her was right after he shot David. But he talked tough. He said he was in the Mafia and had killed people before. Tefft and Young were getting itchy to meet this Ronald Barker, this tough guy who intimidated an eighteen-year-old girl, and blindsided a man with a gunshot to the head.

The rest of the interview consisted of tying up loose ends and clarifying things to make sure they understood exactly what Nourn had told them. She relayed she and Barker moved to Texas and stayed for a short time. Barker had relatives there.

Nourn appeared to be relieved at getting the story out and not having to keep it in any longer. She appeared tired, too. During a lull in the interview, Young asked her if there was anything she would like to tell the Stevens family.

"I'm sorry. I should have said something earlier instead of hiding it. I was worried about my, me and my family, concerned. But then again, I do think about David. I'm not an evil person. I'm really not. I never had any . . . I've never hurt anybody in my life."

Nourn went on, changing from being sorry about being involved in Stevens's death to talking about how Ron Barker used her for himself. Instead of concentrating on the real victim, David Stevens, Nourn made herself a victim during her statement. She said Barker took her father's credit card and made purchases for his wife and child. Barker's wife had delivered a second child within weeks after David Stevens's murder. That meant Barker had started his affair with Nourn even while his wife was pregnant. Meeting Ron Barker would definitely be a treat.

"I guess the thing I'm most curious about is, is why today? I mean after three years almost. What, why today?" Detective Young asked. "What, what was the catalyst that brought you forward? I mean was it the, uh, the thing with the wife on Monday, or what?"

"He wanted me to quit my job and take me away. I don't want to be hurt anymore. I told him I didn't want to lie to him that I love him anymore. I don't love him. If his wife knows [about the killing], I might as well tell the cops. I can't lie to my family anymore. I just feel like there's no way out of this. I might as well come clean. I don't want to go on with my life, 'cause . . . for three years I'm never truly happy."

Detective Young looked intently at Nourn as their eyes locked on each other. "Okay," he said. For once during this interview, something made sense to Young.

"He took over my life, and that's what he did. From seventeen to twenty-one, now. He took the best years of my life."

"Is there anything that you're afraid to tell us? Because you know once we get him, he's gonna have a whole different story."

"He's gonna say I told him to kill him [Stevens]. He's gonna say I told him that I'd pay. 'Cause he told me Monday when I talked to him. He say if he go down, he gonna tell them everything. He gonna say I hired him to kill David. He just some guy I hired to kill him."

Nourn said shortly after the killing they went to Texas. She really didn't know why. They visited his aunt and stayed for several months. They abandoned the Lincoln Town Car in Texas, near Arlington. Nourn explained she had an accident. They simply walked away from the car. She didn't know what became of the car. Eventually, they settled back in San Diego.

Detective Young brought her back to his original question. "Well, you never really did answer the question of what do you think ought to happen to you? I mean, here's David. He's gone. He's dead. His family's agonized for three years. The kid never did anything wrong."

"I feel—I feel guilty that it's my fault. I should've done something about it."

"Okay," Young said. "But what do you think society ought to do?"

"I'm only twenty-one. I need to have my own life. I never had my life. I never had a chance to live my life, because he took it from me. And now I feel as if David's telling me to do the right thing and David's telling me to turn [my]self in."

Young solemnly nodded. "Okay."

"I don't know, but I don't want to go to prison. I have a lot to live for. I've never done any bad in my life, just that."

Since they had covered the most important points, Detective Tefft decided to alter the mood in the room. He explained they needed to get samples of her hair, saliva, and fingerprints. She agreed. "We'd like to have you show us around to the various places of significance that night: the apartment where Stevens lived, the gas station, stuff like that." Nourn agreed, unaware of the anger growing in Detective Tefft's mind.

Nourn said Barker still called and paged her constantly. The detectives asked if she would be willing to call Barker while they recorded the conversation, talking about the killing. She agreed.

While they were on a break, one of the other detectives handed Tefft a San Diego Police Department crime report. In the report, dated July 30, 1998, Nourn complained that a man in his late twenties in Garden Grove, California, a city about an hour and a half north of San Diego, was making threatening phone calls to her. Tefft read the report with rapt interest. In the report, Nourn related she had met the man over the Internet and "had a relationship" with him before breaking up. When they broke up, he began pestering her over the phone to get back together. The detectives would look into this later.

"As I understand it, you and Ron's wife work at the same place. How did that happen?" Tefft asked.

Nourn said she did not work in the same building as Barker's wife, but did work for the same company. She had started there as a temporary worker, and it progressed into a full-time job. She did paperwork on real estate foreclosures.

They asked her about details that had come up during the interview; they had not wanted to alter the pace of the interview by asking before. They asked about what had happened to the gas can after David was burned. Did Ron toss it into the car, or did he bring it with him? She could not remember.

CHAPTER 18

A few hours later, at 6:51 P.M., at the request of the officers, Ny Nourn initiated a tape-recorded phone call to Ron Barker.

After a greeting, Barker asked if Nourn was okay. She said she wasn't, that she had been thinking about what happened. Barker seemed to know Nourn was agitated. Barker scolded her, saying he was ready to kick Tran (his wife) out and now she (Nourn) was acting funny. Why was she acting funny when they were ready to begin their lives together without the wife in the picture?

Nourn told him she felt bad because she learned he had told his wife about what had happened, and the wife told Nourn she knew what Barker and Nourn had done.

Barker seemed desperate, talking rapidly. He accused Nourn of doing things to put him into a depression. Nourn told Barker he had hurt her. Tefft noted both Nourn and Barker were portraying themselves as the victims in this case. Tefft wondered about David Stevens. Did either of them care about him?

"Babe, you—you put me, you put me in this situation," Barker said. "It's very hurt me. You know right now, Ny, right now, I'm so tired. You know what I'm gonna do? I'm gonna go to the fuckin' police; just forget about this shit."

"Tell them what?" Nourn asked.

"I'm gonna tell 'em what happened. Why you do this to me, Ny?"

"Because Tran [Barker's wife] told me I'm the one responsible."

Barker backpedaled, telling Nourn he had told his wife only a little bit about what had happened. When pressed by Nourn, he said he told his wife he and Ny had done some bad things a long time ago. He insisted he didn't go into detail about what the "bad thing" was when he told his wife.

Nourn wouldn't let him off the hook. She told him his wife had specifically told her Barker said they had killed someone.

Barker sidestepped that by saying his wife had no evidence of anything, only what he had told her.

The phone line became disconnected. Barker called back twice to her phone and left messages. In the first message, it seemed as if Barker knew the authorities would soon be notified. He tried to scare Nourn by saying the police were going to arrest her. Barker added he was going to have the police come and arrest her parents, too, for harboring her. His last words on the first message: "Good night. I love you."

Shortly thereafter, a second message came in. "Ny, you hurt me real badly. Guess what, babe? I'm gonna go straight to the police right now. I'm gonna take care of this. And you know what, Ny? They gonna . . . I'm gonna have them come to your house and they gonna—they gonna—they gonna hold you whole parents for, for custody until they get hold of you. I'm really deep hurt right now. I couldn't believe you'd do this to me again. Good luck, babe."

Nourn finally called him back. She asked him why he kept saying he was going to the police. He kept repeating *she* was hurting *him*. He expressed disbelief that she would hurt him like that. Tefft wondered if either of them, as long as they were talking about people who were hurt, might mention David Stevens, just once. David Stevens? The guy with two holes in his head. David Stevens, the guy whose only transgression was having sex with a willing, unmarried woman past the age of consent.

Nourn told him if he was going to the police that she would go, too.

"I'll tell 'em it wasn't me," Barker said. "What you tell, what I tell, it doesn't matter. The story is, man, we both, we both committed it. We both going down."

Nourn said, "No, I didn't kill him. You did."

"You bring him to me, Ny. I do it for you."

"You're the one who shot him."

"You asked me to do it."

"No. I didn't ask you to do it. I never told you to kill him, did I?"

"Ny, you bring him to me. You set this up."

"Did I tell you to shoot him?"

"We both goin' down. It doesn't matter who did it. You set this up, Ny. I did it for you."

"You didn't do it for me. You did it for you. It wasn't for me."

The phone disconnected again. Again, Barker left a series of messages on Nourn's phone, which the police recorded. In them, Barker rambled, begging her not to do it [go to the police]. Alternately, he was threatening to go to the police himself. Finally, he said she had thirty minutes to change her mind. If she didn't change her mind in a half hour, he was going to "say something."

He finally closed by saying, "I'm on my way, trust me . . . I'm gonna tell the truth, everything. Whatever happens, you're involved, Ny. You're the one."

That was the last phone call between the two. Ever.

Before heading out to have Nourn show them the deadly points of interest—David's apartment, the murder scene, the gas station, the burn scene—they decided to continue going over details. The police had a feeling that when they left Ny Nourn that night it might be their last chance to talk with her. They didn't want to release her to her death. The detectives discussed renting a hotel room, with San Diego detectives or investigators from the district attorney's Witness Protection Team posted next door in an adjoining room, in order to ensure her safety. If Barker did anything to hurt Nourn, Sergeant Martin, the man responsible for the operation, could envision tomorrow's headlines in the *Union-Tribune:* "Arson-Murder Probe Leads to Murder-Suicide. Police Screw-Up." No thanks. He planned to play it safe and have her watched, even if the exhausted Team III had to stand vigil.

She detailed the abuse Barker had heaped on her over the years. One point that proved to be significant later on was that he never hurt her *before* the murder. In the months and years after the murder, Barker began getting violent with her. He hit her with a baseball bat, burned her with an iron, punched her with his fists, and pulled a gun on her. After the gun-pulling incident in his garage, he made her give him oral sex while they were in the garage. "Even when he beats me, I can tell he's getting, you know, a hard-on just by doing that . . ." Barker never broke any of her bones or required her to have stitches. Barker knew where to land the punches, and on a woman, no less. They *really* wanted to meet this tough guy.

She told them that on the night of her senior prom, Barker didn't want her to go. In order to control her, he took her out to dinner and rented a room at the Doubletree

Hotel. He kept her from her friends and convinced her she was having a good time with him instead of being at the prom with a bunch of kids. During the early days of their relationship, she really was having a good time. It didn't last. She now realized she wanted to do "kid" stuff, like go to a school dance, or picnic, or to the prom. Instead, he sheltered her from her friends and kept her for himself.

Nourn detailed how they perpetrated a credit card fraud on her parents for several thousand dollars. He also stole goods from Home Depot and returned them for cash.

They asked her where the Lincoln Town Car was now. She said in the summer of 1999, or even 2000, she couldn't remember exactly, they went to Bedford, Texas, to visit Ron's aunt. They stayed there for a few months. One day Ny was involved in a traffic accident. Barker told her they should walk away and leave the car. She thought he feared someone might be looking for them in connection with the murder. They abandoned the vehicle in Texas.

With the interview at police headquarters finished, the only thing left was for Nourn to take them to the various places: give the *murder tour* they had talked about. The detectives had to decide what to do with Ny Nourn. Her phone calls to Barker revealed a desperate, almost irrational man. They had promised to release Ny after the interview.

She said she wanted to be with her family. Sergeant Martin made arrangements for a team of officers to be posted outside her house around the clock, until Barker was taken into custody.

While the officers were having Ny Nourn show them all the vital locations of the night of December 23, 1998, Detectives Dee Warrick and Joe Cristinziani drove to the residence of Deputy District Attorney Chandra Carle, who had gone home for the day. The detectives had the tape of

Nourn's phone call to Barker. The detectives had previously told Carle they were sure they had the right people. This woman knew all the details of the murder. Carle stood in her kitchen staring at the cassette recorder on her shelf. She listened to Barker deny nothing. Instead, he pleaded with Nourn to keep quiet. Carle smiled when she heard Barker say, ". . . We both did it. We both going down." Carle's mind was already making preparations for a court battle many months down the road.

At 9:45 P.M., Sergeant Martin notified Tefft and Young that Ronald Barker was turning himself in to the Oceanside Police Department. Oceanside is a city about forty miles north of San Diego, and ten miles north of where Nourn told them Barker lived.

Oceanside police notified them that Barker was physically under arrest at 10:25 P.M. Nourn said it wasn't necessary to have the police protect her, as long as Barker was going to remain in custody. Tefft assured her Barker would be kept in jail. They dropped her at her vehicle at the mortgage company at 10:45 P.M. She agreed to call them the next day.

As they drove back to police headquarters, Young and Tefft mused how they had tried to solve a mystery for three years. Now that they knew the answer, the real work was to begin anew. Knowing who killed David Stevens was one thing. Having a successful effort in court was another. They had a helluva lot of work left.

CHAPTER 19

Ron Barker had become acquainted with a Marine when he worked at an automotive repair shop in Ocean-side. Gary Truscott eventually retired from the Corps after thirty years to become a rookie Oceanside police officer. Truscott and Barker remained in minimal contact.

In the early evening hours of November 7, 2001, just after hanging up from his disturbing phone conversation with Ny Nourn, Ronald Barker phoned Oceanside Police Dispatch asking for Gary Truscott. The rookie was with his training officer, Phil Dumas, out in the field going through the phases necessary to let Truscott handle patrol work on his own. Police administrators frown on rookies getting personal calls while undergoing training. The dispatcher sat up straight when Barker said he had in-formation on a murder and wanted to give it only to Truscott.

The two patrol officers met with Barker at his resi-dence in Escondido, a few miles from Oceanside. After learning they were dealing with the real thing, the two phoned the San Diego Police Department. Sergeant L. D. Martin made arrangements for Joe Cristinziani and Dee Warrick to pick up Barker from the officers.

The exchange of Barker from the Oceanside patrol officers to Detectives Joe Cristinziani and Dee Warrick was made at a gas station on Interstate 15 at Via Rancho Parkway. Barker was searched, handcuffed, and put in the back seat of the detectives' car. Officer Dumas had placed a tape recorder in his patrol car to preserve what Barker had told the officers and what they had told him. When Barker saw the recorder, he told Dumas to turn it off. Dumas complied. Dumas did not give the tape to the SDPD detectives because it only contained Barker telling Dumas to turn the recorder off. Dumas and Truscott had not questioned Barker.

While Cristinziani and Warrick drove Barker to police headquarters, Tefft and Young had dropped off Ny Nourn and were also making their way back to 1401 Broadway. Other detectives had queried the crime computer for hits on Nourn and Ronald Barker. Among the things located was the restraining order Ny Nourn obtained against Barker. It was dated October 30, one week earlier. Under the "Description of Conduct" section of the restraining order, Nourn's own handwriting detailed the violence she had told to the detectives. She wrote, "He stated he would kill me and bury me in the desert." She also wrote about the slapping, hitting, threats, and fear she felt.

Other computer entries interested the detective. There was a warrant for Barker in the system for real estate fraud. The District Attorney's Economic Crimes division had initiated this case. Homicide detectives would have to wait until tomorrow to find out details. Another warrant existed for perjury. The complaining entity was the California Department of Motor Vehicles. The detectives remembered Ny Nourn said Barker had driver's licenses in two different names, a felony in California.

They also learned Barker was implicated in a kidnap for ransom case back in 1994. The victims were family members of Barker's wife. The family paid the kidnappers over $50,000. A handwriting expert had identified the ransom note as having been written by a man under suspicion. When confronted, the man said he wrote the note at Ron Barker's insistence. Barker had failed a polygraph test. The detective doing the research wondered why Barker had never been arrested and charged. That case had strong evidence of Barker's involvement. The answer possibly lay in the fact that the FBI had taken over the case. Sometimes the feds want not only a smoking gun, but also videotape, and two eyewitnesses before they will pursue a criminal complaint.

When asked about the case years later and why nothing was done to prosecute Ron Barker, the city police officers shrugged and said, "Well, you know. The feds . . ." They didn't finish the sentence.

The homicide detectives, all of them, Cristinziani, Warrick, Young, and Tefft, had worked this most serious of crimes for many years. They had seen many killers during that time. Maybe it was the experience of attending movies, or the Hollywood influence, but almost every time they met a killer, the detectives often thought, "He (or she) doesn't *look* like a killer." The reason for that is because anyone can kill. Killers come in all shapes, sizes, colors, and sexual persuasions. Central casting never provided the detectives with a killer.

When Tefft and Young first saw Ron Barker that night in the interview room, they couldn't help think the thought they often thought: *He doesn't look like a killer.* Barker was five-foot-six, 160 pounds, with short hair and a smooth, dark complexion. He didn't look strong, menacing, evil, or any different from someone you would see shopping at a department store or in line at a fast food restaurant. Barker had a large mouth with thin lips, which he held stretched to the sides to give him a perpetual grimace.

The detectives led Ron Barker into an interview room at 11:10 P.M. The room was set up for audio and videotaping. Tefft and Cristinziani had been working since 7:00 A.M., the start of their regular shift. Their world had turned upside down when the call came in to the word processor operator at 1:15 P.M. They were tired but didn't know it yet.

Detective Tefft went through the preliminaries of obtaining vital information from Barker: name, date of birth, address, etc. He learned Barker's wife's name was Ng but she went by the name of Tran, and he had two sons, aged seven and almost three. Barker wasn't currently employed.

Whereas Tefft had explained to Ny Nourn that she was not under arrest during their interview but might be arrested at a later date, they explained to Ronald Ely Barker that he was under arrest. Tefft, more for the record than for Barker's benefit, explained that he had been handcuffed, transported, and locked in a police holding cell.

"I know what I'll be facing. I know all that stuff, yeah," Barker said.

Even though Barker said he knew what he was facing, Tefft had to make sure this interview withstood the test of time and appeal in a series of writs Tefft knew would be coming in this case. "We'll get into everything that you want to talk about, and, and we'll go from there, okay? And you can pick and choose questions you want to answer, or you can quit anytime. Whatever you want to do," Tefft said.

Since this was a custodial situation Tefft needed to advise Barker of his Miranda warning.

Detective Tefft read the rights to Barker from a card. The rights are rather simple:

1. You have the right to remain silent.

2. If you give up the right to remain silent, anything you say can and will be used in court against you.

3. You have the right to have an attorney present during this conversation, either an attorney of your own choosing, or if you cannot afford an attorney, one will be appointed for you free of charge.

4. Do you understand these rights?

5. Having these rights in mind, do you give up your right to an attorney and agree to talk with us?

Sometimes the police will recite the rights from memory. All of them can do it. But when pressed in front of a judge, jury, and often television cameras, the memory might be hampered by stage fright. That is why John Tefft read Barker's rights to him from a card. If questioned by a defense attorney about how he gave the defendant his rights, Tefft could say, "Excuse me while I *whip this out*." Then, Tefft would casually produce his card and read the rights he had previously read to the accused. It was sure-fire and fail-safe.

Barker said he understood all of his rights by answering "yes." He also said he was willing to talk to them. But first, Barker had some requests. He sat across from the detectives, his hands clasped behind his head like a boss interviewing some kid to work in the mailroom. Barker looked casual and relaxed. He looked like he was in charge. He treated the detectives like subordinates. That was okay with Tefft and Young.

Barker had a habit of continually puckering his lips like someone about to be kissed, then stretching them. He did this with such frequency that one of the detectives dubbed him "The Grouper" because he looked like the fish of the same name.

Barker sat there, legs crossed, hands clasped behind his

head, puckering his lips, looking relaxed and informing the detectives who had him under arrest for murder that he had "some requests." In spite of having been in the United States for most of his life, Barker spoke in broken, but understandable English. He understood the language well. His concepts were clear. It was his grammar and pronunciation that were horrible.

"So far, you don't know what's going on until I tell you," he said, a slight smirk on his face. Barker was establishing control, letting the cops know how this interview was going to play out. "I can still be a free man because you don't know nothing yet." J. R. Young was quietly boiling inside. Who the hell did this asshole think he was?

John Tefft was equally angry. But the two professionals had been in similar situations before. *Let the guy talk. Let him think he's running the show. Let him think he has the hammer. When the hammer does come down, he won't know what hit him.*

"I'll tell you this all the way because I want to bring another person down with me. This person hurt me so much. I'm tired of it." Barker didn't know Tefft and Young had spent the last ten hours with this "other person" and they had considerably higher regard for her than they did for him. They pressed on, took notes, asked questions, their faces expressionless.

"I'm not going to run away or anything. But after I tell you all this, I'd like to have a few days where I can go home and get my family situation arranged."

Sure, Ron. Whatever you say. You're the man. Take as long as you want. How about a few days in Palm Springs? Fine with us. I don't think so.

The detectives never answered. They nodded their heads and wrote in their notebooks.

"The other thing is I don't want this case brought up on TV. I want my family protected. I want me protected from

TV. I'm willing to go down. I left my family just like that [without explaining why I was leaving], and I want to get some things squared away. I can either keep my mouth shut and get them all done and come back, or I could request and deal with an attorney. But the main thing is I want to deal with my family. I don't want my wife to lose any face."

Barker did not ask for an attorney. He did not invoke his right to silence. He merely informed the detectives of what he wanted. This statement of his "conditions" would be the subject of furious debate in the months to come.

Tefft patiently explained to Barker that he couldn't give him any assurances or comment on his request because he wasn't sure what Barker was going to tell them.

"What I'm going to tell you is murder," Barker said. "It about killing somebody. It involves me and another person. It a serious crime, and I'm willing to face this. I've had a good life. I'm thirty-seven years old. But this person has pushed me so far that I need to do this. Because this person has hurt me, I really can't enjoy myself with my family like I used to." Tefft and Young, solemn expressions on their faces, shook their heads affirmatively as if they understood.

"But if I don't tell you anything further, you'll have no clue where to go, and it [the information] won't do you any good." Tefft and Young knew this statement was wrong and they had plenty of evidence; they just didn't have as much as they wanted.

Tefft told Barker that he had the police at a disadvantage. Barker smiled between grouper fish puckers and nodded his head. Tefft told Barker he didn't want to make any commitments to him without knowing exactly what they were discussing. Tefft said Barker was a grown man and could make his own choices. Tefft asked Barker to tell them what was going on. Once the detectives knew, they would figure out how the requests could work, or *if* they could work. Tefft said he didn't know what Barker was going to tell them, and couldn't say anything about the requests Barker had until Barker told them his story.

"But if I tell you all these things, next thing you know I get charged, and then I don't get my requests. You'll have to trust me. I will tell you honestly all the details."

Tefft again told Barker to tell them the story so the police could figure out where to go with the requests.

Barker danced around the topic of his previous requests of taking care of his family and the ban on television. He said he knew he had the right to talk to an attorney. The attorney might be able to work on his requests. Barker told the officers he could just walk out right now and nothing would go on and the police couldn't charge him.

The detectives were treading on dangerous ground. If a court would say that Barker had actually requested an attorney, the case would be in trouble. They would have to settle for what Ny Nourn had told them as their proof of Barker's guilt.

Tefft and Young were experienced homicide detectives. They had undergone extensive training in the art of interviewing. They had attended classes and read books on the Miranda warning and admissible statements. They kept current on the latest Supreme Court decisions regarding the voluntariness of suspect statements. They knew when a suspect didn't want to talk, and when a suspect wanted an attorney. This guy wasn't there yet. He was playing games. He was walking the thin line, but he had not yet said he wanted the interview to stop unless he had an attorney.

What it boiled down to was two sides playing each other. Barker thought he was playing games with Tefft and Young. The detectives knew they were playing a word game with Barker. But until Barker said, "Stop. Interview over," they were still in business. If Barker wanted to play games, they could play, too. And play they did.

The report Tefft wrote later detailed what was going through his mind. The report also summarized what Barker was saying. "Again, Barker makes reference to an attorney. Barker informs us he is fully aware of his right to have an attórney present. Barker informs us of what he would have an attorney do. Barker also informs us he could walk out of this room at any time. Barker speaks about the topic of an attorney, demonstrates he knows the abilities of an attorney, but does not ask for an attorney. Barker does not invoke his right to an attorney. Barker continues speaking with us."

Tefft told Barker they would not give the media his photograph, nor would they talk to the media about the case. He told Barker he and Young couldn't control the actions of others in the department. Tefft explained that the case had received extensive media coverage in the past. The department had a media specialist whose job it is to keep the media informed of big cases. Tefft and Young might not have any control over press releases.

Once again, Barker felt in control. With hands still clasped behind his head like an executive, Barker said, "Well, if I have to talk to somebody else who can control the media, that's fine. If I have to talk to a big guy, I'll talk to a big guy about the media. I've been around long enough. I know what my right is. I know what I can and can't do. I'm very serious about this. I called my buddy [the rookie Oceanside officer]. I'm not playing a game here. They are very simple requests, and I ask that you follow those requests."

Yeah, let's see now about those requests: You want to talk to a "big guy." You want to keep this story out of the press. The story that's been on the news for months, the story that's been on America's Most Wanted *not once, but twice. It's been on* Crime Stoppers. *It's been in* The Reader *and the* San Diego Union-Tribune, *not to mention* Testosterone Magazine. *You want the papers and television to walk away from that. Oh, and about your buddy, the cop. He's a rookie cop. Rookies have a lot of pull. Yeah, pal, you've got some requests, all right.*

Tefft and Young never committed one way or the other to the requests; they simply deflected the requests and moved on. If Barker wanted to say, "Interview over," he could. He didn't. They asked him to tell them about this case he kept referring to.

"Well, I don't even know if there is a case. I don't know the guy's last name, but I do know his first name. My partner would know the name. My partner would know more about that. I'm tired of this person. We're battling back and forth and she threatened me, so I'm going to threaten her. I told her that I'd bring us down. The person I'm talking about is a female, and she twenty-one years old. It an ex-girlfriend, and this happened three years ago. Originally she just my friend and she got me involved in this. She's giving me a lot of stress, and she decided that she just going to walk away, and I'm not going to allow that.

"I got involved in this because of my commitment to her. Then all of a sudden, she is now threatening me with this. But I know she wouldn't do it. She wouldn't want to throw her life away. She only twenty-one. She lies and she manipulates. You can call my friend on Oceanside police, and he can tell you what kind of guy I am. She betrayed me, and she's walking out on me. She's been playing games with me. I decided I'm going to go down, and I'm going to take her with me."

Tefft suggested that Barker tell them the story without mentioning any names. That way, if Barker later changed his mind about coming clean, the poor police wouldn't know what Barker had been talking about. After a few seconds of lip puckering–stretching and grouper fish thought, Barker continued.

"I met this girl and we went out. She liked me a lot. I found out she was fooling around with another guy so I told her to get out of my life. She got mad when I told her that. She said the guy was at her work and threatened her to lose her job if she didn't do it with him [sex]. She wanted to get rid of the guy and asked me how I'd go about doing it. I told her if she really wanted to do this, I had a plan.

"We drew up a plan, and then we did it. I was the main guy, but she helped me do it. After we did it, she promised she would be with me. She would be on my side forever. She owed me some money. She did some credit card fraud against her parents. She realized there was a situation with my ex-wife, and she started to threaten me. So I decided to grant her wish. I told her I was getting a divorce. After I did all that for her, she just turned around and blow me in the face."

Tefft and Young continued to take notes, nodding, occasionally saying, "Okay, um-hmm, yeah," comments like that.

"She tells people I hit her, abuse her, and control her life. I told her if what she say was really true, would I go turn myself in? Would I go throw my life away for her? I told her if I scare her so much, why she with me and by my side all the time? I helped her get a good job, a good education, and then she still threaten me. She say she was going to the police and I say, 'Go ahead.' So, I'm here. That's it. That's the whole nine yards.

"Two persons commit a crime, and now these people hate each other. They turn each other in. You understand what I'm saying? Do you follow my story now?"

The detectives sat there, taking notes, listening, watching, nodding, their eyes seldom moving from Ron Barker's.

"I want to bring her down. I've had a [guilty] conscience about this ever since I did it. I'm tired of all the lies. I'm tired of her manipulating me. One day she tells me she loves me, and the next day she says she doesn't. I'm an old guy. I love her. I care for her. You know she is playing with my mind. She uses this against me.

"She went and lured him to me. She pretended like her car was broken down, and this guy gave her a ride. This guy is an idiot. I guess he has also been taking advantage of her. She lured him to me. She told him I was her brother. She went to his place. She went out with him, and then she met me at a certain point.

"I got in the car with them and she told him I'm her brother. We took him to a desolate area and then we stopped. I was sitting in the back. When we got to that area, I just took care of him, you know, shoot him. I shot him. I shot him in the head. We took the body to another spot. She went and got some gasoline. We got another car. We burned up the body and the car. That's it. We kept quiet ever since. That the reason why I got burned."

Barker rolled up his sleeves, showing Tefft and Young the scars on his forearms. "Yeah, I got burned in the fire. She poured the gas, and when it got lit, BOOM! It never healed. I never went to the doctor for it.

"We always kept quiet about it. I knew there was no evidence. I know exactly where it happened and how it happened. She tried to talk her way out of it. She kept saying, 'You're the one who did it.' But it doesn't matter. I told her she was the one who lured him to me. It doesn't make any difference if I did it, or she did it. She knows we both got to pay for the crime. There's no such thing that just because I did it that she go free. I did it for her. She's the one who brought me into it."

Tefft and Young thought Barker might be done. He wasn't.

"The reason she wanted this guy dead is because she

wanted to be with me. She wanted to gain my trust. When she found me, she felt secure with me. She told me this guy from her work wanted sex from her. He was going to threaten her with losing her job if she didn't. That's the reason she had sex with him, and now she hates herself. I told her to get out of my face. I didn't want to deal with that kind of a girl. She cried. She begged me. She said she'd do anything. She said she would kill him if she could. I asked her if she really wanted to do that. She said, 'Yes. I want to do it for you.' She said she hated him. We sat down and made a plan. The next thing you know, it's done.

"I basically did what she wanted. She begged me. She said she needed me to help her. Of course, I was angry at the guy, too. I didn't know him, but I was still mad at him. You know, why did you go fucking do that to somebody's girlfriend? I'm actually a little scared right now, knowing what I know about her. She might go get another guy and have him do that to me. You see what I'm saying? She's capable of having me killed."

From there, Barker got into specifics that cemented his involvement. He told them the burning happened in La Jolla, right off Highway 52, and that the victim's first name was David, although he did not know the last name. He told them "she" (he still had not given them Ny Nourn's name) had pulled the trigger first. He said he wasn't sure that her shot killed him, so he took the gun and shot a second time. He added that "she" was the one who planned the whole thing, and she was the one who took Stevens for the ride. (Tefft and Young inferred Barker meant she asked Stevens to take her in the car.)

They asked Barker about the gun. He told them it was "hot" and that he had bought it on the street some time ago. He told them he had thrown it off the Coronado Bridge. Tefft wryly remarked that there were probably so many guns in the bay beneath the bridge it was unlikely any Navy ships could still get through the channel. Disposing of guns off the Coronado Bridge was a common crime aftermath occurrence in San Diego.

Barker explained they took the body to La Jolla because it was quiet there and not many people were around. They burned David up in order to "be cautious." Barker wanted to get rid of Stevens's fingerprints.

When questioned about the gun, Barker first said it was a .38 revolver. Then, he changed his mind, describing a semi-automatic instead. He said it was a .380, seven-shot. They asked Barker to make a simple drawing of the gun. Barker made a shape that looked like a semi-automatic as opposed to a revolver.

Barker waxed philosophically about keeping quiet. "When you do something with another person, this is what happens. I'll bet you 50 percent of the crimes you solve is because people get pissed off and come down and confess."

Barker was partly right. Disgruntled employees and scorned women are the cops' best friends.

"I'm not all that sophisticated about crime. I watch a lot of TV movies. You know, I watch the *Case Files*. I watch Discovery Channel. It doesn't take a genius to know this. It just takes a person smart enough to figure it out. It's not a habit of me to do that kind of stuff [killing someone]. I haven't killed anyone since. It's not really my style. I'm a very nice guy. But even nice guys, if you push them too far, will do things. I mean, that's what happened to me."

As part of his regular interviewing protocol, Tefft asked Barker what he thought should happen to him since he had confessed to being involved in a killing.

"Well, I know I will go to prison for a long time and so will she. My wife is very angry. She just recently learned about the relationship [between Nourn and Barker]. Today I told her [about the killing] before I came down to confess what I did. I didn't tell her the same things I told you. I just told her briefly that me and this other person committed a crime. I told her it happened about three years ago. Of course, my wife is very mad at this person because she's going to ruin our family. My wife just has to continue on and take care of things. This isn't like I'm going to do six months and then come home. I'm going to be gone a long time."

At least Barker had a good grasp of what loomed in his future. Tefft asked him how he felt about what he had done.

"I kind of think the guy might have had it coming. He really didn't deserve it. You know whose fault it is? It's her fault. You know she's a good-looking bitch. She's the kind of girl who would create situations where guys kill each other.

"I mean, why would I go kill you if I didn't even know your last name? I would kill you if you messed around with my woman. I don't need to know your last name. I don't care what your name is. She was my girlfriend. Yeah, I was married, but I was married only off and on.

"She had one other boyfriend when I met her. He was making threats to her, and he was going to bomb her house. I called the guy and told him to leave her alone. I didn't do anything but threaten him. Then, this other guy [Stevens] comes along, and he's screwing with my girlfriend. Beating him up isn't good enough. She's the one who said she wanted to kill him. She's the one who wanted to kill him so we could continue on. I told her I couldn't do it alone. She had to do her part. I told her she had to act as bait. She had to bring him to me."

Barker's response to whether he thought he had done something wrong was completely self-serving. He talked more about how wrong it was that the victim was messing with his girlfriend than how wrong it was to ambush, kill, and burn someone merely for going out, and having sex with, an unmarried, unengaged, willing woman.

"Do you want her name now? I might as well." Barker then removed some folded, slightly tattered papers from his right rear pocket, handing them to Tefft. The papers were the restraining order written by Ny Nourn.

"Here she is," he said, pointing to her name. "I think you should go out and arrest her. You can keep the papers. What pisses me off the most is that she tells me she loves me and cares for me. Then she goes and does this [gets a restraining order]. You know, I have a feeling she's fooling around somewhere else with somebody else. You know what? She just might set me up, too [to get killed]."

Barker told them they could go over to her house and arrest her right now. He told them where she worked and what kind of car she drove, things the detectives already knew. They wrote the information down as if they were hearing it for the first time.

"Look, I'm willing to walk you through this detail by detail. But I kind of want to know where I'm going to stand on this, you know, with my family and the TV thing."

Barker reached over and tapped Tefft on the leg. "Hey, John, can I have something to drink? Water's okay," he said, sounding more like an old buddy than a guy under arrest for murder.

Tefft left to get water. Barker continued to talk to Young. "Are you guys going to let me see my family?"

Young danced around the answer, but hinted it didn't look like he would be seeing his family. Barker's mind began to work.

"You know, the cop who arrested me didn't read me my rights. When you arrest someone, you have to read them their rights. If you don't read them their rights, even if they are a criminal, they can walk away. Anytime you handcuff somebody, you have to read them their rights."

(Author's note: Barker's belief that every person arrested must be read his rights is a myth. A person under arrest must be admonished *only if he or she is questioned.*)

Young sidestepped correcting Barker's erroneous belief, instead informing Barker he had two felony warrants for his arrest. One was for forgery. Barker was not buying it. "I don't have any warrants for my arrest. Forgery is not a felony (another factual mistake on Barker's part). That's with the DMV. That's with the paperwork. I changed some names. I'll work it out with the DMV. There's no felony warrant for that."

Barker still seemed relaxed and in control. His situation with the DMV was that he had another driver's license in the name of "Ron Aragon" with his picture on it. He had two driver's licenses in two different names, and he had signed a document, as everyone does, that the name on the driver's license is his true name. The document is signed under penalty of perjury, perjury being a felony.

Barker's other warrant was for real estate fraud, where he had swindled two acquaintances out of several thousand dollars on a bogus house deal. Young told Barker he only knew what the warrant specified. He did not know facts about the cases involving the warrants. He said his job was to investigate homicides, not judge people.

Barker was incensed at the fraud charges, but did not seem to mind telling them about the killing of David Stevens, although his was a self-serving version. Over the years, Tefft and company seldom saw a truly repentant killer. Most of the time, the perpetrators thought up things to justify their actions. That the victim "had it coming" was one of the most popular, and the one Ron Barker used. Killers often also minimized the act itself. "Hey, he was in the wrong place at the wrong time." Ron Barker did mind being told he had warrants for fraud, however.

"If that's the case [that I have warrants], I would like to

have an attorney. I want an attorney present. I'll deal with an attorney, and we'll just go from there. My suggestion to you guys is that you arrest her quick so she doesn't escape. She might go to Mexico. Her parents are the key. She's not home now. She's hiding right now. She might even be at a police station right now, trying to do the same thing I am doing."

Tefft entered the room with Barker's water. Young told him Barker had asked for an attorney. No more questions were asked of Barker.

The detectives would have loved to go through a blow-by-blow account of everything that had happened on December 23, 1998. They also wanted to talk about the aftermath of the murder, how Barker and Nourn had occupied their time for the past three years, how their romance began to flicker and die. But it wasn't to be. Once Barker said the magic words that he wanted a lawyer, it was over. The detectives had a lot of information. But they wanted more.

At eighteen minutes after midnight, Barker was sent to the lab to be processed, fingerprinted, and photographed prior to being booked into county jail. It had been a long day. There was much more work to be done. Barker decided not to give a handwriting sample, which is required when someone is arrested for homicide. Through experience, John Tefft knew he would have to get a court order for handwriting and any judge would sign that order.

CHAPTER 20

After a couple hours' sleep, Team III assembled in their office at 7:00 A.M. Over coffee, Tefft and Young brought all the detectives on the team up to speed on the case. When Young and Tefft left Ny Nourn the previous night, they asked her to call them the following day. She wanted the detectives to meet with her parents and explain to them what had happened and what was going to happen. Even though she had not called by 10:00 A.M., the detectives weren't too concerned. They had much to do, anyway.

At 10:30, Young received a phone call from a representative of the law offices of Kerry Steigerwalt. This attorney was well known in law-enforcement circles. He was also known in the community at large due to numerous television appearances as a commentator on various high-profile cases in town. If Steigerwalt wasn't commenting on the big cases, he was representing accused criminals on other serious cases.

In spite of being a thorough, hard-hitting, take-no-prisoners type of defense attorney, Steigerwalt was respected by cops and deputy district attorneys alike because he was a decent guy who represented his clients vigorously. If his client's guilt was overwhelming, Steigerwalt cut the best deal he could. If the guilt was in question, Steigerwalt was there to make the district attorney jump through every hoop available to the defense and prove every fact alleged against his client. On top of that, Kerry Steigerwalt was a nice guy who was a Little League coach and an entertaining person with whom to have a drink.

Steigerwalt's assistant asked questions of Young about Nourn's legal status. That is, was she going to be arrested? The assistant told Young he thought Nourn might be coming to the police station to keep an appointment. Young kept his cards close to his vest, not revealing anything substantive. They directed Steigerwalt's assistant to phone Chandra Carle because she would be the one making the legal decisions.

When the conversation was concluded, John Tefft phoned Nourn at her home. He asked her if she still wanted the officers to come to her house to speak with her parents. Nourn was guarded in her response, saying she did not want them to come right now. Tefft said they had talked with Ron Barker after Ny left, and they needed to clear up some things Barker had said. Tefft asked to meet with her. Nourn said she was leaving and would be back in the afternoon. She told Tefft she had his number and would call him when she returned.

When Nourn hung up, it was "Oh shit" time around the Homicide office. On the one hand, Nourn had been completely truthful, they thought, in her statements to them. On the other hand, the detectives thought she might have gathered up a few belongings from home and fled. Yet the experienced investigators knew she was only a young girl without financial resources. There were not many places she could go. If she were an heir to a large fortune, for ex-

ample, they would have notified their law enforcement
friends at the airport and the border. Tefft was confident
she had no place to go and would call them in the afternoon. The others weren't so sure.

At approximately 3:00 P.M., Kerry Steigerwalt himself
phoned Detective J. R. Young. Steigerwalt, ever the gentleman, made some social inquiries of Young. Then, he
told Young Ny Nourn was sitting in his office that very
moment. Steigerwalt asked about her status vis-à-vis
being arrested. Young told him Chandra Carle was handling the case and it looked like an arrest would be made
very soon.

Steigerwalt thanked Young, telling him to have patience for a while because he had some work to do.
Steigerwalt told Young not to worry. When some defense
attorneys told you not to worry, you immediately checked
to see if you still had your wallet; then you began worrying. Not so with Steigerwalt. They sat at the office patiently. Well, almost patiently.

At 4:00 P.M., Steigerwalt phoned Young again. He said
he would bring Ny Nourn to police headquarters immediately. A half hour later, Ny Nourn surrendered at 1401
Broadway, accompanied by Steigerwalt.

Steigerwalt spoke with Tefft and Young. He said he
was not certain whether he was going to represent Nourn.
The detectives didn't ask, but they knew it was a matter of
money. Kerry Steigerwalt, in spite of being a good guy,
was not a nonprofit organization. Kerry didn't come
cheap, and that was because he was worth it. Since he
didn't know if he was going to be the attorney of record,
he was reluctant to allow the police to interview Nourn,
even with him present. If, for example, he allowed her to
be interviewed further and did not represent her, the attorney who ultimately did represent her would be able to
give a valid criticism of Steigerwalt for allowing police
access to Nourn. It was an ethical issue. Cops often joke

that defense attorneys don't have ethics, but in this case, the issue was ethics.

Therefore, Ny Nourn was not questioned. She was processed as a homicide suspect and booked into the Las Colinas Women's Detention Facility for murder.

Fans of murder mysteries would close the book, get up, and go get a snack. The mystery was solved. Years of uncertainty, confusion, frustration, even anger were now resolved. Two killers were in jail. It was time to go shopping for a new mystery book. Not so with the police and prosecutors. Now was the time to get into detail. Everything that had been done so far by the police would not only be put under a microscope, it would be put under the Hubbell telescope—not only the things they had done, but the things they would have to do in the future.

There is moral guilt, and there is *legal* guilt. Ny Nourn's and Ron Barker's statements cemented their respective moral guilt. Yet there would undoubtedly be a helluva fight about their legal guilt.

Ron Barker's wife was a good place for the detectives to start tying up loose ends. Joe Cristinziani and Dee Warrick spoke with Tran Barker on November 8, 2001. The cliché about getting information from a passively uncooperative person is "it was like pulling teeth." In this case, getting information from Tran Barker was like pulling teeth with eyebrow tweezers. She was polite, but that was all.

Ms. Barker told Warrick and Cristinziani Ny Nourn's name. They asked if Tran knew Nourn. "A little bit, but not too much," was her answer. Ny Nourn had actually lived in the same house with Tran.

Cristinziani: "When did he introduce you to her?"

Barker: "Uh, couple months ago."

Cristinziani: "Couple months ago?"

Barker: "Yes."

Cristinziani: "And how did that come about?"

Barker: "Just a friend."

Cristinziani: "Just a friend?"

Barker: "Yeah, just a friend because, um, you know, he's trying to help her out. Just a friend."

Cristinziani: "And how did he try and help her out?"

Barker: "By, because, um, she told me that she's, you know, she want to be like, um, to become a, a good person, 'cause I guess she was bad before, like drinking or something . . ."

Cristinziani: "So now what is it that he told you just a couple of days ago?"

Barker: "He told me that he involve something bad."

Cristinziani: "Okay. Did he tell you what that was?"

Barker: "He told me that first, well, I kind of see her as having affair with my husband."

Cristinziani: "How did you figure that out?"

Barker: "By, she's all . . . you know, she like introduce him, you know, like doing this and doing that."

Cristinziani: "I don't think I understand what you're, what you're trying to tell me."

Barker: "Like, you know, like, want him, like, you know, like, everything go to him."

Cristinziani: "Did you know for certain they were [having an affair], or you just suspected it?"

Barker: "I—I kinda notice."

Cristinziani: "Did you ever confront Ron with this?"

Barker: "A little."

Cristinziani: "What did he say?"

Barker: "He denied it."

If Joe Cristinziani was getting frustrated, he did not show it. He pressed on.

Cristinziani: "So then, getting back to the other day, what is it that he told you?"

Barker: "He told me, he told me that, um, he had, he, he was, uh, killing someone."

Cristinziani: "He told you he killed someone?"

Barker: "Yes, but she told him to do it."

Cristinziani: "Ny told him to kill someone and he did?"

Barker: "Yes."

Cristinziani: "Did you ask him why?"

Barker: "So I told him I don't wanna know. I don't wanna hear it."

Cristinziani: "What else did he tell you?"

Barker: "That's about it."

Cristinziani pressed on in the interview, trying to find out how the marriage worked. Tran Barker told him she didn't ask Ron very much. She trusted him "to go here and go there." He let her know about family things, but very little else. She said she didn't question Barker about what he did or where he went. It was the way their ten-year marriage had gone.

Although Tran Barker and Ny Nourn worked at the same mortgage company, they worked in different buildings and seldom saw each other.

Cristinziani: "Did you confront Ny with this information that Ron just told you [about killing someone]? Did you go and see her and try and find her and talk to her about it?"

Barker: "Little bit."

Cristinziani: "What did you guys talk about?"

Barker: "I told her to leave my husband alone."

Nourn tried to ignore Tran Barker at work. The day of Nourn's phone call to the police, Barker finally told Nourn she knew what Nourn and Ron Barker had done. Nourn again denied it to Tran Barker.

Tran Barker told the detectives she knew Nourn had obtained a restraining order against her husband. She never asked Barker why such an order existed. Nor did she ask Nourn why it was necessary to get a court order to make her husband stay away.

Ron Barker had told the detectives Ny Nourn lived in their garage for a time. When the detectives asked Tran if she knew about that, she didn't seem to know another woman was living in her garage.

Tran told them she, ". . . kinda knew, I kinda go in the garage and see, you know, clothes and things, but I didn't know who it is."

When asked, Barker said she never asked her husband who the woman's clothing in the garage belonged to. When asked if she thought having strange women's clothes in the garage was unusual, her answer was, "A little bit."

They asked about the burn scars on Ron's arms. At first she claimed not to remember them. Joe Cristinziani reminded her that he had seen the scars himself and they were substantial, even three years later. The burns must have been very noticeable when fresh. Tran did remember Ron coming home with burns, but said she never asked about them. Cristinziani incredulously asked her if Ron had given her an explanation on his own. Her answer was painfully vague. She said Ron had some gasoline and it caught his arm on fire. That was it. No questions from her, and no explanations from him. The detectives mentally changed places with Tran Barker. All these weird things were going on: a strange woman living in the garage; your husband comes home with an arm that is split like grilled Polish sausage. Nothing is asked of him nor offered by him. In the eyes of the detectives, the world of Tran Barker was certainly a strange one.

They tried to nail down the time period when Ron burned his arm. They used dates of significant events such as Halloween, Thanksgiving, Christmas, the birth of Tran and Ron's second son. It was no use. She couldn't, or wouldn't, remember. Since they had obtained all it looked like they were going to get, the interview was concluded. In terms of humanitarian purposes, the detectives understood the confusing demeanor of Tran Barker. She had to raise two young sons on a meager salary. Her husband was in jail and likely going to prison for a long time. She really didn't know much about the killing, and didn't want to know because her world consisted of her two sons and surviving. The more she knew about the murder, the more immersed she would be in the process. She wanted to stay out of the process and take care of her sons.

Years later, when interviewed regarding the demeanor of Tran Barker, Tefft was philosophical, if not empathetic. "Her husband got her involved in this by telling her about it. She didn't know much and didn't want to know more. She wanted to get on with her life and raise her boys. Part of it might be a subservient Asian culture, and part of it maybe was that she only cared about her boys and surviving herself. While it was strange to us, we [homicide detectives] don't judge people."

Since Barker no longer had possession of the Lincoln Town Car, the police needed to locate it to determine if additional evidence might be inside it. They had a lot of evidence, but they could always use more. Defense attorneys can neutralize seemingly strong evidence by planting a little doubt in jurors here and there. When everything was over, a single juror might have been won over by the prospect of a small weakness in the case, even though a ton of other evidence was available. They wanted to bury the defense in evidence, so much so that a guilty plea and a request for mercy would be the only alternatives available.

Through a series of computer searches, they learned the car had been impounded as abandoned. On November 28, 2001, Joe Cristinziani and forensics expert Mike Callison flew to Ft. Worth, Texas. The following day, they went to Bedford and met with the new owner of the 1996 Lincoln, who had purchased it at a police auction. He was cooperative, allowing Callison to process the vehicle for evidence in the driveway of his home. Nothing of value was ever found in the car.

After talking to Barker's wife and checking into the whereabouts of the Lincoln Town Car, Joe Cristinziani and District Attorney Investigator Ron Thill went to Garden Grove, California, to talk to the man who had made the annoying or threatening phone calls to Ny Nourn necessitating her to make a police report.

The man, in his late twenties, explained to the detectives he met Nourn in an Internet chat room. He invited her to Garden Grove, giving her directions to his house. To his surprise, she knocked on his door six hours later.

The man said he was very embarrassed about the whole thing. Cristinziani asked why. "Well, it just didn't seem right, I guess. I'm kind of ashamed of myself," he said.

"Why were you ashamed?" Ron Thill asked.

"Well, you know. She came up here, and you know, it just didn't seem right."

"What didn't seem right?" Cristinziani asked.

"Well, I didn't even know her. The next thing I knew we were having sex."

"How long after she knocked on your door?"

"About fifteen minutes. I feel so bad."

In the spirit of professionalism the detectives decided not to look at each other. They continued on in the interview. Fifteen minutes after knocking on his door, Ny Nourn and the man were engaged in sexual activity that went on, according to him, for several hours.

"Why do you feel so bad?" Thill asked.

"I didn't even know her. I never spent any money on her. It was just plain sex. We didn't even get to know one another. It just didn't seem right." The man gave the detectives a photo he took of a nude Ny Nourn. She was reclining on her side, leaning on her left elbow. She was sticking out her tongue with a playful, flirting expression. In spite of her slight stature, she was definitely a sexually provocative woman.

Ever the professionals during the interview, Thill and Cristinziani could barely contain themselves until they got back to their police car. Once safely inside the car they burst into laughter. "I couldn't stop laughing," Cristinziani said later. "Here this woman drives over one hundred miles to see him and to have sex with him, no strings attached. He doesn't spend a dime on her. After they have sex for hours, she leaves. And, he's upset at that. Even though we maintained as professionals when talking with him, Ron and I did get a few laughs over that one on the way home."

Privately, the detectives wondered about Ny Nourn. What was wrong with a woman who was reasonably attractive and reasonably intelligent, that would make her have sex with a virtual stranger? Later, when Nourn met Ron Barker, the scenario was almost the same. Meet him, go to a movie, have sex. Although they were not psychologists, they believed Nourn's must have been a lack of self-esteem problem. Ny Nourn was good-looking and smart enough in her own right. Why did she have to have immediate sex with strangers? Was it to get their approval? They were cops, not shrinks. Someone else would have to decide.

CHAPTER 21

When Barker and Nourn were arraigned three days
later, the court appointed Public Defender Rachel Carey
to represent Barker. Carey had gone up against Chandra
Carle several times during her career. Both women were
mutually respectful of one another. Carle knew she would
be in for a fight, but it would be a fair fight. Carle's phi-
losophy is to work with, and not against, an adversary.
She knew a contentious case was a waste of energy for
everyone. Sometimes a defense attorney is unfriendly, uncooperative, and underhanded. Carle would always try to
be pleasant and professional, no matter what. Conversely,
sometimes prosecutors take cases personally and snarl at
defense attorneys, foregoing even the most rudimentary
efforts at politeness. Most prosecutors, in spite of being
dedicated to the good they are doing, are friendly and professional when dealing with the opposition.

Ny Nourn's family retained private attorney Marc Carlos. Carlos, also a well-respected defense attorney, had a
reputation for thoroughness. The University of California,

Berkeley, 1983 undergrad had finished law school at the University of Santa Clara in 1986. He had been practicing criminal law for over fifteen years. Marc Carlos had handled high-profile cases in the past, and had television exposure commenting on cases as a legal expert for Court TV, MSNBC, Fox News, PBS, and *The Today Show*, along with many of the local San Diego television stations. One of his cases had been written about in a book entitled *Living Between Danger and Love* by Dr. Kathleen Jones in 2000.

Marc Carlos was a very busy, successful attorney. He had toiled in the trenches of the public defender's office for many years. Clients now paid him for his services, and they paid him well.

Carlos had not had a murder trial in over a year. Someone referred Ny Nourn's family to him. Carlos said he was taken by the sincerity of these humble, hard-working people. Nourn's father was a short, thin man with long hair who always sported a baseball cap even in the hallway of the courthouse. Her mother had a plain, drawn face, which no doubt had become more drawn at the recent fate of her daughter.

Years later Carlos admitted he took the case for about a quarter of his usual fee. Sometimes people and things affect attorneys and their way of doing business, he said. The Nourns touched his heart.

Chandra Carle knew she had two formidable opponents. Fortunately, Carle knew she had a good team of detectives and plenty of evidence. More important, she knew she was on the right side.

Since both defendants were in custody, they had the right to a speedy preliminary hearing, within ten days. Neither side wanted the hearing so soon. Clerks from the District Attorney's office had boxes of reports, called "discovery," to copy and turn over to the defense. The defense attorneys needed time to prepare for the hearing.

The reality of courtroom life is that seldom is a case dismissed at the preliminary hearing. Nor does a defendant plead guilty to a murder charge before the preliminary hearing. The prosecution puts on a "bare bones" case, detailing only the minimum amount of evidence that will bind the defendant over for trial. While the defense will cross-examine the prosecution's witnesses, an affirmative defense is rarely launched at the preliminary hearing. When the prosecution has finished presenting its evidence, the defense will say, "Your Honor, the prosecution has not met its burden of proof." This is said even when a ton of evidence has been presented. The judge will note for the record that a dismissal has been requested and usually deny the motion.

Preliminary hearings for homicide cases rarely go forward on the day they are originally scheduled. Mutual continuances are asked for, and granted. The defendant has to sit in jail, but that is the price one must pay for a thorough defense.

Before the preliminary hearing, which was scheduled for March 2002, Barker's defense attorney Rachel Carey phoned Chandra Carle. Carey, according to Carle, seemed happy. She was getting off the case because she was pregnant. Or was she happy because she was getting off the case?

Public Defender Terry Zimmerman was assigned to take Carey's place and defend Ron Barker. Among prosecutors, Zimmerman is known as a "true believer." This term is not derogatory. It means that true believers present passionate defenses for their clients. Does it mean they believe their clients? Not necessarily. Being a true believer is a way for defense attorneys to explain, often to themselves, how hard they work for their clients.

Defense attorneys never ask their clients, "Did you do

it?" If the defendant answered truthfully, the answer would invariably be, "Yeah. I did it. Get me off anyway."

Being a true believer means you do not approach your job in a cynical fashion. It means the defendant is going to get the best, most thorough, comprehensive, and meticulous defense available, even if he or she is the guiltiest person in the world. Sometimes defense attorneys are embarrassed in the end if they lose a case while expending so much futile effort. But, because they are true believers, that is how they cope with defeat. A true believer can say truthfully, and with pride, "I did the best job I could."

Chandra Carle did not mind that Terry Zimmerman was appointed to defend Barker. Who did mind was Detective John Tefft. "I don't know what it is about her," Tefft said. "I get along with all defense attorneys, except her. I never did anything to her, but she hates me." Tefft explained he had a previous case where Zimmerman wanted to question him. For legal reasons, it was not proper for her to ask them during her cross-examination of him because the questions were not related to what Tefft had testified about. The judge ruled Ms. Zimmerman would have to call Tefft as a defense witness later in the proceedings instead of questioning him on cross-examination as a prosecution witness.

"She made me sit in the hallway outside the courtroom for a week. I couldn't believe it. There was no reason for it. We're professionals doing a job. I had a lot of work to do in the field, and at my office. She made me wait for no reason."

Tefft said he finally asked the deputy D.A. Augie Meyer to ask the judge to make Zimmerman allow Tefft to remain on standby. He had a pager and a cell phone. Tefft angrily recounted that he could be raising his hand to be sworn in thirty minutes from the time he received word he was needed in court, instead of sitting on a bench outside a courtroom for a whole week.

Tefft said, "When the judge asked her to accommodate me she told the judge she didn't know exactly *when* she wanted me, so she needed to have me right there, outside the courtroom. It was nothing but a crock, but the judge let her get away with it. I work with everyone in the system. It was a waste of time and money, and it was vindictive and unprofessional on her part. I don't know what her problem is." (Terry Zimmerman did not respond to a written request to be interviewed for this book.)

Before the preliminary hearing of Nourn and Barker, Chandra Carle busied herself with other new cases that came across her desk. Prosecutors and attorneys from the public defender's office are not "one-trick ponies." They all juggle numerous cases, working on others when they get a window of time. Carle had a good grasp of the physical evidence she was going to present, and she had a good idea of what she wanted to present. She listened to the interview tapes of Nourn and Barker over and over. She admitted that new information and insight came from each repeated listening.

The preliminary hearing of Ny Nourn and Ronald Barker began on March 19, 2002, in the courtroom of the Honorable Judith F. Hayes. It was decided the defendants would have their preliminary hearings together. Possible motions for separate trials might come later. But the two alleged killers would sit next to each other at the defendants' table for now.

Gerald Stevens, David's father, and Dan Stevens, David's brother, traveled from Nebraska to attend the hearing along with Mark Stevens, David's cousin from Las Vegas who was an attorney and police officer. The family members would not testify, but would observe the proceedings. Carle met with them to prepare them for what they were about to see and hear. She told them the evidence would disturb them. They would hear how David died. They would hear the interview statements of both defendants, including the callousness of Ron Barker's words just before he shot David in the head. They would hear about pouring gasoline on David's lifeless body before lighting it on fire, making him unrecognizable and unidentifiable except for his teeth. Carle wanted to prepare the family for the impersonal approach used in court. David would not be their son, cousin, or brother. He would only be "the victim." Carle wanted to make sure they knew this and were prepared for it, and would not hold the detached, impersonal approach against her. Carle was aware of the problems private investigator John Stevens had caused the police department and didn't want them running to Division Chief Jim Pippin, clamoring to get her off the case.

"I don't blame the family at all," Carle said, referring to the turmoil brought upon Sergeant Martin and Team III. "I blame private investigator John Stevens and all the things he tried to inject into this case. John Stevens was in this for himself, and he took advantage of those poor people. I don't know if they paid him or not. I hope they didn't. John Stevens did nothing but cause trouble. And for what? None of his ideas amounted to anything."

In a trial, hearsay evidence is not allowed. Hearsay is based on something the witness heard someone else say. Hearsay evidence makes the court rely on the veracity and competence of someone other than the actual witness who is before the court. The court would rather have the actual speaker of the words in the courtroom instead of someone who merely heard the witness say the words.

While hearsay evidence is not allowed in trials, California has made an exception for preliminary hearings, which are presided over only by a judge. The reason for the exception is for the sake of expediency. For example, if someone in Los Angeles has his car stolen in Los Angeles, and the thief is arrested and charged in San Diego, the court proceedings will usually be held in San Diego. Rather than make the car's owner come all the way to San Diego merely to say, under oath, "I did not give anyone permission to drive or take my car," the investigating police officer can make a statement in court for the victim.

After being sworn in, the police officer will take the witness stand and say, "I interviewed the victim over the phone two days ago. He told me he does not know [the name of the defendant]. And he said he didn't give anyone permission to take his car. He locked and parked it at the mall at 7:00 P.M. When he went back to his car at 8:15, it was gone."

That is hearsay evidence, yet it is allowed at preliminary hearings. If the defendant continues to plead not guilty and the case eventually goes to trial, the owner will have to come to San Diego to testify in person. In cases as simple as the one illustrated, the defendant will most likely strike a plea bargain. Inconvenience is held to a minimum, and the crook gets a conviction on his record. Justice, although weakened slightly by a plea bargain, is nonetheless served.

Witnesses are routinely excluded from the court proceedings until time for their testimony. This is so the witness's testimony will not be tainted by what they hear another witness say. Chandra Carle designated J. R. Young as her "investigating officer." This means that even though Young might testify himself, he could remain in the courtroom at the prosecution table providing assistance to the prosecutor.

Some prosecutors rely heavily on their investigating officers, asking them for feedback from time to time and having the officers run last-minute errands as the need arises. Some prosecutors don't like to have investigating officers sitting next to them. These prosecutors prefer to have the jury see them "go it alone." Some prosecutors have an investigating officer sit next to them merely as window dressing. It is true that if a detective is particularly handsome, or has a certain sex appeal, a prosecutor will have that detective at the table merely to impress the jury. No members of Team III would be used as window dressing, not in this case, and possibly ever.

Chandra Carle had only two witnesses slated for the preliminary hearing. Captain Michael Merriken, an arson investigator from the Metro Arson Strike Team, testified first. Merriken, along with being a firefighter, is also a sworn police officer. He has undergone extensive training in law enforcement, interview techniques, arrest and control, and court testimony. Merriken had been a firefighter for over twenty years and an arson investigator for over seven years. He knew his stuff.

In this case, Merriken testified that the fire to David Stevens's vehicle was not electrical in nature: not electrical from under the hood, nor electrical from the atmospheric elements such as lightning. He testified that the vehicle windows and the convertible top were in the "up" position, based on what he saw at the scene. From his experience, Merriken believed the fire started in the front seat. This conclusion was based on the severity of the burning to the front seat.

Captain Merriken refused to speculate on his impressions at the time of whether or not an accelerant was used. He said at the scene, he thought the use of an accelerant was a possibility, but didn't want to box himself into a corner absent laboratory results. Lab results would eventually confirm the presence of gasoline, but Merriken was testifying about his initial opinion.

Carle asked about his conclusions. A lay witness cannot give conclusions. But Merriken had established himself as an expert in the field, and the laws of evidence allow experts to give their opinions relating to the subject of their expertise.

"Based on your education, training, and experience, and your examination of the scene as you saw it on December 23, 1998, did you form an opinion as to the area of origin of this fire?" Carle asked.

Merriken said the fire started in the front seat. Crime-scene photos showed paint was still on the trunk and rear fenders. The finish had been scorched off down to the metal at the front of the car. He couldn't be positive whether it started on the driver or passenger side, although he was leaning toward the passenger side as the point of ignition. He did say with certainty that the fire was intentionally started.

Merriken's testimony was short and sweet. Carle sat back and let the defense attorneys cross-examine him.

Both Terry Zimmerman and Marc Carlos went after Merriken with the zeal of ravenous carnivores. The only problem was that there was nothing to go after him for.

Zimmerman asked whether there were other vehicles in the area, or any civilians. Zimmerman wondered if the fire was out when Merriken got there, or still burning. She asked if he was there when the body was removed, and what time that was. She asked whether Merriken thought it was significant that the windows were up.

Zimmerman asked how Merriken ruled out electrical causes such as faulty wiring or environmental causes such as lightning. His answers were routine, boring, and accurate. She asked how long after the incident he wrote his report. She circled and parried, like a fighter looking for a twitch in the opponent, or a slight dropping of a boxing glove to provide an opening. There was none. Merriken kept his guard up. His testimony was complete, believable, and professional. Zimmerman didn't land a punch on the fire investigator.

Marc Carlos got up, straightened his suit coat and cordially greeted the police-fireman. While neither Ny Nourn nor Ron Barker would have been picked to portray murderers in a movie, Marc Carlos could definitely get a spot in a Hollywood film. He was dark and handsome, with the lean, athletic look of a runner, which he was. His engaging smile had no doubt charmed many a juror over the years. He exuded confidence that came from many years of success. Carlos asked Merriken whether the car was sitting on dirt or asphalt. The answer was both. The driver's side wheels were on the pavement, and the passenger wheels rested on the dirt shoulder. There was no curb in this part of the road. Carlos asked basically the same questions as Zimmerman, probably to see if he received the same answers. He did.

Carlos asked, If gasoline had been used as an accelerant, how much would be needed to produce the damage Merriken saw? His answer was less than a gallon.

Carlos asked, If someone did pour gasoline into the car and then struck a match, would that person get burned in the process? Zimmerman jumped to her feet to object. She didn't want anything to point back to her client, Ron Barker, since she knew his burn scars would be introduced into the proceedings later. Chandra Carle sat there, staring impassively, but smiling on the inside. She was glad to let these two defense attorneys attack each other's clients rather than the prosecution witness. Carle could see where this prelim was heading, and she liked it.

Merriken could only say that if the person was standing next to the open door when the gasoline-soaked car was ignited, the person might get burned. If a fuse, or some kind of delaying mechanism had been used, the person would not be burned. Of course, everyone knew about Barker's statement to the police about his burns and the existence of the burn scars on his arms. The attorneys were all just "playing the game."

When the defense attorneys were finished, they

weren't really done. Ms. Carle asked a couple of clarifying questions on redirect examination. Then, both defense attorneys went back at it to re-cross-examine Merriken. Zimmerman, who represented Barker, reminded Merriken that he said less than a gallon of gas could have caused the fire. Zimmerman then asked him if a woman could carry a gallon of gas? Both Marc Carlos and Chandra Carle jointly objected to the question as calling for speculation. The objection was sustained, and Merriken did not answer. The point Barker's attorney was clearly trying to make was that Ny Nourn could have carried the gasoline. It was a stretch, but if that was all an attorney had going for her . . .

The nitpicking by the defense attorneys continued for several minutes. In truth, they had demonstrated they were competent, thorough, imaginative attorneys. The final score was that they had not done one molecule of damage to the prosecution's case. Both defendants should have been proud of their lawyers. The defense result, however, was comparable to a football team getting beat 35–0, but still playing hard.

In criminal cases, the People, or the prosecution, puts on its witnesses and evidence first with direct examination. Then, the defense figuratively attacks the prosecution with cross-examination. When the prosecution is done, the defense rebuts the prosecution's evidence by putting on its own evidence. A defense is rarely presented at a preliminary hearing.

Detective John Tefft was the second, and final, witness for the prosecution. Before Tefft testified, Chandra Carle asked the court to stipulate to certain facts that both she and the two defense attorneys had agreed upon.

Judge Hayes listened to the stipulations.

1. That Dr. Brian Blackbourne, the Chief Medical Examiner of San Diego County, had performed the autopsy on David Stevens on December 23 and 24.

2. That Dr. Blackbourne would have testified the cause of death to Mr. Stevens was two perforating gunshot wounds to the head.

3. The first wound was to the right temple and went right to left. He could not pinpoint the exit area due to fractures and fire damage to the skull.

4. The second gunshot wound also went right to left, and the exit area could not be identified due to skull damage.

5. There was no evidence of smoke inhalation (meaning the victim was dead before the fire started).

6. That Dr. Norman Sperber made a positive identification of David Stevens based on dental records.

7. That Jeff Graham from the San Diego Police Department's latent fingerprint unit lifted Ny Nourn's fingerprints from the headboard of David Stevens's bed.

8. That Tanya Dulaney did a gas chromatograph analysis for the presence of accelerant on the clothing of David Stevens and detected gasoline on cloth taken from the right arm and torso.

Both defense attorneys agreed to this because they knew they could spend hours taking that testimony apart and still end up with the same result: The above evidence would be admitted anyway. If the defense attorneys might want to confuse a jury sometime down the road at a trial, they could try. For the purposes of this hearing, the evidence would be admitted.

The court went for a short recess and began anew at
11:00 A.M. with the testimony of John Tefft. At the time of
the hearing, Tefft had been a police officer for twenty-
seven years, seven of those spent in homicide. Chandra
Carle led Tefft through the phone call from Ny Nourn and
her subsequent interview with him and J. R. Young. She
not only had Tefft tell what happened, she made sure he
brought out Ny Nourn's involvement. She made sure Tefft
brought out that Ny went to David Stevens's apartment
and lured him out, and that Nourn could have told Stevens
what was going on once she was inside his apartment. She
could have told Stevens that Barker was following them
when they were on the road and told him not to stop, to
keep on going; to escape. She could have told David of
the plan to kill him.

Although none of them would have been in the courtroom unless Ny Nourn had come forward, the truth still
was that the murder would not have happened without her
cooperation and efforts. Ron Barker would have had to go
to considerable trouble even to identify David Stevens unless Ny Nourn helped him.

Terry Zimmerman, Ron Barker's attorney, grilled her
former adversary Tefft on why Nourn was not arrested
right away when she made the incriminating, corroborated
statements about the homicide. After all, Ny Nourn was
allowed to go home, settle things with her family, then
voluntarily return to be arrested.

Tefft, ever the seasoned veteran, remained calm while
saying they were not done with the investigation. While
Nourn was saying things that checked out according to
what they knew, they still had to check on other aspects of
the investigation.

Zimmerman, acting like she had a bomb to drop on
Tefft, pointedly asked the detective why, if they let Ny
Nourn go home, did they arrest her client. Zimmerman
hoped to show unfair and biased treatment against her

client. Tefft relished giving his simple answer: Ron Barker
had two felony warrants on other matters in the criminal
justice system. Had the police known the whereabouts of
Ron Barker, they would have arrested him even if they
had never heard of Ny Nourn. It is unlikely Tefft, or any
of the homicide detectives, would have arrested Barker,
but some police officer would have, because two warrants
were out there.

Later, Tefft smiled when he recounted this exchange
with Zimmerman on the witness stand. "Here she thought
she was going to make a big deal out of unequal treatment
against her client. We had the perfect reason to book him
and we did book him." Tefft said getting to Zimmerman
like he did wasn't nearly enough of a payback for her
making him sit in the hallway for a week, but it was pretty
good.

Marc Carlos, when it was his turn, tried to save Ny
Nourn. He harped to the court how cooperative Ny Nourn
had been. Even though Carlos was asking Tefft questions,
the questions were posed in such a way that Carlos was
making a statement, singing the praises of Ny Nourn.
After all, the San Diego Police would not have solved the
case without her.

Then, Carlos had Tefft relate that Nourn had told him
how obsessive and possessive Ron Barker was; how
Barker wouldn't let Nourn go to her high school prom;
how he was jealous and threatened her; that he was in the
Mafia, and was married, and had felony warrants; how she
had to sneak out to be with him, and she damn well better
stay with him. The litany went on. Carlos reiterated how
Ny Nourn had no ill will toward David Stevens. She actually liked Stevens and found him attractive. She was only
afraid of being confronted by Ron Barker because she
knew what Barker was like. On top of that, Nourn's fears
were realized when she got home from her sexual en-

counter with David and found Barker waiting for her, lurking outside her home like a predator.

Marc Carlos asked Tefft about Ny Nourn's statement to Tefft. After Barker badgered Nourn to admit having sex with David Stevens, didn't *Barker make her have sex with him in the back seat of the car before he went over and killed David Stevens?* Although Nourn was a willing participant in sex with David Stevens, she was not a willing participant in the sex in the back seat of Barker's car. Marc Carlos didn't say the word *rape,* but he made every inference the sex between Barker and Nourn was not consensual.

Barker was the one who said Nourn was no longer pure and he needed to kill Stevens to cleanse Nourn. Carlos intimated that killing Stevens was all Barker's idea. It was, Tefft said, but Nourn could have stopped the escalating events at any time, a detail Carlos conveniently left out. Tefft set the record straight. Although Barker made Nourn have sex with him in the back of the car, it was before *they both* went over and killed David. The killing could not have taken place without Ny Nourn.

Carlos said, "But Barker made the plan. Based on his control of her she just went along with it."

Tefft could only shrug. He had made his point very clear that if Nourn had not cooperated and even assisted, the murder would not have taken place. Nourn set it up and participated at many levels even though Barker pulled the trigger.

Ron Barker sat at the defense table fuming over the questions Carlos was having Tefft answer, glaring at Marc Carlos. His "grouper fish" lips were puckering and stretching at a rate difficult to calculate. Ron Barker was angry. When Ron Barker got angry, things happened.

Carlos reiterated through artfully posed questions to Tefft that Nourn spent nine hours with the detectives, helping them out, supplying details. She didn't ask for anything in return. She was telling them the truth because she was a good citizen. Sure, she was there at the crime scene three years ago when something bad happened. But Barker thought up the plan, went to his house to get the gun, shot Stevens twice, bought the gas, and lit the fire. Ny Nourn was terrified of him.

Tefft shrugged again. The slant Carlos applied to the story of the murder and the relationship between Nourn and Barker was interesting. Yet the facts were the facts. Ny Nourn was an integral part of the murder. Remove her from the equation by her refusal to help, and David Stevens would be alive today.

Terry Zimmerman got up on re-cross-examination and reminded Tefft that Barker said Nourn wanted to kill Stevens. And Nourn initially told Barker that Stevens had raped her. Tefft had already testified to that. He shrugged again. The repetitious testimony was for the judge's benefit, he guessed. Besides, just because Ron Barker said something, it didn't mean what he said was true.

While Tefft sat there with both attorneys going on about how each respective client was the victim of the other defendant, Chandra Carle sat there with a professional gaze on her face. She was still smiling on the inside. *Let these two blame the hell out of the other's client,* she thought. In her opinion, both were almost equally guilty, and a judge and jury could sort things out. Sure, Barker pulled the trigger. But he would not have known where to aim the gun unless Nourn had told him.

Marc Carlos made another pitch to ensure for the record that Ron Barker forced Ny Nourn to have sex with him in the back seat of his car.

Terry Zimmerman countered that Ny Nourn continued to stay with him for the next three years. Her inference was that if Barker were so evil, Nourn would have left a long time ago.

When it was over, the only thing Terry Zimmerman could argue was that "special circumstances" did not exist. There are several ingredients to the concept of "special circumstances." Only one of the many ingredients need be present in order to make the case qualify as special circumstances. In this case, the special circumstance was the "lying in wait." David Stevens was truly set up and ambushed by Nourn and Barker. Other special circumstances in California include murder during the commission of rape, robbery, or other violent felonies. Murder for financial gain is another. Lying in wait was the ticket in this case. The result of special circumstances is that the guilty defendant will either get the death penalty or life in prison without the possibility of parole.

The most serious degree of murder is first degree. In California, first-degree murder merits the defendant twenty-five years to life in prison. A parole hearing is usually allowed after two-thirds of the sentence has been served, or fifteen years. Since a gun was used, an additional two years would be tacked on, making it twenty-seven years to life, and making the parole hearing seventeen years away instead of fifteen. Under recent California political administrations, first-degree murderers are not let out of prison at all. The parole hearings are often thought of as mere formalities. The press will cover the parole hearings of famous convicted killers such as Charles Manson and Sirhan Sirhan. Garden-variety killers rarely rate any newspaper space unless their original crime generated media interest. Political climates change constantly, especially in California. But "life without" parole is exactly, and always, that. No parole hearings are held for "life without" convicts. Chandra Carle was alleging both defendants set the defendant up and were truly "lying in wait." If the judge bought the special circumstances aspect of the case, Carle would bring the case be-

fore the district attorney's "death committee" for it to decide the ultimate fate, if a conviction was earned.

While Terry Zimmerman hung her hat on the theory
that special circumstances did not exist, Marc Carlos went
for the brass ring. He stood up, with testicles of steel, and
moved for dismissal on the part of Ny Nourn. He said the
evidence was "speculative at best as to Nourn's intent, or
as to whether she agreed with Barker to engage in any
type of activity that caused the death of Mr. Stevens."
Chandra Carle noticed Carlos didn't say David Stevens
was *murdered*. He said his death was *caused*.

*Yes, Mr. Stevens. I'm sorry to inform you your son's
death was caused by two bullet wounds to the head and a
gallon of gasoline.*

This was a very subtle defense ploy. People don't get
shot, stabbed, strangled, mutilated, or tortured. Instead,
their deaths get *caused*.

At issue was who had lured David Stevens to the fateful place and who had pulled the trigger twice before in-
cinerating his lifeless body. The answer was both of them,
working as a team. There were more issues, but those
were the dominant two. Lawyers!

Chandra Carle had the last word. She stood up, cleared
her throat, shuffled a few papers in her hand, and said,
"Both defendants were present, waiting for the opportune
moment to complete the killing they had conspired to
complete. Special circumstances had been more than adequately shown." Then she sat down.

Judge Judith Hayes, a veteran trier of fact, married for
many years to another Superior Court judge, wasn't about
to be flimflammed by anyone or any speculative theory.
She hesitated only a second or two before saying, "Substantial cause exists to believe the offenses have been
committed, including special circumstances, and the
herein named defendants are guilty. The matter is therefore referred for further proceedings."

The "further proceedings" she mentioned are a trial. In other words, the two would have to undergo a real trial. Their only alternative would be to ask the People for a plea to something less than first-degree murder with special circumstances. Things did not look good for Ny Nourn and Ron Barker.

In a last-ditch effort to help her client, Terry Zimmerman asked the judge to set bail for Ron Barker, a nearly futile dream. Judge Hayes denied bail, as expected.

As murder preliminary hearings go, this was rather routine. It took one day to put on. The prosecution only called two witnesses. The defendants were clearly guilty. The defense's only hope was to spare the life of the defendants, or maybe get the jury to disregard the special circumstances and get a straight twenty-five-to-life sentence. Maybe, in a burst of optimism, the defense attorneys might hope for a second-degree-murder verdict based on Ron Barker's uncontrolled rage. Stranger things have happened. Remember a guy named O.J. Simpson?

Ron Barker was pissed off to the extent that his anger was off the charts. He didn't like what went on at the preliminary hearing, and he wasn't about to sit back and see this little bitch, Ny Nourn, portray him as a killer. In his own mind, he had rescued her, and purified her after she went to bed with another man. Ron Barker had a plan.

CHAPTER 22

The next scheduled court date was April 2, some three weeks away. Nothing of consequence was scheduled to happen at that hearing except the official charges would be read to the defendants, and a date for trial would be set. It was time to start preparing for trial. It was also time to pay attention to some other cases that had piled up on Chandra Carle's desk. It was time to prepare to go before the district attorney's death penalty committee and tell the whole story. The district attorney himself would then make the final decision on the ultimate punishment for the two, if they were convicted. The committee is made up of experienced deputy district attorneys, many who had put on death penalty cases before.

But something happened to temporarily derail things. Ron Barker, as mentioned earlier, was extremely angry after the preliminary hearing. He didn't like it that Marc Carlos tried to portray *him* as the real bad guy. Carlos was trying to make it look like that slut Ny Nourn only went along for the ride, and was somehow controlled by Barker.

How dare Marc Carlos say that? Ron Barker had done *everything* for Ny Nourn. He had taken care of her for over three years. He had loved her. Not only did she turn on him, her defense attorney was trying to exonerate her just because she was barely eighteen years old when the killing happened. Barker knew he had done wrong. But *he had done it for her!* Sure, he had killed a man. But he had done it to cleanse his woman, who was unclean due to her sexual appetite. *She was the sole reason this whole thing happened, and her attorney was blaming him.* Something had to be done.

Nine days after the preliminary hearing, on March 28, 2002, a jailed client of public defender Liesbeth Vandenbosch had been approached to assist in a murder of one person and a kidnapping and possible murder of two others. The person soliciting Vandenbosch's client was Ron Barker. The first proposed murder victim was Marc Carlos. The secondary targets for kidnapping and possible murder were Ny Nourn's parents.

Tim Chandler, Chief Deputy of the Alternate Public Defender's Office, and Dan Mangarin, Assistant Chief Deputy, phoned former colleague and current friend, Marc Carlos. Chandler was insistent that he and Mangarin get together with Carlos immediately. Chandler suggested lunch at The Panda Inn, a popular Chinese restaurant in downtown's Horton Plaza. Carlos was busy. He was preparing for another trial, and wanted to go for a run instead of eating lunch. Chandler would not be deterred, telling Carlos it was very important. Sensing something in Chandler's voice, Carlos decided he could run after work.

Both Chandler and Mangarin were grim-faced as they broke the news of the contract hit to Carlos. Carlos didn't seem to take them too seriously. After all, Marc Carlos had handled many difficult cases and had been the target of threats before. While he didn't like being threatened, Carlos had taken past threats in stride. Nothing had ever happened to him.

Mangarin bore in on Carlos, as if to make sure Carlos realized the importance. "Marc, this asshole means business," Mangarin said, referring to Ron Barker. "He's got some guy from Sinaloa (Mexico) named 'Psycho' who's coming up here to kill you and maybe Penny." Carlos is married to an Assistant U.S. Attorney who was eventually appointed as a Superior Court Commissioner.

Carlos knew the significance of having someone come from Sinaloa. The area, in the interior of Mexico, is a hotbed of narcotics and violence. The baddest of the bad reside there. Stories of violence and mayhem from Sinaloa were legendary, and true.

"He's got letters with your office address. He wants this 'Psycho' character to follow you home and kill your ass. Barker's pissed at you for what happened at the prelim. Marc, this is a viable threat against your life."

"You're not kidding, are you?" Carlos asked. He couldn't believe his ears. He had merely done what any other defense attorney would have done at the preliminary hearing: represent his client to the best of his ability.

Mangarin and Chandler seemed upset at Carlos for not grasping the magnitude of what they were saying. Both Chandler and Mangarin had represented ruthless killers in the past. These alternate public defenders were not corporate attorneys who dealt in wills, estates, and corporate mergers. Every day they dealt with people who killed other people, often without a sidelong glance or second thought. If Mangarin and Chandler were concerned, Carlos eventually thought maybe he should be concerned, too.

Carlos became somber, thinking of the implications involving his wife in this mess. He thought of his daily vulnerability of coming and going to work without a thought of his personal safety. He had weathered halfhearted threats from pissed-off clients, former clients, and competing witnesses before. Suddenly, this seemed different.

The enormity of the situation started to sink in just as the waiter brought their food. Suddenly Marc Carlos didn't have an appetite. He glanced up to see Mangarin and Chandler devouring their food.

"You guys come down here, scare the hell out of me, then eat your lunch like nothing's happened," Carlos said, pushing his food at them. "Here, you might as well eat mine, too. I'm not hungry."

Years later Carlos laughed when recounting that story. "It's just like a couple of public defenders," he said. "I used to work with them. That's what we're like. I have to tell you, it scared the hell out of me, though."

Carlos told Patrick O'Toole, his wife's boss at the U.S. Attorney's Office. Carlos and his wife spent a sleepless night. Both Marc and Penny were experienced attorneys, not easily shaken. Now they were.

Carlos altered his daily routine. He parked his vehicle in a different place. He avoided his office for several weeks, working out of the courthouse. He constantly looked in his rearview mirror and over his shoulder. "Do you know what it's like looking for a Mexican in San Diego named 'Psycho' when you don't know what he looks like?" Carlos asked years later when interviewed for this book. "*Anyone* and *everyone* could be that guy. I was scared."

The Special Operations unit of the District Attorney's Office handles high-profile investigations, those involving politicians, police, and sensitive prison or jail cases. Investigator Patrick Espinoza and Deputy D.A. Craig Rooten met with Vandenbosch and her client at the county jail's George Bailey Correction Center in Otay Mesa, located in San Diego near the Mexican border.

Nothing was asked for by the inmate, nor offered by

the D.A., in the way of benefits, for this conversation. In fact, the district attorney representatives didn't know what the inmate had to say or what he wanted in return. If the inmate did have something of substance and he was going to get a reduction in sentence, or other benefit, considerable work had to be done.

If the meeting amounted to anything, the district attorney representatives would have to fill out a "Confidential Informant Benefit Request." The packet would contain information on the inmate about to testify. The packet would spell out what the inmate was getting in return. All of this information would be turned over to the defense attorneys for Nourn and Barker, especially Barker.

If the inmate finally did testify and Barker's defense attorney was not made aware of any benefits received, Barker's defense attorney could trumpet to the jury, or the court of appeals, that the inmate was getting an abundance of benefits to *"Come forward and tell the lies you are telling today. Isn't that correct?"* In the long run, full disclosure of benefits is in the best interest of justice. It would not be fair to learn, after the fact, that an inmate had cut a sweet deal in exchange for his testimony in a criminal case. The jury deserved to know the motivations of one inmate testifying against another. Failure to disclose benefits could result in the overturning of a case.

The San Diego District Attorney was embarrassed by not disclosing benefits to an inmate-witness in a 1999 trial. The court of appeals overturned a murder conviction for failure to disclose inmate benefits to the defense. Without the inmate's testimony, the case was weakened. Rather than have another trial without the inmate's testimony, both sides reached a plea bargain to a lesser charge. The suspected killer pleaded guilty to a manslaughter charge and was released after being given credit for "time served." Paul Pfingst, then the district attorney, abhorred the negative publicity the case generated. Pfingst, an elected official, did not get re-elected. That case, trumpeted by his opponents as one of his many indiscretions, did not help his campaign efforts.

But, this meeting on March 28 would be a "free talk" session. The inmate could give his statement in generalities. If the district attorney was interested, the office would make some kind of offer about what the inmate might get in return for his testimony, if the inmate even wanted anything at all. He usually did.

The inmate began the free talk by saying he had met Ron Barker in a strip bar in Tijuana a few years earlier. Since being in jail, Barker continually talked about his case to his old friend. The inmate didn't especially want to hear about the case, but he had no choice. Barker talked constantly.

Barker asked the inmate why he was in jail. The inmate lied, saying he was in for kidnapping. As Barker asked more questions of the inmate about his crime history, the inmate made up story after story as he went along. He portrayed himself as a rather violent person, when in reality he was in jail for a property-related crime. Claiming exaggerated incidences of violence is a way to gain respect and possibly protect yourself in jail.

Barker told the inmate he was desperate. He needed to have Ny Nourn's family kidnapped and maybe killed. He needed someone to kill Ny's defense attorney, Marc Carlos. That son of a bitch Marc Carlos was putting all of the blame on Barker and none on Nourn. Barker said he had a friend named "Psycho" from Sinaloa, Mexico, who would do the kidnapping and the killing, because it was obvious Barker wasn't getting out of jail in the foreseeable future. What Barker needed from the inmate was to have someone show "Psycho" around various points in San Diego where his services would be needed.

According to Barker's convoluted plan, when the killer came to town, Barker wanted someone the inmate could trust, to show the killer where Ny's family lived and where Marc Carlos's office was. From there the killer could follow Carlos, learn where he lived, and take care of business as the killer saw fit.

The kidnapper would somehow nab Ny Nourn's family and hold them hostage. Someone would contact Ny in jail and tell her if she didn't take full responsibility for Stevens's murder, her family would be killed. Barker gave the names, addresses, and vehicle descriptions of Ny's family to the inmate.

Barker gave the inmate the name and office address of defense attorney Marc Carlos. Barker wanted the local contact person to follow Marc Carlos home from the office and find out the size of his family and where he lived.

Barker asked the inmate to find someone to act as a guide for "Psycho." The inmate told Barker he would get back to him. "Now, what should I do?" asked the inmate.

Investigator Espinoza was a thirty-one-year veteran police officer, having spent twenty with the sheriff's department, and eleven with the district attorney. He gave the inmate a "cool" phone number within the DA's office, one where anyone could leave a message without knowing Espinoza was connected to the district attorney's office. Espinoza also gave his cell phone number, saying he would pose as the guide. Espinoza said his undercover name was "Lamont." Although in his fifties, Espinoza has the swarthy, dangerous good looks and chiseled build of an organized crime "hired muscle" tough guy.

At this point, it was too early to formulate an elaborate plan to snare Barker. Espinoza would have to wait for Barker to make his move. Depending on what Barker said, they might be able to go forward and build a case against him.

The inmate brought letters, purportedly written by Barker. An examination of the handful of papers revealed a kind of "code" thought up by Barker. The code was easy to crack, since Barker wrote the key on the first page. In essence, Barker told the inmate to find someone who would show Barker's hit man friend where the targets lived. Espinoza collected the letters to be logged into evidence.

March 29, 2002, the following day, at 1:40 P.M., someone called Espinoza on the "cool" phone in the DA's office, leaving a voice message and a phone number. "Hey, Lamont, this is Chino. I'm trying to get a hold of you. I'll try you later on your cell phone." Chino left a number for Lamont to call. A search revealed the number was a phone at the apartment complex in Escondido where Barker lived prior to his arrest.

Espinoza called the number as soon as he learned of the message, at 2:30 P.M. Espinoza asked to speak to Chino. The person answering the phone said Chino was not available and could not be reached. The person in the apartment in Escondido said Chino had called him, and he had forwarded the call to Lamont (Espinoza) because Chino had problems calling Lamont directly. Espinoza asked the guy to have Chino call him direct next time.

At 3:40 P.M., Espinoza's cell phone rang. Espinoza was on Interstate 5 heading north. The caller said, "Hey, Lamont, this is Chino. I wanted to call you this morning when I got your number from [the inmate informant], but they had us on lockdown this morning and we couldn't call out. And then I called you on your cell phone, and I couldn't get you."

Espinoza told Chino he was in a bad cell phone reception area and he was trying to head for higher ground. Espinoza said if they lost communication to call him back immediately, or wait until 9:00 P.M. when Espinoza would make sure he was in an area where he could receive the call.

Chino started to tell Espinoza it was difficult to get to phones. The line went dead. Chino never called back.

•   •   •

Espinoza and the lawyers later learned Chino was upset
that the reception went dead. Chino (Barker) was also
upset that Lamont was telling him when to call. Chino
was supposed to be directing when things would be happening, not Lamont. Chino liked to be in control.

Later, Espinoza listened to the taped interview between
homicide detectives and Ron Barker. Espinoza had no
doubt that Barker and Chino were one and the same person. Since Barker never called back, the district attorney's
office had no choice but to let the investigation lapse. Any
attempt by the police to contact Barker to go forward with
the plan would make it look like the authorities were
badgering Barker to commit a crime, and would raise the
specter of entrapment. However, Marc Carlos had better
watch his back. Ny Nourn's family had better stay vigilant, too.

With this most recent adventure disclosed to him, Marc
Carlos removed himself from the case. The district attorney had a duty to disclose the purported plot to Carlos.
Once Carlos knew about the plot he had to get off. He
hated doing that. He felt a duty to Ny Nourn. Carlos believed deep within his heart that the real culprit was Ron
Barker. If Barker had not controlled Nourn, she would not
have been involved.

Craig Rooten told Carlos that, since he wasn't a witness for the prosecution, the district attorney's office
could not provide protection for him.

Since the district attorney could not help Marc Carlos,
Marc Carlos decided he had to help himself. He went over
the names of those convicts in the same tank as Ron
Barker in the county jail.

Carlos saw the names of two guys who owed him favors. Carlos later said these were not merely favors owed
to him, they were "big-time favors." Carlos had done ex-

cellent defense work for them. Although they were presently in jail, without Carlos's help they would be in a worse place.

"These were two very bad guys," Carlos said years later. "They were violent. I don't want to say they were Mexican gang members. But, they were not strangers to violence. Hurting people didn't bother them. They told me Barker was trying to figure out where he should fit in at the jail. He was Asian, but tried to fit in with the Mexican guys in the tank. Everyone called Barker 'Chink.' Nobody wanted anything to do with him. He was a punk.

"My former clients confirmed with me that 'Chink' had fifteen to twenty thousand dollars he was trying to use to hire someone to kill a guy. My clients didn't know I was the intended target. These guys were going to tell Barker they'd do the hit, but were planning just to rip Barker off for his money. If he complained, they were going to beat his ass.

"Anyway, when they heard I was the one Barker wanted killed, they told me not to worry. They said, 'Don't worry, Marc. We got your back,' was what they told me."

Years later Carlos was asked what he thought happened between Barker and his former clients since Barker never contacted Pat Espinoza again. "I don't know," he said. "They probably told Barker that if anything happened to me, he'd be dead, or worse. Maybe he'd wish he was dead."

It's nice to have friends with influence.

CHAPTER 23

As murder cases go, this didn't appear to be a most difficult one for the prosecution. After all, they did have confessions, admissions, and some nice burn scars on Ron Barker. At issue in the case against Barker was a potential Miranda warning problem. Barker would undoubtedly say he wasn't advised of his rights properly. And, after being advised of the rights, he would claim he did ask for an attorney, but the police kept plowing forward with their incessant questioning, rendering anything he said inadmissible.

If the police obtained Barker's statements illegally, the case against him would be in trouble because his words constituted nearly all the evidence against him. The prosecution couldn't use the statements of Nourn against him because the former lovers were co-defendants. In order to convict Barker, without Barker's statements, the district attorney would have to give Nourn immunity, or strike some kind of deal for her to testify against him, both unlikely events.

The case against Nourn was very strong. But the district attorney didn't want to lessen the charges against her or give her immunity. She was every bit as guilty as Ron Barker. Both defendants should stand trial and be convicted, according to the prosecution.

The first order would be to find new attorneys for the two. Barker's attorney, Terry Zimmerman, was from the Public Defender's office. She badgered Carlos to tell her why he was getting off the case. Carlos could only tell her he had a conflict. Since Barker was bringing in his *third* attorney, the Private Conflicts Counsel would have to be brought into the fray.

A complex formula exists for appointment of someone from the Private Conflicts Counsel. The appointed attorney must have the requisite credentials to fit the crime. Since this case was a capital one where the defendant faced death or life in prison without parole, an experienced attorney would be brought in. In this case, private attorney John Mitchell was appointed to take Zimmerman's place and represent Ron Barker, at public expense. Mitchell, an elder statesman and dignified gentleman with a law degree from the University of Michigan, had an excellent reputation among the Bar in San Diego. He was thorough, intelligent, diligent, and played fair. With Mitchell, there would be no dirty tricks or subterfuge in this trial. Chandra Carle was happy to learn of Mitchell's appointment. Mitchell was a consummate professional.

Carlos drove to Las Colinas, the women's detention facility in eastern San Diego County to break the news to Ny Nourn. She was inconsolable, crying and begging him to stay on the case. Carlos was very upset, too. He did not want to abandon this woman and her mother and father.

Carlos knew of a former associate in Santa Monica named Bruce Cormicle who was an excellent attorney. Carlos wrote Cormicle a check from the retainer he had received from Nourn's parents. Her family would have to come up with the remainder to pay Cormicle, but Carlos felt it was the least he could do to help this poor young girl, and her desperate parents.

Carlos was bothered for several months about having to relinquish his duties. He couldn't tell anyone why he was off the case. Years later, when interviewed for this book, Marc Carlos was still visibly affected when recounting the events of telling Nourn he had to get off the case.

The district attorney's death committee met to decide whether to seek the death penalty against these two accused killers. They examined the case from every possible angle, looking at the victim, the defendants, the severity of the crime, and the viciousness with which the crime was completed. They factored in whether David Stevens may have, by his conduct, contributed to his own murder. They argued and pushed their points, as lawyers do. They voted. More than half of the assembled attorneys believed Ron Barker deserved to die. None of them wanted death for Ny Nourn. Because of the split vote on Barker's fate, neither Barker nor Nourn would face the possibility of the death penalty. Although Ron Barker was clearly the "heavy" in this matter, only half wanted him to die. The net result was no death penalty would be sought for either.

The next court proceeding started on October 22, 2002. Seventeen motions for the defense were the order of the day. The Honorable Frederic Link, a twenty-two-year veteran of the bench, was appointed to preside over the case. He was flamboyant, not shy (read: *loud*), humorous, articulate, energetic, knowledgeable, and gifted. Link ran his courtroom in every sense of the word. Although not against publicity, Link controlled everything in his courtroom. He courted the media, but did not kowtow to them. He was no Judge Lance Ito. If Link had presided over the

O.J. Simpson case, things might have been different; although maybe not, given the Simpson jury. Nobody walked on Fred Link. If someone tried it, he tried only once. His old license plate used to read, LINXLAW, and he meant it. More important, everyone knew it. Link relished the adulation everyone gave him, but did not abuse it.

Link was a sound jurist, rarely overturned on appeal. He demanded punctuality from everyone. He expected the attorneys to be prepared. Link expected his juries to be intelligent and follow the law. Link didn't look at the wall above your head when he addressed you. He looked at you. He looked *through* you. Cops who came to him with arrest and search warrants had better be prepared to discuss finer points of the affidavit with Link. He knew his stuff and expected everyone else to know his or hers. It was Link's Law.

Most of the motions on the Barker/Nourn matter came from the defense. The defense wanted two different trials so their clients would not have to be in the same courtroom. Chandra Carle was opposed, for the sake of convenience. She didn't want her witnesses forced to make two separate appearances. An alternative was to have one trial, with two juries, one for each defendant. There would be times when one jury would be excused from the courtroom so they wouldn't hear restricted testimony about their defendant. In spite of being cumbersome, the two-jury plan was ultimately the most expedient.

Also, Judge Link wanted to get rid of the fraud and perjury charges against Barker. He didn't necessarily want them dismissed forever. He merely did not want the fraud case issues to muddy up the murder trial and possibly distract or confuse the jury. Barker had been accused of committing perjury with the California Department of Motor Vehicles by having driver's licenses in two different names, Ronald Barker and Ron Aragon. Also, Barker had been accused of real estate fraud for cheating two of his friends out of several thousand dollars by deception. If Link allowed the real estate case to go forward, Steve Robinson, the attorney from the District Attorney's Economic Crimes division, would present the facts. Real estate fraud cases are complicated and convoluted, containing forgeries, questionable notarized forms, and improperly recorded documents. If Barker was able to perpetrate a real estate fraud, he had to have some intelligence.

Real estate fraud is much more complicated and difficult to pull off than the usual street con. The average crooked dice-player-in-the-alley doesn't do real estate fraud, nor do the guys on the trolley who try to entice people to play Three-Card Monte or the shell game. Chandra Carle took note and made sure she did not underestimate this darkly glaring man puckering and stretching his "grouper fish" lips at the defendant's table.

Steve Robinson later said, "I can understand why Judge Link wanted to separate the real estate fraud from the murder charges. They are two separate crimes. The jury might get hung up and confused on the real estate case, and their thoughts could bleed over to add confusion to the murder charge. If the murder case somehow didn't end in a conviction, then I could have put on the real estate case.

"I had a very hard time dealing with Barker's real estate victims. They were nice people who actually befriended Barker, who was known to them as Ron Aragon. He left them with nothing. It was about $600,000 he cheated them out of. I explained to them that if he was found guilty and sentenced to life in prison without parole, it wouldn't matter if he had five or ten years tacked on for the fraud case.

"They understood that part okay. They just wanted Barker, or whatever the heck his name was, to say he was sorry. I had already explained to them that restitution was out of the question since Barker didn't have anything. They understood, but were still angry. All they really wanted was an apology. They had lost everything."

Judge Link handled most of these motions by listening and talking with the attorneys. No witness testimony was required except for the motions regarding the admissibility of Ron Barker's incriminating statements to the police.

Barker's statement to his friend Oceanside police officer Gary Truscott, was the first to be considered. Although a retired thirty-year United States Marine Corps top sergeant, Truscott had been a rookie police officer when Barker phoned the Oceanside Police Department that fateful night, November 7, 2001.

Barker's only hope during the motions proceeding of October 22, 2002, was that Judge Link would believe Barker gave inadmissible statements to Truscott. After being sworn in, Truscott testified he received a call from dispatch that Barker had phoned the station asking to see Truscott because the subject was murder. Truscott and his training officer left the city of Oceanside to go to nearby Escondido to speak with Barker. They never would have left Oceanside but for the fact that Barker had told the dispatcher he wanted to give information about a murder.

Barker told Truscott and his partner he had killed a man a few years ago and wanted to surrender. Once training officer Phil Dumas and Truscott learned the investigating jurisdiction was San Diego, they made arrangements to transfer Barker to San Diego Police. Truscott testified Barker contacted him voluntarily. Truscott did handcuff Barker, but only because Barker said he had killed a man and he would be getting in the back of the police car, standard procedure for every police department everywhere.

Barker's attorney, John Mitchell, asked Truscott if he had questioned Barker during their brief time together. Truscott had not. Barker talked a lot, but it wasn't in response to any questions. Dumas had a tape recorder playing, but turned it off when Barker told him to. Barker noticed the recorder as soon as he was put in the police car. Dumas said the only sounds on the tape were that of the door closing and Barker asking if that object was a tape recorder. When Dumas told him it was, Barker ordered Dumas to turn it off.

The defense made no headway with Gary Truscott. San Diego detective Joe Cristinziani testified next. In response to John Mitchell's questions, Cristinziani said he and his partner Dee Warrick did not admonish Barker during the ride to police headquarters for the simple reason they did not ask him any questions. Unbeknownst to Barker at the time, Cristinziani and Warrick already knew what Ny Nourn had told John Tefft and J. R. Young. They didn't need to ask Barker any questions.

Cristinziani testified during the ride to police headquarters Barker did all of the questioning. The cops only gave answers. Barker asked them if there were prisons in California. He told the detectives he knew he was going to prison. He asked them how much time he was facing. The detectives said they didn't know. It depended on many things. Barker told them he wanted to stay close to his family so they could visit him. When Barker did bring up the murder case, Warrick told him they did not want to discuss the case or the penalties. She said he could speak with the detectives who were going to handle the interview, and they would arrive downtown shortly.

John Mitchell asked Joe Cristinziani why the police didn't advise Barker of his right to silence and an attorney. Cristinziani's answer was simple: "This was not a Miranda situation, because we didn't ask him any questions. He gets in our car and he told us he was going to prison. He asked us about where the prisons were, and if he could be close to his family. We don't have any answers about where he might go, and for how long. That's why Dee told him we didn't want to talk about that. We made small talk unrelated to the case with him. We didn't ask him any questions about anything."

Attorney Mitchell wondered to the court if Barker understood what was happening. By the look on Judge Link's face at that question, Mitchell could tell that Link thought Barker understood very well. Mitchell knew he had an uphill battle in defending Ronald Barker.

All the parties had gone over the transcripts of Barker's interview with John Tefft and J. R. Young. Having been a defense attorney for fifteen years, Link had been around the block a few times. He could see the word game Barker was playing during the interview. Nonetheless, Link had to allow the defense to get its objections in for the record.

John Mitchell told Judge Link, "The police should have done something [to let Barker know what he was facing, or to tell him he needed an attorney], and they did absolutely nothing, and there's a reason they did nothing." Mitchell tried to blame the police for Barker's confessing. He tried to accuse the police of withholding an attorney until they received the necessary incriminating information.

Chandra Carle stood up to address Barker's references to the attorney, which he did make. Barker talked a lot about an attorney, yet never asked for one. He merely danced around the issue. "We can't take Mr. Barker's statements in a vacuum," Carle said. "We have to combine them with his tape-recorded phone conversations with Ms. Nourn. We have to consider Barker's saying he was going to the police first so he could get some kind of advantage.

"Mr. Barker set these things in motion. He called the Oceanside Police Department. He confessed to Gary Truscott. Barker knew he was going downtown [to the police station]."

Carle said, "Look at Barker's body language on the videotape of his interview with Tefft and Young. He's

very relaxed. His hands are clasped behind his head. He
taps Detective Tefft on the leg. 'John, can you get me
some water?' Barker's acting like he's running the interview. He had never met Detective Tefft before, yet he's
addressing Tefft like they are old friends. He knows he's
in trouble because he already told Officer Truscott what
he did. He now wants to make sure Ny Nourn is in trouble, too. Barker wanted to make sure the police officers
knew up front that he might even be smarter than they
were, in terms of what the law required. Ron Barker knew
exactly what he was doing and what he was saying.
Barker wasn't tricked by anyone. The tape speaks for itself."

Judge Link handled that motion as if it were a routine
ground ball. In terms of legal procedure, it was. "Mr.
Mitchell, you know the police don't have to explain to the
defendant what would happen if he did, or did not, have
an attorney. . . . The question is, Did Mr. Barker invoke
his constitutional rights, and did the police in this case engage in coercive activity to either violate those rights or to
somehow talk him out of it?"

Link paused for effect, looking at everyone, making
sure they were following him. Looking *through* them, as
he was wont to do. "Barker was on a mission to 'get to the
chapel' before Nourn, because he didn't know Nourn already talked. Just when it looked like Barker was going to
invoke, he stopped short and kept on going [talking]. The
police don't have to prevent him from talking." Link ruled
Barker's statements to all of the police officers, from both
departments, would remain in the record.

Even though Chandra Carle expected that ruling, she
breathed a sigh of relief. There are no "slam dunks" in a
courtroom. There was a slight possibility Judge Link
could have ruled in the defense's favor. Predictably, he
didn't. That was one prosecution roadblock out of the
way.

On the other motion, Judge Link ruled there would be one trial and two juries. The three sides discussed jury questionnaires.

On October 31, 2002, nine days later, all parties were in court again. They were together because Ron Barker brought a Marsden motion against his attorney, John Mitchell. Simply put, a Marsden motion seeks the removal of an attorney. The possible reasons for such a proceeding are numerous. There could be a major personality conflict between client and attorney. There could be a claim of incompetence, of illegal activity, or any similar reason. The majority of Marsden motions are brought by the defendant. Defendants have access to a plethora of inmate "jailhouse lawyers" in every penal institution everywhere. Also, a Marsden motion is a good delaying tactic because, if new counsel is appointed, the new attorney must start at square one and review the files. While delays mean a defendant sits in jail longer, it also means that in the ensuing delay, witnesses might move, die, forget, or, heaven forbid, even get killed.

What is said in a Marsden hearing has the same code of secrecy as the Catholic sacrament of Confession. The prosecution is not allowed to be present at a Marsden hearing, usually held in the judge's chambers with only a court reporter, the judge, defense attorney, and defendant. The judge will listen to what the defendant has to say about the professional relationship. The attorney responds. Invariably, the motion is denied. Insiders in the defense bar of San Diego laughed when informed John Mitchell was the subject of a Marsden hearing. Mitchell was a thoroughly professional, conscientious, ethical attorney who loved and respected the law, and who treated his clients, both appointed and retained, with great respect and courtesy, whether they deserved such treatment or not.

Not surprisingly, Judge Link denied the motion. Since it is unknown what was said in the meeting, one can only speculate. However, those who know Link could not help but think he offered his opinion to Ronald Barker about what he thought about Barker's claims against John Mitchell. On the other hand, Link simply may have said, "Motion denied." Everyone doubts Link's ruling was that concise and lacking in personal input. The personal input was a feature of Link's Law, free of charge.

Another Marsden hearing was held on December 6, 2002, at the insistence of Ronald Barker. Again, no one knew what his claims against John Mitchell were. When this new motion was denied, Barker added another twist. He demanded to represent himself. When Barker spoke conversationally, his grammar was fractured and his speech accented. If the jury couldn't understand his sentence construction, they would be equally confused by his pronunciation.

The Marsden hearing was held in closed chambers. The motion for Barker to represent himself, however, was held in open court. No one would have blamed John Mitchell for being hurt, or even angry. The man sitting next to Mitchell wearing jail blues, was an alleged punk killer. He had accused Mitchell of professional incompetence, or worse. Now, Barker wanted to represent himself.

When a defendant opts to represent himself, the judge is obligated to obtain a Lopez Waiver from the defendant. A defendant named Lopez once embarked on the road of In Propria Persona (otherwise known as "pro per," or acting as one's own lawyer) and, not surprisingly, lost the case. Another lawyer appealed that Mr. Lopez didn't know the pitfalls of self-representation. Because of that ruling, judges must now specifically look the defendant in the eye and tell him, or her, the road that lies ahead is fraught with pitfalls, potholes, and dangerous curves that will probably result in a loss of the case.

Judge Link tried to inject Barker with a dose of reality. "Mr. Barker, if you do represent yourself, you'll get no help from the court. You must act as an attorney. You'll get no special privileges. You'll have to make motions like an attorney." Link paused for effect, looking first at those assembled, to confirm their comprehension, then looking through Ron Barker. "Mr. Barker, do you understand it is very unwise for one to be his own attorney?"

"Yes," Barker answered.

"Mr. Barker, look up at the picture of that ugly guy on my wall."

Barker first looked behind Link at the array of Chicago Bears memorabilia adorning his courtroom. Link pointed to the picture on the wall above the jury box. By the questioning expression on Barker's face, he did not recognize who was in the picture.

"Mr. Barker, that man is Clarence Darrow. Darrow once said, 'He who has himself for an attorney has a fool for a client.' Do you know what that means?"

"Yes."

"Do you still want to represent yourself?"

"Yes, and I want to file a motion for a continuance."

"I'll deny the motion . . ."

"But, I need—"

Judge Link established the line of demarcation immediately. Link's volume rose to the "you better pay attention" mode.

"The first rule here is *Don't talk while I'm talking.* I don't let the attorneys interrupt me, and I'm not going to let you. Remember, you have to conduct yourself like an attorney."

When Link allowed Barker to speak, Barker said he needed a private investigator to do some work for him. He also needed a runner to obtain legal documents and pick up research from the law library.

Getting back to the self-representation issue, Link said, "Personally I wouldn't grant a right to *pro per*. It's like leading a lamb to slaughter. I've been in this business for thirty-five years, twenty-two on the bench. The end result [of a *pro per* case] is a disaster. One hundred percent of the time! But the appeals court says we must allow it if a person is competent."

Link explained that "competent" didn't mean competent to practice law. In this context, someone was "competent" if he could read and write. Barker told Link that he had graduated from high school and went to auto mechanic school for a few months. This meant that Ron Barker, in the eyes of the law, was competent to represent himself.

Link, after ensuring the requirements of the Lopez Waiver had been fulfilled, granted the motion for Barker to represent himself. Link appointed John Mitchell as his advisory counsel, and John Lane as his private investigator.

Barker wasn't done. He wanted John Mitchell removed as his advisory counsel. This removal of Mitchell would mean a continuance while other advisory counsel was appointed. Link denied the motion to have Mitchell removed.

"But I don't want him," Barker said.

"I don't care what you want," Link said, leaning forward, showing just the faintest evidence of testiness. "He's your advisory counsel."

Meanwhile, Chandra Carle sat there, taking in the proceedings. She would put on the case based on her evidence. But a *pro per* defendant represented a minefield for her. Perhaps a jury would feel sorry for a person representing himself. In this case, however, Carle believed Ron Barker was so inherently unlikable, it was doubtful anyone would feel sorry for him. Yet, as evidenced by the O.J. Simpson case, anything could happen in a courtroom.

Because Ron Barker was now representing himself, Link had to change one of his previous rulings. He reversed himself without request by any of the parties. Link granted separate trials for the two defendants. There would no longer be two juries and one trial. There would be two trials.

Although initially opposed to two trials, for the sake of expediency and the convenience of witnesses, Chandra Carle was now in favor of two trials. She witnessed how Barker handled himself in the courtroom; how intractable he was; how controlling he could be, if given a chance. Barker was not awed by the judicial presence of Frederic Link, one of San Diego's most respected jurists. Barker was barely respectful of him. If Ron Barker had been allowed to defend himself in the trial with two juries, Ny Nourn's jury would see what a control freak Barker was. They would see, as Carle had seen during the court proceedings thus far, Barker had a need to control everything. Link's strong admonitions to Barker, although obeyed by Barker, had no effect on Barker's demeanor. When Link raised his voice to real attorneys, the attorneys cringed. When Link raised his voice to Barker, there was no visible reaction. Barker acted superior to Link. Nothing dissuaded Barker from running the show. He was in control, even though he came in to court every day shackled and wearing jail clothing. At noon, when the judge and attorneys went to their favorite San Diego eateries for lunch, Ron Barker munched on his traditional jail-issue bologna sandwich. This disparity in living conditions had no effect on the outlook of Ron Barker. In his mind, he still sought to control.

Carle believed a jury would look at slim, quiet, dainty, compliant, subservient Ny Nourn and come to the conclusion that maybe Ron Barker *was* solely responsible for killing David Stevens. Carle suddenly remembered that this case was still about David Stevens. That's why they were here. It wasn't about Ron Barker and the events he strove to control. This was about David Stevens—his brutal murder. Carle chided herself briefly and vowed never to forget about Stevens again, even for one minute.

Carle had to make sure Ny Nourn's jury realized, but for the fact of Ny Nourn leading David Stevens to Ron Barker, David Stevens would be alive today. Carle remembered Barker casually announced he was going to kill David Stevens shortly after Nourn admitted having sex with Stevens. Nourn knew she was taking Stevens on his way to Eternity when she told Stevens the lies that lured him out that night of December 23, 1998. During the ride when they were alone in Stevens's car, Nourn could have told Stevens what Barker planned to do. By her silence, she helped kill David Stevens.

All parties were back in court on December 19, 2002. Ron Barker had filed a written motion for a continuance. Link had to rule on it.

"Your Honor, I've been given nothing by Mr. Mitchell in the way of discovery." (Discovery means "discovery documents.") These are police and evidence reports that the police and prosecution generate. Defendants have the right to examine the documents in advance of court proceedings in order to prepare a defense.

Chandra Carle stole a quick glance at John Mitchell when Barker accused him of not giving the documents. Mitchell, in a rare display of emotion that undoubtedly illustrated his inner thoughts, tilted his head back and rolled his eyes upward. Judge Link appeared to catch the body and eye movement.

Barker continued, telling Judge Link that John Mitchell had told him nothing about what was going on.

Barker said Mitchell told him just to sit there and not say anything. He was asking for a continuance to get a new legal advisor.

"Mr. Barker, you're trying to delay the case," Link said. "Motion denied."

CHAPTER 24

January 7, 2003, was showtime. *The People of the State of California versus Ronald Ely Barker.* San Diego Police Department Case 98-088720, District Attorney Case AAO 882, Superior Court Case SCD 163772. It was the day for which they all had been preparing. Before jury selection began, there was some legal housekeeping to be done. Chandra Carle made a motion to dismiss the real estate fraud and perjury complaints against Barker. Judge Link granted the motion, which was not opposed by the defense. On the chance Barker was acquitted of murder, the district attorney could refile those cases. If the jury found Barker guilty of first-degree murder with special circumstances, he would get life without parole, rendering the other charges moot. Who cared if he lied to the Department of Motor Vehicles, when compared to killing a man? Since Barker had no money, it wouldn't serve the real estate fraud victims any solace to add that conviction to the murder conviction. The real estate victims wouldn't get any restitution.

Prior to the bailiff bringing the jury pool into the court-room, Ron Barker, not surprisingly, had some motions to give Judge Link. Sounding like anything but a real lawyer, Barker informed Link he had rights as an American under the Sixth Amendment to the United States Constitution and the California Constitution, Section 15. Some court observers doubted Barker had ever read the Sixth Amendment or the California Constitution. Some wondered if Barker even knew independently that California had its own constitution in addition to the United States document. Barker's statements sounded like more coaching from a jailhouse lawyer.

Barker said he still had not received any discovery documents. None of Barker's witnesses had received subpoenas. Barker asked for another continuance.

Judge Link looked at John Mitchell. "Mr. Mitchell, have you provided discovery material to Mr. Barker?"

"Yes, Your Honor, I have."

"I also filed a complaint against Mr. Mitchell with the State Bar," Barker said, speaking out of turn but, surprisingly, getting away with it for now.

With widened eyes, Link stared at Barker. Link didn't comment.

"I also have brought a Pitchess motion against Detectives Tefft and Young," Barker said. A Pitchess motion is named after former Los Angeles County Sheriff Peter Pitchess. In the "old days," defendants were not privy to obtain personnel material on police officers relative to citizen complaints against the officers for brutality, dishonesty, or other negative factors. The law was changed when an accused person sued Pitchess, to allow defendants to obtain certain items in an officer's personnel file.

Link denied the motion for two reasons, but not without comment. First, Link said the Pitchess motion was not timely. One couldn't file such a motion the day before the trial. The date of a trial never comes as a surprise. It had been scheduled for months. Second, Link cited a court case, *City of Santa Cruz v. Municipal Court,* (49 Cal. 3D at pages 85 and 86). This case said, in part, "The defendant must demonstrate the relevance of the requested information by providing a specific factual scenario which establishes a plausible factual foundation for the allegations of officer misconduct committed in connection with the defendant."

In his request for a Pitchess motion against Tefft and Young, Barker didn't specify any citable wrongful conduct committed by them against him, only that they engaged in misconduct. He did say they were "coercive" in their interview of him, and denied him a lawyer when he asked for one. Link had already viewed the videotape of the interview and had already ruled on that issue. Barker lost the Pitchess motion.

Barker had presented a list of several potential defense witnesses who would testify for him. Chandra Carle had a right to know approximately about what they were going to testify. Would they be alibi witnesses, saying Barker was with them in the early hours of December 23, 1998? Would they be character witnesses, trumpeting his excellent character?

Barker indicated they would be character witnesses. Carle had to get it onto the record that if anyone came in to testify about what a great guy Barker was, the door would be opened for her to bring in the kidnap victims in the old case the FBI did not bring forward for prosecution. Those victims, blindfolded and held at gunpoint for several days, would also talk about Ron Barker's character. Also, the information about the aborted "contract hit" on Marc Carlos would become fair game, even though the case was not charged. If anyone tried to say Ron Barker was a nice guy and would never do anything violent,

Carle had people waiting to tell the jury exactly the opposite.

Judge Link looked at Barker, or through him, and told him how it would go. He could have someone testify he was nonviolent, but he was, at the same time, opening the door for the floodgates of accusatory witnesses who would testify to the opposite. It was something for Barker to think about.

Ronald Barker wasn't ready to begin jury selection just yet. He asked for a hearing without the prosecutor being present. Carle, with a wide-eyed "whatever!" expression on her face, gathered up her papers and walked out of the courtroom. The court reporter stayed.

Barker said he needed some things. He asked Judge Link to:

1. Appoint a burn expert for him.

2. Appoint a new private investigator.

3. Hire a jury selection expert.

4. Appoint a fire expert.

When Judge Link asked why he needed these people, Barker responded that a burn expert would help his case. Barker was referring to the burn scars on his arms, which would undoubtedly become a point of evidence against him.

Barker continued that he needed a new private investigator. John Lane, the appointed investigator, "did nothing," according to Barker. "Every time I want to interview someone, Lane says this person is not relevant to my case," Barker complained. (Note: John Lane is an experienced private investigator with many years of court and investigative experience.)

"When I called John Mitchell and asked what is his

(Lane's) job, Mitchell said he didn't know," Barker continued. Barker again asked for another legal advisor. He
accused Mitchell of not liking him and being prejudiced
against him.

Judge Link waited for Barker to finish his rambling
accusations. Link, for the record, told Barker that John
Mitchell had done a very good job for Barker. Link
pointed out that Mitchell had even filed an appeal of a ruling Link had made. This appeal had been denied by one of
the most liberal judges on the Court of Appeals. This
judge was notorious for granting appeals favoring defendants. When this judge ruled against the defendant, and
said Judge Link had not erred, the legal community
"perked up its ears," Link said.

"All your motions are denied."

"Is there a motion that I can file that you will not deny,
Your Honor?" Barker asked. Barker laughed at his own
joke. No one else did.

"Bring in the prosecutor," Link said.

Chandra Carle had one motion before jury selection was
to begin. She asked that Ny Nourn be allowed to make a
physical appearance before the jury. Nourn would not testify in Barker's trial; she would only appear for the jury to
see her. Link asked for an explanation.

Carle said they had a photo of Nourn for the jury to
view. Carle said she wanted the jury actually to see a person, instead of a mere photo. Nourn could walk in near the
jury box, the jury could view her, and Nourn would leave.

Link granted the motion. The jury would see, but not
hear, Ny Nourn.

One other problem existed for the prosecution. Carle
was fearful Barker would try to muddy up the waters.
Since he had access to discovery documents, which included the San Diego Police reports, Barker now knew all
about Kita Jones, Jason Van Dusen, all the other strippers,

Kathie Newkirk, and the Santerian voodoo fiasco. By reading the reports, Barker also knew about steroids, vitamin strength supplements, and lawsuits within that industry. Those theories sounded good to deflect blame from Barker. Barker knew nothing about these topics before he saw the case file.

The legal concept of blaming someone else is called "third-party culpability." Since there was not one scintilla of evidence that pointed toward any of the third-party theories having any credence, Carle moved to head them off at the pass and disallow Barker from bringing them forward. Even though the police worked those possibilities as leads, the possibilities didn't work out toward solving the case. Barker couldn't even mention the possibility that strippers or anyone else was responsible because it would only be speculation.

John Mitchell knew Barker had a friend who was prepared to testify that Barker did not have burn scars on his arms a month after the killing. Mitchell hoped to introduce this witness's testimony and dovetail it with the theories of strippers, steroids, and the other false leads the police had tracked down and refuted. Mitchell believed once Barker's friend said he didn't have burn scars, the defense should be allowed to present third-party culpability theories. It wasn't to be—not in this case anyway.

CHAPTER 25

Carle and Barker, with John Mitchell's input, selected a jury on January 7 and 8, 2003. The jury selection process can be elaborate and time-consuming. Often, when issues or evidence is complicated, attorneys strive to find the "right" juror, who they think will give their client the benefit of the doubt, if a doubt may exist. If sympathy is a possible issue, defense attorneys will try to find jurors in the "touchy-feely" professions, such as social workers or schoolteachers. These occupations often deal with people who have had a tough time and have not had fair opportunities and need that one break to make their lives a success. In Carle's opinion, Ron Barker's trial was not a "sympathy" case. This case stood on the merits of evidence: who did what, to whom, when, and why. The clerk swore the jury in, and it finally really was showtime.

Chandra Carle's opening statement was simple and direct, with only a hint of passion. She would "bring David Stevens to life" later in the proceedings. Carle promised the jury that many true, incontrovertible facts would soon

be set before them. There would not be innuendo, speculation, or hearsay. There would be solid evidence. Much
of the evidence would be circumstantial but would be
strengthened by statements from credible witnesses. The
jury would not have to make any leaps of faith or perform
any great feats of deduction. The evidence would be right
there, and it wouldn't be confusing. It would be clear.
When she was done, the evidence before the jurors would
be sufficient to convince them, beyond a reasonable
doubt, that Ronald Barker had killed David Stevens with
malice, premeditation, by lying in wait, and by use of a
firearm. After Barker killed Stevens, Barker committed
arson by setting Stevens's car and body on fire.

Then, she sat down.

Barker, wearing civilian clothing, which he put on
every day in the back hallway, stood up to address the
jury. Although slightly nervous at the outset, he soon
came into his own in front of the jurors and alternates.
Barker told them he didn't expect sympathy. He said they
were probably wondering why he was representing himself. He said it was because he wanted the jury to hear the
truth from the same man who was accused of a crime he
didn't commit. By representing himself, the jury would
never have to wonder how come the defendant didn't
speak up.

Barker continued on, interspersing legal terms that
sometimes fit but often did not, a product, undoubtedly, of
his conversations with the jailhouse lawyers who watched
legal shows on television, or had been on trial many times
themselves.

Even though she didn't want to, Chandra Carle was
forced to object several times that Barker was presenting
arguments instead of giving an opening statement. Carle
didn't want to object for fear the jury might think she was
bullying the poor, untrained man who was trying to represent himself. She had to object. She won every objection,

with Judge Link continually telling Barker to stop arguing and confine his remarks to an opening statement.

With confidence that some said bordered on smugness, Barker informed the jury there were neither fingerprints, DNA, nor any weapons that connected him to the crime. Only *words* connected him to this case. And those words were lies.

Barker informed the jury he would prove "the prosecution case is built on a foundation of trickery, lies, and deception." He told the jury he gave an interview to the police as his ploy to have the true criminal arrested. He told them that portion [where he mentioned the existence of the true criminal] of his statement to the police was taped, but purposely disposed of by the police. The tape was gone, and the police would lie that Barker never mentioned any real killer. The police didn't *want* the real killer. They wanted to blame Ron Barker for a crime he didn't commit.

When Barker was done with his opening statement, Carle began calling witnesses for the prosecution's case. She went through the chronology of events in an orderly fashion. Detective Terry Torgersen described the crime scene. The forensic dentist, Dr. Norman Sperber, explained how by comparing known dental X rays of David Stevens, sent by David's dentist in Nebraska, to the X rays of the homicide victim, he was able to determine that the charred corpse was, in fact, David Stevens. Dr. Brian Blackbourne, now retired, testified as to the path of the bullets, where the bullets entered, and how long the victim might have lived after being shot. The corpse Blackbourne examined stayed alive only a matter of minutes after the shooting but would not have been aware of anything, or felt pain. Mr. Gerald Stevens sat in the gallery of the courtroom. He would testify later about his son, David, and what he was like.

Officer Gary Truscott, the longtime friend of Barker,

testified about being contacted by Barker, driving to Barker's apartment, listening to Barker's story, and subsequently arresting him and turning Barker over to the San Diego Police detectives.

Detective John Tefft testified about Ny Nourn's controlled phone call between Nourn and Barker. Then, he told about the interview with Barker; how Barker laid out the chronology of the murder. Tefft talked about burn scars on Barker's arms, and Barker's statement that his eyebrows were burned off in the flash. Tefft identified photographs of Barker's burned arms, pointing out the prominent scars caused by the gasoline fireball.

Tefft brought up how Barker admitted to the killing on tape. Barker told how, when, and why he killed David Stevens. He told the detectives where and how he disposed of the body.

As each of the witnesses was cross-examined, the defense sought to poke holes in memory, to deflect blame from Barker, to somehow cloud the issue of Barker's involvement. That was the intent of the defense. It didn't seem to be working very well. Carle believed the questions by the defense had not damaged her case.

The evidence against Ron Barker was piling up steadily and impressively, according to court watchers. As court cases go, this was neither a complicated nor a difficult one. The prosecution amassed a ton of evidence.

When summoned by prosecutor Carle, Ny Nourn stepped inside the courtroom from the private hallway where the judges' chambers are located. She appeared in civilian clothing, wearing silver-rimmed eyeglasses, looking shy and demure, as was her usual appearance. Although now twenty-one years old, Nourn, at four feet, eleven inches tall and weighing nearly one hundred pounds, looked more like the high school girl down the street you would hire for a babysitting job than a woman facing life in prison for murder.

Carle completed the case for the prosecution. Now, Ronald Barker would put on his defense, sometimes with the assistance of attorney John Mitchell.

CHAPTER 26

Chandra Carle dreaded Ron Barker's defense presentation. She knew he would screw up frequently, necessitating her objections. She didn't want to object because the jury might perceive her actions as crushing the poor, uneducated auto mechanic who was putting on a valiant fight for his freedom, and, according to Barker, his fight for justice.

Called by the defense, Detective John Tefft took the witness stand on January 15, 2003. Ron Barker acted as if he were going to make a fool of Tefft, exposing the lying detective for what he was: a coercive, deceptive, dishonest cop.

Barker referred to himself as "Barker" when addressing Detective Tefft. "Is it true you told Barker you would go arrest Nourn if Barker would place himself in the crime somehow?" he asked.

Tefft wouldn't buy into referring to Barker in the third person. "No. *You* told us how both of you killed David

Stevens. She led him to *you*, and *you* shot him." John Tefft
looked over at the jury. Their expressions were like stone.

The questioning continued in that same fashion: Barker
would refer to himself as "Barker," and Tefft would look
at the jury and say, "You told us . . . You said . . . You
brought up the fact that . . ." And so it went.

In the interview with detectives, Barker had said Nourn
shot Stevens first and then Barker shot him the second
time to make sure he was dead. The police doubted that
version, but it didn't matter anyway, not legally.

When Barker didn't seem to be scoring any points with
Tefft's testimony about the confession, Barker shifted
gears. "Detective Tefft, is it true that you have a history of
police misconduct and bad coercement (sic)?"

"No," Tefft said, before Carle could object.

Carle wished she could have entered Tefft's excellent
personnel record before the jury. She wished she could
have presented his numerous commendations, both from
the department, and from the families of victims over the
years. It wasn't appropriate, however. She hoped the jury
could see, and hear, that John Tefft was a pro's pro and a
cop's cop. She let Tefft's patient demeanor, even in the
face of being maligned now, speak for itself. She hoped
the jury saw Tefft as she saw him.

Barker called a Vietnamese friend to the witness stand.
The friend was at Barker's house approximately one
month after the December 23 murder. The friend could
not remember seeing any burn scars on Barker. Nor did
the friend notice Barker's eyebrows missing. In terms of
points scored, Chandra Carle didn't think Barker was on
the board yet. Carle didn't know if the friend was lying,
not observant, or stupid. Even if he really didn't notice
Barker's burn scabs or scars, it didn't mean they weren't
on his arms. The photos revealed the scars were evidence
of some previous serious burns.

• • •

During the prosecution's portion of the case, John Mitchell handled the technical questioning of the experts such as Dr. Blackbourne and Dr. Sperber. When it came to the defense portion of the case, Barker handled most of the questioning himself. Barker wanted to examine himself when he took the stand. Mitchell had to go along with this tactic, because he was only the legal advisor. Ron Barker requested permission to testify in a narrative fashion. That way, he wouldn't have to ask himself a question and then answer it, an obvious distraction.

After being sworn in, Barker testified to the jury that a friend of his, Ny Nourn, told Barker a friend of hers from work [David Stevens] was killed. Nourn told Barker her fingerprints were at the dead man's house because she went there to help him do some computer work.

Nourn told Barker her other boyfriend, with whom she was having a sexual relationship, became angry because he learned Nourn was also having sex with David Stevens. Barker said he was "only a friend" of Nourn. One night Barker was at a movie with her. Someone paged her. She examined her pager and told Barker a male friend of hers had sent the page. Barker told the jury he had said to Nourn, "Okay, I'll leave." Barker said if Ny Nourn wanted to have another boyfriend, he would bow out of the picture, a far cry from the controlling, jealous Ron Barker everyone involved in the case had known him to be.

Barker said he left Nourn because he knew he didn't have a future with her anyway. After all, he was married, and his wife was a "sweetheart." As a method of damage control, Barker did say that he had sex with Ny Nourn the first time he met her. He knew Chandra Carle would bring this up. Barker rationalized having sex with Nourn because she was "easy."

Barker said he knew about Stevens's death. He told the

story of the murder, but substituted another male, Nourn's other "boyfriend," whose name he didn't know, as the real killer. When Barker asked Nourn about the killer after the murder, she wouldn't tell him anything more.

Regarding officer Gary Truscott, Barker said he asked the officer, "Should I confess to something I didn't do, or turn the other person in?" Barker said Truscott set him up, telling him to confess in order to ensure Nourn's guilt. He said the two Oceanside officers asked him a lot of questions. He said the Oceanside officers had a tape recorder on, but destroyed the tape because the tape contained the real truth.

In previous testimony, the officers had said they had a tape recorder, but Barker told them to turn it off. Since they did, and there was nothing on the tape, they turned it off. The tape was subsequently discarded.

Barker said he kept asking John Tefft for a lawyer. He testified Tefft said, "We don't know what you're going to say." In reality, as evidenced by the tapes, Barker had said he had some conditions he wanted met before he gave a statement. He also told the detectives he didn't know if he needed a lawyer. Barker turned these two factors around. He said the detectives tricked him into thinking his conditions would be met, and then the police reneged on the deal. He turned the lawyer statement around to make it sound like he wanted a lawyer. Even though Barker's convoluted story sounded good, it fell apart when stacked up against what he really said on the tape.

In terms of points, a liberal scorekeeper might have given Ron Barker a point, his first of the trial. This would presuppose that one or more of the jurors weren't too smart. In the grand scheme, however, Chandra Carle thought it was unlikely any of the jurors had been tricked.

When Carle questioned Barker during cross-examination, she did not allow him to skip over his relationship with Nourn. During Barker's testimony, he characterized Nourn merely as a friend he was trying to help. Carle bore in on him to get the salacious details of their living together, and their sexual relationship. Barker tried to gloss over the relationship as one person assisting another to get her life together. Regarding the sex, Barker continually said, "She was easy." He wanted to convey to the jury that she had deep, aggressive sexual urgings and he was merely there, a man not strong enough to decline her seductive advances. Barker rationalized and otherwise dismissed the fact that Nourn lived with him and his wife and they traveled across the country to Texas where the two of them lived together for several months. Barker, in answering the questions, acted as if none of that was important. Carle believed it was very important.

In her cross-examination of Ron Barker, Carle asked him, "Would you agree that someone who sits behind someone then shoots them in the head, has planned the crime?"

Barker answered, "I didn't do it."

"I didn't ask you if you did it. I asked you, generally, if someone sits behind someone in a car and shoots another in the head, has the shooter planned the crime?"

"I didn't do it," Barker said.

"I didn't ask you if you did it," Carle said again, patiently. "I'm only asking if you think someone who would shoot someone from behind had planned the crime?"

"No."

"Okay," Carle continued. "Would you agree that someone who shoots someone twice in the head intended to kill the person?"

"I wouldn't know. I didn't do it."

"Not you," Carle said. "Just generally. If someone

shoots someone else twice in the head, do you think the shooter intended to kill the person he shot?"

"No," Barker said.

"All right, then," Carle mused, pausing to make sure the jury absorbed that last exchange. "How about if someone poured gasoline into a car and set it on fire, do you think the person intended to burn the car?"

"I didn't do that either."

"I don't mean *you*. I mean if someone put gas in a car then lit it on fire, did they intend to burn the car?"

"No."

Carle decided to change the course of the cross-examination. She had inflicted enough damage on the stumbling Barker. She didn't want to evoke any possible sympathy from the jury.

"Mr. Barker, were you coerced by Detective Tefft into making statements against yourself?"

"Yes."

Carle walked to the tape machine and hit the PLAY button. She played part of the interview tape again, where Barker was going over his conditions, telling the police they really didn't have anything without him. The tape was of the conversation between Tefft, Young, and Barker. There was no coercion or anything except three men talking.

When the tape was done, Barker said, "Something is missing from the tape to show I was coerced."

"Okay, Mr. Barker, please tell me exactly how Detective Tefft coerced you."

"He just did."

Carle played several more portions of the taped interview, none of which showed any evidence of coercion, force, trickery, or deception. Carle didn't want to numb the jury with overkill. If the jury didn't get the message that Barker was making things up, her case was in trouble.

When Barker was done testifying, his defense case was

complete. Barker had possibly scored in only two areas, and his weakening of the evidence was not one of them. The crime scene spoke for itself. Bullet holes, a burning car, and a dead man could not be disputed. The tapes were pretty good, too. Barker could only hope one juror bought his story that a phantom boyfriend of Ny Nourn killed David Stevens. If the juror, or jurors, bought that prospect, it would mean the juror believed also that Ron Barker had been tricked and lied to by both Gary Truscott and Detectives John Tefft and J. R. Young. Barker's hopes were slim.

Nonetheless, John Mitchell whispered to Ron Barker, who said, "The defense rests, Your Honor."

It was time for summary arguments for both sides.

CHAPTER 27

Ron Barker began his closing argument on January 16, 2003. The jury heard a sincere, if inarticulate, rendition of how he had been in jail for fourteen months, and life in jail was difficult. After all, Barker explained, gesturing with his open hands, he was married, a father with two children. During the trial, Barker was allowed to display a professional studio photograph of his family, and subsequently enter the framed picture into evidence. Barker did not call his wife, Tran, to testify. Chandra Carle would have loved to ask Mrs. Barker a few probing questions.

Barker told how difficult it was being away from his wife and children, unjustly locked up. Barker repeated to the jury that the police falsified evidence and coerced him into admitting things he did not do. The police did not follow proper police procedure or proper constitutional conduct. It did not matter to Barker that the jury had not heard any evidence to back up what Barker was alleging.

Barker said when he tried to tell the police that someone else did the killing, the detectives twisted his statement as if to appear that he [Barker] had killed Stevens. He said he knew Ny Nourn was responsible for the killing, and he wanted to make sure justice was done in that at least one of the guilty people would be arrested. That is the only reason he came forward and played along with the murder scenario. He assured the jury he did not commit the murder.

Even though his grammar was fractured, his pronunciation was distracting, and his logic hard to follow, observers gave Barker credit for sincerity. He spoke passionately. Did the jury buy any of it?

To Deputy District Attorney Chandra Carle, that closing argument was the biggest bunch of bullshit she had ever heard. Her heart pounded wildly as Barker addressed the jury. She wanted to scream. She wanted to shout. She was at least mildly fearful that maybe one of the jurors had bought Barker's line. Then what? She couldn't bear the thought of an acquittal, or anything less that first-degree murder for this guy.

Cautioning herself to remain calm and focused, Carle stood up, took a sip of water, closed her eyes for two seconds, and looked at each of the jurors.

"How offensive," she said, stressing each syllable, her lower jaw barely moving. Pointing at him, she continued, her volume increasing. "How offensive for the defendant, Ronald Barker, to stand before you today and tell about fatherhood when he has chosen to take away someone else's son."

Carle had it under control now. She was angry yet confident she would not be too angry, even though she certainly was too angry inside. She knew the only way to get this conviction was to present this closing argument as systematically as she could. She was offended by Barker's trying to portray himself as a victim, and hoped the jury was, too. The jury had seen Mr. Gerald Stevens in the gallery every day. Carle hoped the jury bristled, as she had, at the mention of "lost fatherhood." The jury only had to look at Mr. Stevens to see the sadness of losing one's son.

"Mr. Barker talked about how tough the past fourteen months have been for him, away from his sons. How about Mr. Stevens's having to go through the past four years? At least Mr. Barker still has his sons. Mr. Stevens's son is gone forever.

"The defendant is living in a fantasy world. You have heard for yourselves the interview that the police conducted with Mr. Barker. You did not hear any coercion. You did not hear any false statements from the detectives."

Carle reviewed the evidence the jury had to consider. The evidence was clear, concise, and right before them. Carle sat down, her job done. She had tried to do the best job she could. David Stevens could not speak. She hoped she spoke for him.

After Judge Link delivered the jury instructions, the jury retired to a room to consider and deliberate the evidence, and discuss the case.

In two hours they were back. They hadn't asked to have testimony repeated, as juries sometimes do. They had not asked to see any exhibits. In two hours they talked about everything they wanted, and needed, to talk about.

The jury foreman handed the verdict slip to the court clerk, who handed it to Judge Link. Link looked at the verdict and handed it back to the clerk to read aloud. Ron Barker was guilty of murder and arson. More important, the jury found him guilty of first-degree murder with the special circumstance of lying in wait, and with the use of a firearm. They could have found him guilty of a lesser degree of murder. For example, if the jury had believed Barker became so incensed at the thought of his girlfriend having sex with another, and that he was so angry at that thought, he might have killed David Stevens without thinking his actions through. That legal term is "heat of passion."

Instead, the jury had considered Barker's words: "You're not pure. You're used goods." Nourn also said Barker told her, "Only way you stay with me is if you kill David or I kill David." His final statement was, "You're mine forever and now that I've did this for you, then you're clean, as in your sin has gone away."

Sentencing was set for February 14, 2003. It wouldn't happen then, however. Barker needed a continuance. He needed to buy time to find a reason to have another trial.

That was well and good for Ron Barker. Chandra Carle had another trial to put on in five days.

To best illustrate the legal and grammatical skills of Ronald Barker, one need only look at the memo he sent to Chandra Carle on February 20, 2003. It is printed here exactly as it was sent to Ms. Carle.

(The word "[sic]" used within brackets to show that a quoted passage, often containing some error, is precisely reproduced, is not used here because "[sic]" would be used several times within each sentence. Suffice it to say that the entire passage should be bracketed with [sic.])

TO: CHANDRA CARLE   DATED: 2/20/03
DEPUTY DISTRICT ATTORNEY.

MY NAME IS RONALD E. BARKER AS PRO-PRIA-PERSONA. Due to the fact that discovery didn't disclose to me until 12/31/2002, and the remain 80% of the discovery is handing over on 1/29/2003. discovery that regarding to my murder case. There are five additional boxes i would like a list of Itemized show what are there suppose to be in the discovery, mr.

Mitchell handing me over the discovery with missing material still. there should be a list of Itemized prepare from day one when the discovery was handing over. so im requesting that the prosecution to give me this list of evidence belong to discovery. this list should show all the witnesses name involve to the case. all the police officer involved. video tape audio tapes. photo how many and what kind of photo. everything that regarding to this muder case or relevant to the case. it seem mr. mitchell may have lost some of the discovery or miss place some of the evidence , or the D.A. did'nt disclose all of discovery. this is the reason why a list of Itemizes should have been done from the start. with this list I can check to see if everything is disclose to the defendant. by law the defendant have the right to compel all of discovery from the prosecution. Thank you for you cooperation. as of now i also would like to remind the D.A. that any respond is need to be done to me directly, not mr. mitchell, im a attorney of record and that mr. mitchell is not my lawyer. but just an advisor. I can be reach at **P.O. BOX 122952, SANDIEGO CA. 92112.** Please once this list is available you can forward to my privated investigator and have him bring it to me or you can mail it to me.

respectfully sumitted

RONALD E. BARKER
PROPRIA PERSONA

Chandra Carle read the memo, shaking her head. And to think the law said Ronald Barker was capable of acting as his own attorney, and in a capital case, no less. She made arrangements to have a clerk copy the memo and send it to John Mitchell.

CHAPTER 28

Ron Barker's trial ended on January 16. Ny Nourn's began on January 21. In terms of difficulty for Chandra Carle, Barker's trial had been worse than she believed Ny Nourn's would be. With Barker, there were challenges each and every day. Barker was a difficult defendant. He presented so many motions that had to be addressed, even though most were frivolous and ridiculous. With Barker's guilty verdict in the books, Carle had no time to exult, not that she ever did when completing a homicide trial. She didn't even have time for a contented sigh or a "glad that's over" thought. It was time to jump right back in that trench and start fighting again.

Ny Nourn's attorney, Bruce Cormicle, was from Santa Monica, near Los Angeles.

John Mitchell was a consummate professional. Cormicle proved to be equally competent, thorough, and formidable. While not surly, Cormicle was not friendly either. He was all business, and rarely offered a smile during the morning greeting. While John Mitchell's face crinkled into a grin from time to time, Bruce Cormicle had his "game face" on from start to finish.

(Author's note: When contacted about giving an interview for this book, John Mitchell said, "I'll tell you what I always tell the press: 'No comment.' But, good luck." When contacted months later at a party, and asked again for a statement, Mitchell laughed, put his hand on my shoulder, and said, "No, I never talk to the press, but I hope you do well." At a chance meeting on the steps of the courthouse one afternoon, Mitchell declined for the third time to talk about the case. He said, "Hey, let me know when that book comes out."

Bruce Cormicle never responded to a written request for an interview or a statement.)

Carle had no doubts about the evidence in this case. Nourn had come forward and pointed to the evidence the San Diego Police had collected. Nourn corroborated what the crime scene revealed. Her lip prints were on the drinking glass. Her DNA was on the lipstick. Her full handprints were on the mirrored headboard of David Stevens. Her long, dark hair was in his bed and bathroom. Nourn's story matched up to the physical evidence in the apartment and was consistent with the fiery scene on La Jolla Scenic Drive.

Chandra Carle's problem in this case was different. Ronald Barker was not an inherently likeable person. Some might say he was contemptuous. When Barker spun a lie, it was fairly obvious to everyone listening. Barker craved the limelight. He loved to swagger in front of the jury. By their quick, yet thoughtful verdict, the jury had conveyed how they felt about Ronald Barker's involvement in David Stevens's murder.

With Ny Nourn, Chandra Carle had to consider the sympathy factor. Her waiflike appearance could evoke feelings of sympathy among the jury.

The other pitfall that lay ahead for Carle was the actual crime she had charged against Nourn. The Barker jury could have considered second-degree murder, or even voluntary manslaughter. With Ny Nourn, Chandra Carle had charged first- or second-degree murder, nothing less.

Jury selection began on January 21, only five days after Barker's verdict. The process went smoothly. Selection would be crucial in that Bruce Cormicle wanted an empathetic jury, while Chandra Carle wanted one that would dispassionately consider the facts. Cormicle wanted social worker, counselor, and schoolteacher types, while Carle set her sights on engineers, scientists, and linear thinkers.

Nourn's incontrovertible, voluntary statements to the police would undoubtedly do her considerable harm when considered by the jury. Nourn's defense was that Barker was responsible for the killing. It was his idea, and he controlled her so completely in every aspect of her life.

Carle presented the evidence exactly as in Barker's trial. She established the physical evidence in the apartment, the burning car, the cause of death, and the identification of the victim, David Stevens. Carle remembered to talk about him as often as possible. David Stevens temporarily came to life: the good son; the high school wrestling champion; the farm boy from Nebraska; the telemarketing supervisor with the clean criminal record whose only fault was having sex with a willing, unmarried woman. For that fault, Stevens had received a death sentence. Maybe first-degree murder was appropriate for Ny Nourn.

Then, Carle brought in Nourn's voluntary phone call to the police, followed by her statement to Tefft and Young. John Tefft testified about the "murder tour" she gave the detectives to Stevens's apartment in Pacific Beach, the murder spot off of Route 52, and the burning scene on La Jolla Scenic Drive. Tefft also testified that Nourn told him the very first time Ron Barker laid an angry hand on her was *after* David Stevens was dead. That angry hand was a slap in the face to stop Nourn's hysterical crying and get her in the car before they drove Stevens to be burned.

Nourn did not testify at the trial. Cormicle pounded home as often as he could that Ron Barker was the controlling person in this relationship. What Barker said, went. His word was law. Barker pulled the strings.

Making a strategic decision, Bruce Cormicle did not mount an affirmative defense during the trial of Ny Nourn. Cormicle had cross-examined each prosecution witness, testing the evidence the prosecution presented. Cormicle did not put on evidence pointing to the innocence of Ny Nourn.

It would have been silly for Cormicle to suggest Ny Nourn did not play a part in the killing of David Stevens. Cormicle wanted the jury, however, to remember that if Nourn had not told the police about her involvement in Stevens's murder, none of them would be in court. She may have had some responsibility for the death of David Stevens, but she was also responsible for solving the crime. Cormicle hoped for one soft heart among the assembled twelve plus alternates.

If Ronald Barker had not knocked Nourn around, hounded her, and attempted to control her life after the murder, both Barker and Nourn would still be free. Nourn, it appeared, feared Barker more than prison.

When the evidence was in for both sides, the respective attorneys had to do their jobs. Cormicle had to generate sympathy for Ny Nourn.

Bruce Cormicle believed his best hope for Ny Nourn would be for sympathy from the jury. He knew he had to fight with everything at his disposal for Judge Link to give jury instructions that would be in Nourn's best interest. Both Cormicle and Nourn knew she was going to prison. They wanted to minimize the term of incarceration rather than undergo the "life without parole" sentence sought by the prosecution.

On Super Bowl Sunday, the last Sunday in January 2003, Carle stood alone in her kitchen watching the game on her small television. Her husband, Jeff, a firefighter, was on duty. Along with watching the game, Carle had another task at hand. She had with her a three-foot by two-and-a-half foot white paper flip chart. Printing in three-inch letters with an indelible marker, Carle printed WHAT NOURN KNEW, and WHAT NOURN DIDN'T DO.

WHAT NOURN KNEW

- Barker threatened to kill Stevens

- Barker said he would get a gun

- Killing Stevens was the only way to save the relationship

- They both went to get the gun at Barker's house

- She believed Barker got the gasoline

- She believed Barker was hiding the gun after he got it

- She directed Barker to David's apartment

- She buzzed David's intercom

- She gained access to his apartment

- She told David she had car trouble

- She asked David to help her

- She told David her brother would help them

- She saw Barker waiting by Stevens's apartment to follow them
- She told David to pull over on the freeway when Barker flashed his lights
- She met with Barker at the side of the freeway while Stevens was still in his car
- She told David to follow Barker when he exited the freeway
- She introduced Barker as her brother
- She sat in passenger seat when Barker got in back and directed Stevens
- She sat there as Barker:
  - *Gave directions to exit the freeway*
  - *Pulled over on the side street*
  - *Pulled out the gun*
  - *Grabbed Stevens*
  - *Shot and killed Stevens*
- She got back in the car in the back seat
- She retrieved Barker's car
- She drove Barker's car while Barker drove David's
- Went with Barker to get a gas can
- Drove Barker's car to the fire site
- Waited for Barker while he set the fire
- Drove to pick up Barker after he set the fire
- Gave her bloody clothes to Barker
- Went with Barker to throw away the keys
- Said she only worked with David when the detective called her after the murder

WHAT NOURN DIDN'T DO

- Refused to take Barker to the victim's apartment

- Leave while Barker was getting the gun

- Seek help from neighbors

- Warn the victim at his apartment

- Call the police to report Barker

- Tell the victim not to go to his car

- Warn the victim in his car when Barker gave the signal

- Tell the victim not to pull over

- Tell the victim not to exit Route 52

- Tell the victim who Barker really was

- Tell the victim that Barker had a gun

- Tell the victim that Barker planned to kill him

- Tell the victim not to stop at the exit

- Warn the victim not to let Barker in the car

On the final page, in large letters, Carle printed: BUT I CAN'T SAY THAT RON MADE ME. IT'S NOT HE MAKE ME OR HE PUT A GUN TO MY HEAD AND TOLD ME TO DO THIS AND THAT. These last words were from Nourn's taped statement to the detectives.

In court the next day, prosecutor Carle went over each of the points, elaborating when necessary. Sometimes, the statement stood alone, no elaboration or explanation from the prosecutor needed. She watched the jury, hoping to see signs of agreement. Their set expressions gave her no clue how they viewed her presentation.

• • •

Bruce Cormicle did the best he could in his closing argument. At one point, Nourn had told the detectives, "I thought he was just gonna scare David, or beat him up." To the detectives, Nourn quoted herself as saying to Barker, "I do anything you say." With the first statement, Cormicle hoped to convey that Nourn didn't know Barker was going to kill David. With Nourn's second statement that she would do anything he said, Cormicle hoped the jury would recognize Barker's control over her.

After receiving instructions, the jury began deliberating on January 27. One and one half hours later, they returned with a verdict of guilty of first-degree murder with special circumstances, and arson.

Nourn cried quietly at the verdict. Someone had told her what first-degree murder meant, given the reality of the special circumstances. It meant life without parole. No chance of parole—ever. Life in prison for as long as you are alive. That was a big bite to swallow for this twenty-one-year-old. Both attorneys had done their jobs the best they could.

CHAPTER 29

Chandra Carle gathered up her binders, putting them in a large briefcase. She shook hands with David's father, Gerald Stevens, who responded with typical Midwestern stoicism. He was solemn and polite. Carle thanked the detectives for their work. A man was dead. Even though his brutal killers were held to answer for the crime, there was still no cause for celebration. The cops gathered up their notes and reports and headed back to the police station.

Carle went to her office in the Hall of Justice. She closed the door, telephoned her husband, Jeff Carle, at the fire station, and told him the guilty verdict was in. After breaking the news to him, Carle said she "lost it," bursting into tears. Months of work, preparation, conflict, and back-to-back trials took their emotional toll on the young mother of two. No matter what she had done, or how much she had done, David Stevens was still dead. She didn't allow herself to be emotional during the process except for the brief anger she allowed herself during her closing argument in Barker's trial. She was incensed at

Barker's attempt to gain sympathy by saying he was a father who had had it tough for the past fourteen months.

There had been some conflicts with Team III when they wanted her to take the case before the grand jury and indict Kita Jones and Jason Van Dusen. Carle had realized back then that the police were frustrated and wanted to try something, anything to get the case solved. The conflict with the detectives was brief. In the end, the police realized their theory wouldn't stand up against scrutiny. They acquiesced to Carle's decision like the professionals they were.

Carle cried uncontrollably while her poor husband could only sit at the other end of the phone and listen. Jeff congratulated her, hoping that is what she wanted to hear. He felt helpless but knew his wife had appreciated his support during the previous months getting ready for trial, and the trial itself.

After that brief display of emotion, Carle fixed herself in the mirror and began preparations for the sentencing.

The February 14 sentencing had been put over to March 5. Before any statements were made, Ron Barker naturally had more motions to file. He asked for a new trial because his legal advisor, John Mitchell, had not given him discovery documents. Mitchell, ever the professional, did allow his eyes to roll again as he looked at Chandra Carle during some of Barker's more ridiculous statements. When asked later, Mitchell would neither confirm nor deny making any eye-rolling gestures. But, with a smile, Carle said she knew "rolling eyes" when she saw them.

Most defendants, if they are smart, will not make a statement at sentencing. Any statements made during those proceedings become a part of the permanent record—the record that will be reviewed for appeal. Anything said at sentencing can and will be held against the defendant when the appellate justices consider the appeal.

If there is something that might aid them, defendants can include that evidence, or statements, in the brief their attorneys file in the appeal. Seldom is there a benefit to making a statement, unless one does not plan an appeal and wants to convey real remorse to a victim's family.

Most defendants who give statements at sentencing are those who possess huge egos. Not surprisingly, Ron Barker stood up to give his statement to Judge Link and those in the courtroom.

Of course, Barker started off by claiming his innocence. He said the crime happened because of all the things the police had concentrated their efforts on before they even heard of Ron Barker. The murder of David Stevens was the result of steroids, lawsuits about vitamin supplements, strippers, voodoo, and the topless clubs and bars the victim frequented.

Barker said he was innocent. Ny Nourn blamed him for murder because he rejected her. Barker added the justice system doesn't allow a *pro per* defendant to win. The deck is stacked against a defendant who represents himself. Curiously enough, Judge Link, in his warning to Barker during Link's admonition at the time of the Lopez waiver, had said defendants who act as their own lawyers usually lose.

Barker sarcastically sneered that prosecutor Carle should be proud because she beat a *pro per* defendant on a murder case, a *pro per* who had no knowledge of his case until six days before trial because his defense advisor had chosen not to give him documents that would aid in his defense. Barker claimed he didn't even know what the case was about, except that someone was killed.

Barker's voice took on an even more sarcastic tone as he told Judge Link what a pleasure it was to have had the experience of preparing for a murder trial in only six days, especially with all of the abuse he had had to put up with from Link's court.

Barker repeated his claim of innocence. Then, he sat down.

Carle knew Judge Link well enough from years of dealing with him that she didn't need to say a lot. The look on Link's face, when Barker was delivering his diatribe, accusing Link of judicial abuse, was enough to signal her to be brief. She didn't need to convince Link of anything.

Carle also didn't need to convince a jury of anything. They were gone. She only needed to make sure her statements were correct for the record. She said, "I never heard 'I'm sorry,' from the defendant. He never said he was sorry. He killed a man in cold blood and never said he was sorry. It was all about him, and how wrongly he had been treated." With a rare expression of disgust, she glanced at Barker, then sat down.

When Frederic Link speaks, he talks like a normal person. He doesn't talk in "judgespeak." He knows how to deliver lofty, formal speeches when necessary. He seldom finds it necessary to be anything other than a normal person.

Link addressed Barker as if Barker were the only person in the courtroom. Link's eyes penetrated Barker. Link's words were clear and delivered with the proper modulation and speed.

Just as Link's look bore through Barker, so did his words. "You haven't been abused by anyone, Mr. Barker," Link began. "You abused all of us, and you abused the system. People like you who commit crimes, like you did, fall into three categories:

1. People who have severe mental problems

2. Crazed individuals

3. Cold-hearted killers

You're the third kind. The evidence convicted you—not me, not the prosecutor, not biased individuals. You convicted yourself."

Link wasn't done with Barker, this killer who accused the respected jurist of abusing him. "You wanted to get out of jail and go home to your little sex nest; home to your wife and your girlfriend." Link paused, probably deciding not to say something he would later regret. After a brief paper-shuffling pause Judge Frederic Link sentenced Ronald Ely Barker to life in prison without the possibility of parole, the site of incarceration to be determined by the California Department of Corrections.

Ny Nourn's sentencing was short and sweet. She, wisely enough, listened to her defense attorney and elected to make no statement.

The sentence for her was the same as Barker's: life without parole. Nourn would get an appellate attorney appointed for her who would appeal some aspects of the case.

CHAPTER 30

Some minor debate took place in the Hall of Justice and places where lawyers gather to talk, and talk, and talk. The consensus was that Ron Barker's sentence represented what he deserved. Ny Nourn's fate was another matter.

Even some police officers, traditionally unsympathetic to any defendants, thought the system was a little tough on Nourn. Everyone involved in the prosecution said Barker got what was coming to him. A lethal injection or a strapdown seat in the first-class section of the gas chamber might even be a good thing for Barker. They weren't so sure about Ny Nourn and her life sentence. After all, without Ny Nourn's coming forward, the cops would still be out there, trying to find the solution to that crime. Many believed Nourn should be given *some* leniency for her part in the resolution of the crime. One of the things considered by the system is if the defendant might commit a similar offense in the future. With Barker, given his narcissistic personality and penchant for violence toward anyone who crossed him, future murder was indeed possible. Everyone agreed it was unlikely Ny Nourn would be involved in the future death of anyone.

Prosecutor Carle and other respected legal insiders could not be convinced Ny Nourn deserved anything less than life without parole because of the facts of this particular murder, how the facts fit into the legal definitions of murder, and the concept of special circumstances. Carle said Nourn was responsible for the entire crime. She cowardly complained to Barker that David Stevens had raped her. This so enraged the volatile Barker that he killed Stevens. And Nourn could have stopped it at any time right up until the end. These legal strategists said she was not the demure coquette she presented herself as, but rather a conniving, manipulative woman who used her sexuality to get what she wanted. Remove Nourn from the equation, Carle said, and there would have been no murder. No matter how sympathetic to Nourn one was, one couldn't argue with the prosecutor's logic.

It didn't matter what anyone thought. The system had worked. The juries had heard the evidence and delivered their verdicts. Down the road, the court of appeals could decide whether or not the system was too tough on Ny Nourn or unfair to Ronald Barker.

Some legal insiders quietly suggested that Bruce Cormicle might have been "hometowned" by Judge Link regarding some of Link's rulings. This is legal slang, meaning that Link possibly "tightened up" his rulings on issues affecting Cormicle's case because he didn't have to see Bruce Cormicle every day. Cormicle was an outsider in the San Diego legal community. He would never run into Link at a restaurant, theater, or on the golf course. He probably would never have another case with Link. It is human nature to be more delicate if you have to deal with someone every day. Link probably would never see Cormicle again.

The "hometown" reference to Judge Link might be unfair. A good judge, and Link is almost unanimously thought of as one, is like a good umpire. He knows he's not there to be loved. He knows he's going to have to make some really close calls and one side won't like a particularly close call. Making those calls are his job. Link's responsibility is to know the law, interpret the law, and make the call. Since he knows the law, as evidenced by his many years of success, he must interpret it with common sense. Frederic Link would not be afraid to face an attorney he had just made a close call against in the local grocery store. Link would undoubtedly greet the attorney and go about his business. Just like a good umpire, when Link made a ruling, there was nothing personal involved.

Link, or any other judge, would not *consciously* "hometown" an outside attorney. It could happen though.

NBC's award-winning reality-based television program *Law and Order: Crime and Punishment*, became interested in the case from the outset. A film crew followed Chandra Carle around the Hall of Justice as she made final preparations for the case. The nearly invisible camera was in the courtroom during all of the proceedings. Jurors were never filmed during the course of the show. The defense is always given the opportunity to be featured and interviewed for this show. As is most often the case, the defense declined.

Hundreds of hours of film were distilled down to approximately forty-six minutes for the production. The program, which aired June 8, 2003, did a good job of showing the criminal process. The audience received a fair and accurate glimpse of Ron Barker and his efforts to be a criminal defense attorney. The cameras even caught his incessantly puckering and stretching lips that caused him to get the nickname "Grouper fish." The viewing public was never let in on this inside joke of the San Diego cops and the people from the district attorney's office about Barker's personal foibles.

The program, thankfully, did not air the roadblocks experienced by the San Diego Police Department, more specifically Homicide Team III, during the investigation. The program did not show the existence of the newspaper articles generated by private investigator John Stevens. That dirty laundry was kept away from the viewing public. Neither did the public see the blind alleys Team III went down nor the red herrings they were forced to consider until all possible leads were exhausted.

A&E's *Cold Case Files* featured the murder of David Stevens for the first time on October 26, 2004. During their half-hour treatment, the program stuck with the facts of the case. Viewers saw the somewhat cooperative Ronald Barker telling the police how the murder happened. They did not see his courtroom shenanigans where he accused the police of destroying tapes that would exonerate him.

Gerald Stevens refused comment for both the *Crime and Punishment* and *Cold Case Files* programs. His reasons are understandable. A letter was sent to Mr. Stevens's attorney, Lance Carlson, in Nebraska, seeking an interview with Mr. Stevens and requesting a statement for this book. The correspondence was never answered.

Private Investigator John Stevens phoned me from Portland, Oregon, on March 26, 2004. We had tried to speak before that time, trading phone messages for a few days.

Although I am a thirty-four-year veteran police officer currently employed as an investigator for the San Diego District Attorney's Office, I had no involvement in the David Stevens murder investigation or trial. I barely remembered reading about it when it happened, and had forgotten about it by the time the trial started.

My interest in writing about the case came about in May 2003, when I attended the annual awards banquet put on by the Deputy District Attorneys' Association, the bargaining and social unit for the Deputy D.A.s. My close friend, Alexander Lutzi Jr., was being honored as the Investigator of the Year for work he had done in the Insurance Fraud Unit. I had never before attended the attorneys' banquet.

At the time, I had known Chandra Carle for approximately ten years and had worked with her in two criminal divisions within the office, the South Bay branch and Insurance Fraud. I had not spoken with Carle in several months. As she made her brief acceptance speech for winning the "Outstanding Achievement Award," Carle gave a *Reader's Digest*–type sketch of the crime. Having written over one hundred murder stories for now-defunct various true crime pulp magazines over the years, I became interested in the story of David Stevens. I began preparations to write this book shortly after attending the banquet.

The San Diego detectives from Team III, whom I had written previous murder stories about over the years for the true crime magazines, urged me to contact private investigator John Stevens. "You'll like him," they said, with the cynical, sarcastic humor possessed by many police officers.

The first thing John Stevens asked me, during our phone conversation, was if I had a conflict of interest. Temporarily befuddled, I told him that was really my concern, as opposed to his. The case was a matter of public record. I had gone to the court of appeals and examined the transcripts, on my own time, over a period of a few days, as any citizen, writer or not, could have done. To gain access to a criminal file one tells the court of appeal's clerk the name of the case. The clerk looks it up. A few minutes later, the clerk brings the transcripts. One cannot leave the building, or make copies, but a large reception area is available to spend as much as time as one wants looking at transcripts. One may take notes, which is what I did. I also had interviewed the homicide detectives and Chandra Carle on my own time.

After asking if I had a conflict of interest, Stevens asked me if I had investigated the case. I told him I read about it when it happened and then forgot about it until I read about the verdict. Stevens gave a short laugh that sounded like perhaps he didn't believe me.

I told Stevens I had talked to the prosecutor, and to the detectives, and had a familiarity with the case. Since this was my interview, I asked him how he became involved.

John Stevens said the police contacted him, at the suggestion of David's family, to see if he still possessed David Stevens's fingerprints from David's stint as a private investigator. John did, and sent the prints to Team III.

A short time later, David's family notified John that "the system was not working." David's father told John Team III didn't have a good attitude. The homicide investigators were rude to the family, and they weren't making any progress solving the case. I asked John Stevens what he meant by "rude." He said the police told the Stevens family, "Listen. Get out of here. We'll talk when we're ready." John Stevens said the family wanted him to get involved. They knew he was a private investigator and that David had worked with him.

I was a homicide detective for one of the local police departments for four years in the 1980s. Homicide detectives come in all sizes, shapes, and emotional makeup. Different detectives have different "bedside manners." Different detectives have different levels of directness and smoothness. Each detective has his or her own style, based on one's personality. Some are painfully blunt, and some are syrupy smooth. I have seen and heard a lot over the years. I cannot imagine any member of Team III saying, "Listen, get out of here. We'll talk when we're ready." All the members of Team III deny saying those words, or even similar words, to Stevens's family, or any family, ever, for that matter.

"Tom, I lived with that case for years," Stevens said. "I interviewed hundreds of people. I have hundreds of exclusive documents." Stevens said he had been all over San Diego working on the case. He had interviewed many people the police, for whatever reason, decided not to interview.

So far, I had only been listening to Stevens, not saying a word myself. "Tom, you have a law enforcement background," he said. "I have a journalistic background. The D.A. types, and the police all put [their] spin on things. When I get involved in a case, there is no agenda. I'm doing three murders right now."

Really, I thought to myself. In the four years of homicide investigating experience and the seventeen years I had been with the district attorney's office, I had never seen a private investigator, or newsman, solve even one homicide. I had read plenty of good fiction where a P.I. would break a case, but never in real life.

In August 2004, a California private investigator hired by a family member to locate a young girl who had disappeared over thirty years earlier, was able to locate the girl's mother and boyfriend in the Midwest. He was able to get the police interested enough to follow up on the girl's disappearance. The girl was only three when her mother left California with two other children. The young girl never made the trip. Her siblings said their mother told them never to mention the girl. Murder charges are pending against the mother and boyfriend. While a private investigator might be involved in a missing person case that might have turned into a homicide, rarely does a P.I. crack a murder.

Stevens said he had an idea of what happened during David's murder shortly after he became involved in the case. According to Stevens, Team III told him to stay away from the girls at Perfect Match. "Tom, Tefft told me he had checked all of the girls, and they checked okay. Why weren't they looking at the girls at Perfect Match? The killer was right where I said she was."

John Stevens's statement about Detective Tefft ordering him to stay away from Perfect Match caused me to pause. Stevens, by his own admission, was a tenacious bulldog newshound. If someone ordered him to not do something that was contrary to what Stevens believed would solve a case, or sell a story, nothing could have kept him away from Perfect Match. If one would have *wanted* Stevens to interview the girls from Perfect Match all the person had to do was order Stevens *not* to interview them.

I told Stevens I had read the two articles Bill Manson had written in *The Reader*, and the two columns written by TC Luoma in *Testosterone Magazine*. I said Stevens never mentioned Perfect Match employees in those publications. I recalled Stevens's saying David was investigating some kind of unknown case and that is what got him killed.

My statement to Stevens was deflected. Instead, Stevens told me to check his website and find one article entitled "Huskers v. Southern California." (I subsequently did, but found nothing that explained anything.) Stevens continued on at a rapid pace. "Tom, I was willing to share information with the police. I was willing to forego journalism, Tom, to solve a crime. They just didn't want me to be involved."

"Well, they did solve the case," I offered meekly.

"Tom, if I had a badge I'd have had an arrest within hours," he said. Stevens's pace accelerated. He sounded as if he were giving a lead-in to a story for "International News Service" for the six o'clock news.

I told him I was just gathering information for a book. I had read the articles where Stevens gave his story to Bill Manson. I reminded him that I became involved because Chandra Carle had won an award for her work on the case.

"That is an absolute laugh that she won an award for her work on that case," he said.

Previous to this, I knew Stevens had issues with Team III. I never knew he had a beef with the prosecutor. Since I had read most of the trial transcripts, I said I thought she had done a pretty good job.

"You're kidding, Tom. Aren't you?" he asked.

I still didn't understand where he was going. The evidence fit the incriminating statements by Nourn and Barker quite well, in my estimation. "I'm not kidding. It looks like they arrested the killers," I said.

"Tom, the motive just doesn't fit."

I was getting really curious. "Okay. What is *your* theory about what happened?" I asked.

"Tom, jealousy doesn't fit. The motive of a love triangle doesn't fit. I have hours of taped conversations with Barker from prison. I got it on the record, Tom."

Oh yeah, a statement from Ron Barker, a real good source for the truth, I thought, with appropriate internal sarcasm. I had read the trial transcripts. I believed anything Barker said approximately the same way the jury believed him—not at all.

I wondered what John Stevens's "fit" was going to be if it wasn't the love triangle. I wondered what his "record" was that he constantly mentioned. "Do you mean that Barker didn't do it?" I asked.

"Tom, Barker might have had his hand in it. Someone else was involved. Tom, you have to look at things in totality." His tone was slightly scolding or impatient, or condescending, in that I was lazy, or maybe not too bright in that I hadn't looked at things "in totality." Maybe

Stevens didn't think I was smart enough to grasp his "expert" view of the crime. I wondered how many death scenes or autopsies John Stevens had attended.

I thought I had looked at things "in totality." I had viewed reports and transcripts. I told John Stevens I had read the police interview with Ny Nourn. I had read the transcript of the surreptitious phone conversation between Nourn and Barker. What had happened that early morning of December 23 seemed fairly clear to me.

Stevens brought up the taped phone call from Nourn to Barker, questioning the legality of it. Nourn had called Barker at the suggestion of the police. John Stevens apparently thought the defense attorneys for Barker had overlooked the taped call as a point of contention, and the possible judicial error in allowing the call into evidence. He asked if it wasn't illegal to tape a conversation unless the party being taped was aware of the taping and gave consent. I told Stevens it was legal in California to secretly tape a conversation if one of the participants was the subject of a criminal investigation. A suspected crook need not be notified his or her statements are being recorded. I don't know if Stevens believed me. He didn't press the matter.

My confusion mounting, I asked Stevens what he thought happened to David since he didn't believe the police-prosecution version.

"Tom, I think it was a hit," he said with some drama. He started, or ended, almost every sentence by calling me by my name. Maybe it was an investigative journalist thing. I perceived the contrived attempted personal bonding to be the gimmick of a high-pressure salesman and found it annoying.

Stevens went on, making me think he was still working on the case and presumably trying to solve this "hit." He said he had spoken with Barker's wife, Tran, "on the record," whatever the hell that meant. I could never get

Stevens to tell me why anyone other than Ron Barker wanted David Stevens dead. No one else had had a motive.

"Tom, I've worked the Interstate 5 corridor from Mexico to Oregon and back. There's plenty going on down there."

I was still puzzled. While I sat there holding the phone in one hand and scratching my head with the other, Stevens continued on.

"Tom, law enforcement in San Diego is corrupt."

I asked him to elaborate. He said he had filed a complaint with the San Diego Police Department about Captain Ron Newman. When I asked why, Stevens said Newman threatened him.

"How?" I asked. I have known Captain Ron Newman since he was a working detective, over twenty-two years. He was among the most soft-spoken, thorough, conscientious persons I have ever known. Detective John Tefft had been really angry with Ron Newman, but it was because Newman, as an administrator, was keeping the monetary strings closed on the case when Tefft believed the strings should have been opened to go to Las Vegas to run the sting on Kita Jones. The conflict was purely an internal spat between two people in a law-enforcement organization; Tefft would have defended Newman to the end regarding his ethics and professionalism. Newman would have said the same about Tefft. The feud between Captain Newman and John Tefft was over tactics and money, not ethics.

"Tom, he told me to 'get out of Dodge.' I've never been told to get out of town. I was just getting too close to things. The police lied to David's family, Tom. They had no business telling the family the things they did."

I told Stevens I was still confused about the corruption angle. Did he mean the police were protecting a killer— the "real" killer? Did they accept money? What did he

mean by "corruption"? I have seen police corruption over
the years in San Diego. In each case, the corruption had
been handled immediately, and forcefully, when detected.
Bad cops had been discovered here and there, taking
money, falsifying evidence, tipping off illegal establishments of impending search warrants, or selling contra-
band. Investigations were begun, and cops were fired or
sent to jail, as the cases merited. No police officer I ever
heard of in San Diego got a walk on a criminal charge, or
even on an ethical one. Bad cops were eliminated from the
force.

"They're just plain dirty, Tom. The criminal justice
system was demonized by them [Team III]. The taxpayers
were raped in San Diego. You see, Tom, they knew I was
talking to *48 Hours* [the television program]. They didn't
like that. Tom, the taxpayers were the real losers in this
case. Newman did a lot of damage in this case. He threatened me. My attorney was prepared to sue him."

The word *lawsuit* gets tossed around a lot. I asked
Stevens if he was going to sue Newman, or anyone.

He danced around that question. He did say that it
would be a good idea for me to be correct about everything I wrote regarding the conversation we were now
having. Since he mentioned my accuracy within the context of a lawsuit, I interpreted that to mean if I wasn't
careful, a lawsuit could happen to me, too. Yikes!

"Tom, Team III spent more time worrying about what
I was doing than solving the case. I told them if they
jerked us around, I'd be right on the air with the story. I
told them, 'If you come clean, I'll disappear. If not, I'll
keep going with it.' I don't let up. You don't threaten a
journalist."

Stevens hinted he might also be writing a book but
would not say directly, when I asked. I continued on, trying to find out more about any suspected corruption, or
the "real" motive. The best I could arrive at with him was

that the police were corrupt because they not only didn't cooperate with the family in the investigation, but they also told John Stevens not to be involved. Stevens never gave a reason for his suspected "hit" on David, except for an investigation David might have been doing. There was never any evidence, in any form whatsoever, that David was freelancing an investigation or had been hired to investigate anything.

I told Stevens I had seen the "bullet memo" on International News Service letterhead where he outlined the possibilities for the story. Since he mentioned the program *48 Hours* to me, I asked him if he had anything pending with that program. He wouldn't say anything directly about that subject. I envisioned some soon-to-be-unemployed producers at *48 Hours* if anyone there bought into what I had been listening to for the last few minutes. Stevens said he had six boxes of investigative material. Of what use the tapes were, Stevens never said.

We talked about whom I had interviewed and whom I planned to interview. I mentioned Judge Fred Link.

"That guy," Stevens said. "Tom, I had the most bizarre conversation in the hallway with Link before the trial started. It was just bizarre."

I was real curious now. I asked what they talked about. Stevens wouldn't tell me anything more. I have known Judge Link professionally for over twenty years. He knows what he can and can't do, especially regarding reporters. I would find it very interesting if Link said anything substantive about a case either before, or during, the adjudication of any legal matter.

Judges in San Diego have gotten themselves in trouble for simply joking about a pending case while on the golf course in a foursome made up only of judges. Link is too smart to discuss a legal matter at an improper time, and with an investigative reporter, no less. I put a big star next to Judge Link's name to remind me to try to interview him. I wondered what "bizarre" things Link could have said. The most bizarre thing I could imagine Link saying was, "Get the hell away from me. I can't discuss a case that's pending." I was really getting curious.

I needed to get back to Stevens's original statement that he urged the police to look at Perfect Match, the tele-marketing dating service, to find the killer. Why did he think there was a connection between the killer and Perfect Match?

"Tom, don't you see a clue about the evidence relating to Perfect Match?"

I knew Ny Nourn's fingerprints were on the headboard. I knew the police entered those prints in the state and national Automated Fingerprint Identification System (AFIS) and there were no hits because Nourn's prints were not on file. There was physical evidence at Stevens's apartment, but it wasn't linked to a suspect until after the arrest.

"What clue?" I sheepishly asked.

"A *clue*," he said with exaggerated emphasis, indicating I might not be able to see or detect a train coming if I were standing on the tracks. "Long dark hair, Tom. Ethnic hair. Who had *long, dark hair*, Tom? It was Ny Nourn. Don't you see? Asian hair. Long, dark hair. Tom, don't you see?"

I did know that Ny Nourn had long, dark hair. But I told John Stevens that Nourn and David had taken great pains to conceal their brief relationship from people at Perfect Match. No one knew they even spoke, except for job-related matters. David wanted it that way because of previous sexual harassment difficulties he had. The police had interviewed several people at Perfect Match. Not one person there even suggested Ny Nourn had any contact or connection with David outside of work.

In retrospect, and doing Monday-morning-quarter-backing, the police should have taken fingerprints from

every person who had ever known David Stevens. Cases
aren't run like that, though. It's easy to look back to see
what you *should have* done, after the case is over. Detective Young did speak with Ny Nourn when her phone
number was on David's phone tracker one single time.
Her explanation for the call was plausible. She called him
about her work schedule. What should Young have done,
drag Ny Nourn in and angrily demand that she "give it
up"? Nourn was never a reasonable suspect right up until
she confessed. Besides, if David's murder was a "hit,"
what connection did Ny Nourn have with a hit? She was
a high school girl with no connections to anything.

When John Stevens spoke with reporter Bill Manson
from *The Reader*, Stevens never mentioned his Perfect
Match theory. John Stevens only perfunctorily involved
himself with the dating service. His "investigation" centered on the vitamin supplement company, distributing
photo flyers about David Stevens, even though David
Stevens had not worked there in a year. Because of high
turnover, very few of the employees at the vitamin company even knew David.

In the article, Stevens brought up David's private investigating experience as being related to his death. John
Stevens never mentioned Perfect Match. It is conceivable
he could have mentioned Perfect Match to the police, and
they could have ignored him. If that had been the case, he
certainly would have told Bill Manson about how the police failed to follow up on Perfect Match. He told Manson
the police didn't confiscate the surveillance tape from the
bank across the street. If he told Manson anything about
the dating service theory, Manson would have printed it.

It was second-guessing and Monday-morning-quarter-
backing at its best, nothing more.

John Stevens is an award-winning journalist, having
won the Edward R. Murrow Award for News Excellence

in 2001 in Oregon. He is a hard-working, ever-digging person who believes in what he says about this case.

When he first spoke with me in March 2004 he appeared cocky, almost condescending; a real journalist talking with a hack wannabe writer. I had not yet signed a contract to do this book and was only in the negotiation stage. In September I wrote asking him for a promo picture, telling him I now had a contract with a publisher. When he called me about the picture in September, his tone had changed. John Stevens possibly originally thought I was some dreamer, like thousands of others, who "wanted to write a book," but probably never would find anyone to buy it. My photo request and writing contract changed his tone. John Stevens wanted to know how he would be portrayed.

I told him the book was being written basically from the view of the homicide team, who didn't like him. I told him I had read the articles, talked to the cops, the prosecutor, and talked to him. I told him I was a fair person, but the book had the police slant to it. While his actions never really adversely affected the case, he was a bother to the police.

He repeated his litany of how inept the cops were, what they should have done, how they threatened him, and how the key to the case was at Perfect Match all along. When we hung up I had a headache. He said he'd think about sending me a picture.

CHAPTER 31

On May 13, 2004, the California Fourth District Court of Appeals issued an opinion on Docket Number D041961, *The People v. Ny Nourn*. The opinion is "unpublished," or not certified for publication, meaning that although the findings in this case are binding on this case, the ruling may not be cited as a precedent on other cases. (California Rules of Court, rule 977(a) prohibits courts and parties from citing or relying on opinions not certified for publication or ordered published, except as specified by rule 977 (b). The opinion on Nourn's case has not been certified for publication or ordered published for purposes of rule 977.)

Nourn's appellate defense sought reversal on four aspects of the Ny Nourn case:

1. The trial court erred by instructing the jury that an aider and abettor could act with "reckless indifference," instead of the more stringent "intent to kill"

requirement to qualify for the special circumstances of lying in wait.

2. The court erred in failing to instruct the jury to consider Nourn's possible defense of duress, and instead instructed the jury that duress was not a defense in this case.

3. The court erred in refusing to instruct the jury to consider the lesser-included offense of voluntary manslaughter.

4. The court erred in imposing consecutive terms for the murder and arson counts, instead of allowing the sentences to run concurrently.

The appellate judges agreed only with the defense's first contention. They said an aider and abettor had to have the "intent to kill" before special circumstances could be found. The appellate judges said the jury should not have been instructed that "reckless indifference" was sufficient to supply the requirements for special circumstances.

The end result of the appellate ruling is that Ny Nourn's conviction for first-degree murder remains intact. The special circumstances allegation was removed. Nourn could be resentenced under first-degree murder guidelines (twenty-five-years to life in prison *with* the possibility of parole; twenty-seven to life if the arson charge is consecutive). The prosecution could retry Nourn on the special circumstances allegation. Or the prosecution could contest the appellate court's ruling and take the matter to the California Supreme Court.

The appellate court rejected the defense's other three grounds for appeal. That is, Judge Link was correct in not allowing the jury to consider manslaughter, that duress was not a defense in this case, and the court was correct in allowing consecutive terms for murder and arson.

To find this crime to be manslaughter would have been a big "reach" for a jury, or the appellate court. The murder of David Stevens was planned. It might have been a hasty plan, but a plan was involved. Heat of passion would exist if all three—Stevens, Barker, and Nourn— were together when Nourn broke the news to Barker that she and Stevens had been intimate. Barker would have had to reach in a drawer or some convenient place and pick up the gun, which just happened to be there. Pulling the trigger in that instance probably would have constituted "heat of passion."

Regarding "duress," it had been well established that even though Barker was a controlling type of person, he never used any kind of force against Nourn until *after* the murder. And, duress is not a defense to murder. It might be a mitigation, but not a defense.

Regarding consecutive sentences for the two crimes, murder and arson, it seemed logical. They didn't plan a killing and burning at the same time. The burning was an afterthought of Barker on how to take care of what he had done and conceal Stevens's identity. The last three were relatively easy legal issues.

Prosecutor Chandra Carle experienced a change of scenery—and of salary. The administration of the District Attorney's Office transferred Carle from the downtown Special Operations Unit to be the assistant chief of the South Bay branch office in Chula Vista, about eleven miles to the south. If Carle looked out her southern window from her office on the third floor, she could see Mexico. If she looked out her west window she could see the ocean, and San Diego Bay.

A short time after the transfer, Carle was promoted to Deputy District Attorney IV, which resulted in a slight salary bump. What it really meant in terms of logistics is that every time Carle appeared on the Ny Nourn matter she had to drive to downtown San Diego and hunt for a parking place before going into the courtroom, lugging whatever documents she needed on a rolling cart.

When Chandra Carle first heard of the appellate decision she was upset. It was clear to her that without Ny Nourn's involvement, David Stevens would be alive today. Carle actually blamed Nourn more than she did Ron Barker. Many others did not agree with Carle. In the strictest sense, however, Carle was correct.

Deputy Attorney General Niki Kyle Schafer, who handled the appeal, agreed with Carle. Both prosecution attorneys were technically correct, and possibly too close to the situation.

A few weeks later, after consulting with Prosecutor Carle, the administration of the district attorney's office decided to try the penalty phase of the crimes a second time. The worst that could happen for the prosecution was that Ny Nourn would have to serve twenty-five to life. The best outcome for the prosecution was that life without parole would again be the sentence.

Chandra Carle explained her reasons for believing Ny Nourn should spend life in prison. "I'm really afraid that if she only has a twenty-five- or twenty-seven-to-life sentence, she might still be a young woman when she gets out. It wouldn't bother me a lot if she got out eventually. I just want her to be old when she gets out."

Presently in California most people found guilty of first- and second-degree murder don't ever get out. There is no guarantee that will always be true. Californians have had conservative government leaders for a long time. What would happen if an elected official starts appointing people to the parole board who are soft on crime? Okay, maybe not "soft on crime," but people who will be inclined to feel sorry for a cold-blooded killer because the killer never enjoyed certain advantages as a youth.

"If Nourn serves twenty years she'll be about forty-one when she gets out," Carle said. "To me, that's still young." Carle laughed, then said, "That's close to how old I am, and I think that's young. If she's sixty-one when she gets out, that's different, and it will be okay with me. Remember, she's the one who told Barker David raped her. Sure, she recanted later, but Barker had already heard enough. He had already decided David had to die. She could have stopped the plan at any time."

Once again, Carle was right. Or, more accurately, she was not wrong. You could argue the length of Nourn's prison sentence with Carle, and you could disagree, but her points were very strong.

On September 9, 2004, Judge Frederic Link formally removed Bruce Cormicle from defending Ny Nourn for the retrial. He thanked Cormicle for doing a good job and said it had been a pleasure to deal with a true professional. Since Nourn's family had retained Cormicle, court watchers speculated her family had run out of money. Another attorney, Douglas Brown, was appointed by the Private Conflicts Counsel to represent Nourn, at public expense.

The court of appeals affirmed the conviction of Ronald Barker in its entirety. To quote the cops in a conversation over beer, "Barker is toast."

CHAPTER 32

I interviewed Judge Frederic Link in his chambers on October 13, 2004. Link made it clear from the outset that we could not discuss the Ny Nourn case because he had to hear her retrial in slightly over a month. Link was not skittish about the verdict in Nourn's case because the guilt question had already been answered. Ny Nourn was guilty. The new trial would determine whether her conduct during the murder and arson entitled her to receive the special circumstances punishment of life in prison without parole, or the twenty-seven years to life for only first-degree murder.

I looked around his chambers, which contained as much Chicago Bears memorabilia as his courtroom. Link explained his wife was from Chicago and he was born and raised in lower Illinois. An all-pro Chicago Bear receiver had been Link's fraternity brother. Link's contemporaries constantly teased him about the Bears' insignias, but he never seemed to mind.

I asked Judge Link how much he usually knows about

a case before trial. "I try to avoid knowing outside things so I won't be prejudiced. If I know too much, I might have to get off the case. After hearing all the pre-trial motions I usually know just about everything, though." He explained, for example, in the Ron Barker trial, he knew all about the wild-goose chases involving strippers, steroids, and voodoo Team III went through because Ron Barker wanted those stories in, and the prosecution wanted them kept out. Link had ruled to keep out the third-party culpability issues.

He knew about the Marc Carlos murder-for-hire situation. Link made sure Ron Barker knew that Link knew Barker had tried to get someone killed who was involved in the trial, in case Barker had any designs on a similar contract for Link. Frederic Link is no shrinking violet when it comes to intimidation.

I asked Link how difficult it was to try a defendant who was acting as his own attorney. He said it was not all that difficult. "I'm fair, but I don't bend over backwards to accommodate them." Link said if a defendant-attorney asks an improper question that is objected to by the prosecution, he merely makes a ruling and moves on. Some judges coach a *pro per* defendant, telling the defendant how he had asked an improper question and subtly suggesting how to make it proper. "I make sure from the beginning they know they have to act like an attorney. Then, I treat them like an attorney."

Link has had several of his trials presented on national television for Court TV, and on some local channels. Before the trial begins Link assembles everyone in his courtroom—reporters, camera operators, and even station managers. With everyone present, Link lays out the ground rules, just like a good umpire before the start of a game. Link tells them what he expects of them. He tells them what they can and can't do, where they can and can't go. That way, if someone violates one of his rules and is ejected from the proceedings, the person cannot complain Link is making up the rules as he goes along. Everything is explained at the outset. "They actually appreciate it," Link said, referring to the media learning of his guidelines. "They know what they can do, and they know what will happen to them if they do something they aren't supposed to."

CHAPTER 33

Douglas Brown, Ny Nourn's newly appointed defense attorney, had a plan. In Nourn's case, the clichéd adage of "there's more than one way to skin a cat" applied. Although the court of appeals had decided Nourn couldn't claim duress as a defense, because duress is never a defense to murder, Brown planned to prove Ny Nourn was a victim of "battered woman's syndrome." Brown wanted to prove that Nourn was so psychologically controlled and "battered" by Barker that she couldn't properly form the intent to kill David Stevens, thus removing special circumstances and giving Nourn a chance at eventual parole.

Detective John Tefft had covered the battered woman base adequately when he specifically asked Ny Nourn if Barker had ever hit her *before* the killing. When she said Barker had not, everyone thought it was clear that Nourn had not been a battered woman before the killing. Barker started knocking her around after the murder, but that didn't count, for court purposes, because the post-killing battering had nothing to do with the murder.

Attorney Brown considered the young age of Nourn and her life experience compared to that of Ronald Barker, twice her age. Perhaps some professional out there might believe Barker's controlling influence over Nourn constituted psychological battery.

Court watchers regularly see the "battle of the experts." The defense hires an expert who claims the defendant committed the crime, not because he or she wanted to, but because of fetal alcohol syndrome, child abuse, temporary insanity, previous bedwetting, stuttering, dyslexia, poor self-esteem, no cable TV when growing up, or whatever is the most popular excuse du jour presented at the latest defense attorney seminar.

In the back of her mind, as much as she reviled the actions of Ny Nourn, prosecutor Chandra Carle thought defense attorney Doug Brown might be onto something. She knew where Brown was heading, and she wanted to make sure she was not caught unprepared.

Carle tapped into the prosecution's vault of experts to find a professional familiar with battered woman's syndrome and problematic relationships. Both the prosecution and defense like to hold themselves out as ethical, upstanding, and honest. Yet, it seems each side has its stable of experts who will back the respective plays on a consistent basis. The prosecution knows all about the defense experts, their tactics, their strengths, and weaknesses.

If a defense expert has had a problem in a previous case, the prosecution knows all about the problem, down to the question that tripped him or her up, or about the professional certificate that an investigator had found to be dubious in nature. "Isn't it true, *Doctor* Jones, that the Louisiana State Institute of Psychotherapy didn't even exist in 1989, when you claim you received your certificate of forty hours of 'Advanced Analytical Therapy'?" This kind of discovery has happened to both sides.

The prosecution's informational network is up and running, and works well. The same can be said of the defense's knowledge of the prosecution experts. If an expert gets tripped up in a case, his or her phone might stop ringing for referrals. Both sides have been embarrassed over the years because of meticulous checking on the part of the opponent.

It is more difficult in the hard sciences to find an "expert" who will side either with the prosecution or defense. The previously mentioned forensic dentist, Dr. Skip Sperber, who confirmed the identity of David Stevens through dental X rays, is an example of a hard scientist.

Sperber has testified for both the prosecution and the defense. Sperber said, "It doesn't matter who hires me. I go where the science takes me." Sperber has examined thousands of bite marks, dental impressions, and photographs of bite marks on people who were victims of crimes. He has examined hundreds of dental impressions of victims who have bitten suspects and suspects who have bitten victims. If a scientifically identifiable bite mark is either there, or not there, Sperber will render a studied opinion, no matter who is paying him.

Often, given the age and fading images of bite marks, Sperber may have to qualify his opinion to the extent of showing the jury the similarities and consistencies, and letting the jury make the call. Sperber might say, "It's him" (the suspected person who did the bite), or he may say, "The biter could very well be him, based on the characteristics you can see. I cannot rule him out, but neither can I say for sure it's him. The evidence is not 100 percent conclusive."

In the softer disciplines of human behavior, there are experts out there who can be relied on if it's at all possible to shift or minimize the blame of an otherwise guilty person by finding myriad excuses that will explain the illegal behavior.

In the Ny Nourn case, Douglas Brown hired psychologist Meredith Friedman. Initially, prosecutor Carle didn't know much about her. A background summary revealed Friedman had previously worked at the Metropolitan Correction Center, the local federal jail in San Diego, most likely a good sign for the prosecution. Now in private practice, Friedman had testified for both the prosecution and the defense in the past. It did not appear that Dr. Friedman would be a shill for the defense.

Dr. Friedman met with Ny Nourn two different times on November 8 and 29, 2004, for lengthy sessions at the San Diego County Las Colinas Women's Detention Facility on the outskirts of eastern San Diego. She gave Nourn a battery of psychological tests that included:

- Shipley Institute of Living Scale

- Personality Assessment Inventory

- Millon Clinical Multiaxial Inventory-III

- NEO Personality Inventory-Revised

- Thematic Apperception Test

- Forer Incomplete Sentence and Human Figure Drawing

Dr. Friedman studied these test results, read Nourn's interview with the police, Barker's interview with the police, and reviewed trial transcripts. She interviewed Nourn, wrote a fourteen-page report, and submitted it to the court. Not surprisingly, Ny Nourn was diagnosed as having low self-esteem. She was also submissive, compliant, and needy. Nourn's intelligence was average, and her maturation level was normal. Based on the various test results and information revealed in the interview, Ny Nourn fit within the classic parameters of the battered woman.

Ny Nourn landed in the United States in Jacksonville,

Florida, as a young girl. She and her mother had escaped
with their lives from Cambodia. She never knew her real
father. Her mother married another Asian man, and her
mother had two children with him. Although the man who
raised her was not her real father, he never favored his
own children over Ny. He was strict, and she was somewhat rebellious. According to Dr. Friedman's report, Ny
Nourn told Friedman there was periodic abuse to her
mother, but none that merited police or medical intervention. Her mother and stepfather argued a lot, mostly over
money. Nourn was never a victim of child abuse, but there
was physical punishment. She was never molested, but
was sexually promiscuous from her mid-teens. In short,
Ny Nourn was like a few million other girls in the United
States.

Attorney Douglas Brown then enlisted the services of
another psychologist who dealt with tormented people on
a constant basis to interpret the test results in a way that
would paint an effective and telling picture for the court.

Dr. Mindy Mechanic, an assistant professor of psychology at California State University, Fullerton, was requested to read the pertinent reports and make an
evaluation of Ny Nourn. Dr. Mechanic is a licensed psychologist in Missouri, Illinois, and California. Her credentials are impressive. She is an expert in "intimate
partner violence," a politically correct term that brings
battered men, including homosexual victims, into the
fold, too.

Dr. Mechanic read all of the police reports, especially
Dr. Friedman's interview of Ny Nourn. The psychologist
received additional insight into the relationship between
Barker and Nourn by reading the self-serving police interview of Ronald Barker and his almost comical self-
representation as an attorney during the trial. She saw
Barker's primitive written motions to the court detailing
how he had been wrongly accused. Digesting the text of

Barker's interview with the police detectives, she was able to get an even better handle on what kind of person Banker was. Dr. Mechanic never met Ny Nourn, but based her final opinion of Nourn on the test results, Dr. Friedman's interview with Nourn, the police reports, and how Nourn's actions fit in with Dr. Mechanic's knowledge of human behavior.

Dr. Mechanic was not especially an expert on battered women who were defendants in criminal cases. Her practice and area of expertise dealt with women who were victims of abuse and stalking. She worked with them on how to deal with what they were suffering from and how to protect themselves from future harm. Nor was Dr. Mechanic a shill for the defense.

The psychologist determined that Ronald Barker, because of his age advantage and life experience, had assumed control oven Ny Nourn. Dr. Mechanic's report of January 11, 2005, said that Barker was "possessive and continually controlling."

Barker made Nourn wear a pager so he could keep tabs on her constantly. He picked her up and dropped her off at work. He made her give him keys to the house she shared with her parents.

Barker withheld important personal facts from her, like his real name, and the fact he was married with one child and another on the way. Nourn "suffered severe consequences when she questioned him on his personal life." He only told her what he wanted. Barker "limited her world to just him." Barker's conduct forced her to "live in a climate of fear." He told her he was a gangster, in the Mafia, and that he had killed people before. The subtle inference was that he could kill again, and quite easily, too. Barker continued his "reign of coercive control" by terrorizing Nourn.

As a way of keeping her under his control, he had her commit credit card fraud against her own mother and stepfather. She would hold on even closer to Barker, fearing Barker would expose the thefts to her parents.

Barker's systematic abuse of Ny Nourn predated the act of murder, although he never actually hurt her until after the murder. Nourn knew she should be submissive, compliant, and try to appease Barker. Dr. Mechanic calls this term *survival behavior.* Nourn's actions, then, were not the act of a murderer, but of a survivor, according to Dr. Mechanic.

Prosecutor Carle hired Dr. David B. Wexler to look at the case. Wexler came with the appropriate credentials. He is a clinical psychologist in private practice in San Diego, specializing in the treatment of relationships in conflict. Wexler was designated a "Master Lecturer" by the California Psychological Association and received that group's "Distinguished Contribution to Psychology" award in 2003. Wexler conducts workshops all over the country. He writes extensively, most recently penning the book *When Good Men Behave Badly: Change Your Behavior. Change Your Relationship.* Wexler is nationally known, appearing on the *Today Show* and *Dr. Phil.*

Dr. Wexler runs the Relationship Training Institute in San Diego. He has a full staff of clinicians, a director of forensic services, a training consultant, a neuropsychological consultant, polygraph consultants, and even a child custody evaluation consultant. He has a faculty pool of twenty-eight professionals from various walks of life in the relationship realm from which to choose, depending on the workshop he is conducting. Many of the professionals are from law enforcement—both police officers assigned to domestic violence and prosecutors specializing in the same field. Wexler's group seemed to be a well-rounded collection of truth-seekers.

Dr. Wexler studied the reports and the interviews of Ny Nourn, along with the results of the psychological tests

Dr. Friedman administered to her. He read the transcripts of interviews and testimony of Ronald Barker. Wexler noted that Barker wouldn't let Nourn go to her senior prom. Instead, he took her to dinner and a motel for a night of sex. Nourn was at Barker's mercy once she gave him her pager number. He demanded to know where she was every minute. She had to account for all her actions and conversations. If Nourn were late coming home, she had better have a good reason, and if the reason was that she was out screwing David Stevens, that was not good for her.

On the one night she left her pager off in order to be with David Stevens, it cost David Stevens his life and Ny Nourn her freedom. Going into the study, prosecutor Chandra Carle knew Dr. David Wexler might find that Ny Nourn had less free will than met the eye. No matter what Carle personally believed about Ny Nourn, Carle believed in seeking the truth.

Dr. Wexler wrote his report on February 7, 2005: "The fact that there was not [a] pattern of direct physical abuse during this [pre-murder] period does not discount these conclusions." The "conclusions" referred to simply was the fact that Ny Nourn was a battered woman. Nourn suffered much physical abuse after the murder of David Stevens, but Wexler believed he saw clear evidence of psychological, but still real, abuse prior to the murders. He wrote, "(Nourn) was a victim of a wide range of classic power and control tactics that are characteristic of abusive relationships."

Nourn believed Ronald Barker had previously killed others. He socially isolated her; made her ask permission for nearly everything; limited her friendships; and made decisions about their mutual activities. Barker practiced secrecy and deception about his life, and he controlled her finances.

The fact that Nourn had sex with so many men (approximately thirteen different partners by the time she was seventeen) was a "desperate search for affection, attention, and protection." In spite of Barker's being as bad as he was to her, she was terrified of losing her relationship with him. For people in a normal relationship, it seems incongruous to be afraid of losing a relationship with someone who is terrorizing you. Yet this fear is the norm for someone in an abusive relationship. Almost as an afterthought, Dr. Wexler said Nourn suffered from "low self-esteem."

That made it unanimous, then. All three shrinks agreed. Chandra Carle had to accept that her life-without-parole sentence had just gone out the window.

CHAPTER 34

If Doug Brown was successful in getting Chandra Carle and the district attorney's administration to accept that Ny Nourn was a battered woman, albeit a psychologically battered one, that would only mean Ny Nourn would have to stay in prison from twenty-seven years to life. Given the uncertainties of the California Parole Board, and the different types of citizens who sit on this revolving, appointed council, Nourn might still be facing life in prison forever. In other words, a parole board might never grant her parole even after her initial twenty-seven years were up. (In California, a convicted murderer isn't automatically eligible for parole, only eligible for a *parole hearing*, after two-thirds of the sentence has been served.) Charles Manson and Sirhan Sirhan are only two of thousands of killers who have had many parole hearings but never been paroled.

Brown wanted to do something to get a new trial for Nourn. Defense attorneys, no matter what else they might be, are smart people. The only way Brown could think of to get a new trial was to shift the blame of the loss at trial to her former attorney, Bruce Cormicle. Brown would have to show that Cormicle provided "ineffective assistance of counsel." In layman's terms, it means Cormicle "blew it."

In order to show a defendant was denied effective assistance of counsel, a defendant must prove:

1. [Defense counsel] failed to act in a manner to be expected of reasonably competent attorneys acting as diligent advocates, *and*

2. [Defense] counsel's acts or omissions resulted in the withdrawal of a potentially meritorious defense. (*People* v. *Fosselman* (1983) 33 Cal.3d 572, 581.) "The defendant bears the burden of establishing counsel's ineffectiveness, and the proof must be a demonstrable reality and not a speculative matter; the record must establish that counsel was ignorant of the facts or the law and that such ignorance resulted in the withdrawal of a crucial defense. (*People* v. *Jenkins* (1975) 13 Cal.3d 749, 753 . . .)" (*People* v. *Waters* (1975) 52 Cal. App.3d 323, 330.)

Brown had to get Ny Nourn back to court to show that Bruce Cormicle didn't do a good job. He did this by filing a writ of habeas corpus. Television anchors, reporters, and print media throw around the term *habeas corpus* all the time. Few know what it really means in Latin. They know it means the defense is trying to get someone out of jail.

Habeas corpus means literally, "You have the body." A defense attorney will file a writ of habeas corpus telling the judge to tell the prison warden, "You have the [defendant's] body. Bring the body to court to examine whether the imprisonment is lawful, or the person should be released."

In this case, Brown hoped to prove that Cormicle's alleged poor representation of Nourn had a substantial and injurious effect on the jury's verdict.

Brown's writ, filed February 22, 2005, said that Cormicle "failed to investigate and present a meritorious defense of battered woman syndrome during trial." Brown offered that three experts determined Nourn was a battened woman, one of the experts even being hired by the prosecution. Brown wrote that there were issues of intent and state of mind that Cormicle failed to address. Brown concluded by writing there was no tactical reason for Cormicle not to present the battered woman defense. Since duress was not allowed as a defense, only the battered woman syndrome was available as mitigation, and Cormicle did not use it.

It is unknown what a future court will rule regarding Cormicle's ineffectiveness. When Judge Frederic Link officially allowed Bruce Cormicle to be free of the case, Link congratulated him on an excellent job. If Link didn't think Cormicle was a competent attorney who did a good job, Link could have accepted Cormicle's resignation from the case and said nothing about Cormicle's work. Judge Link, as a judge, doesn't "blow smoke."

Regarding the failure of Cormicle to use the battered woman defense, prosecutor Carle said if Cormicle wanted to use that tactic, he would have had to have Ny Nourn testify in person. She would have had to get on the stand and tell the court and the jury the same things she told the police and the psychologists. The only problem is that Chandra Carle could cross-examine her.

Accused murderer Ronald Barker did testify to clear his name, and he was drawn and quartered by the prosecution for his attempt. The truth is, most attorneys don't want to expose their client to the rigors of cross-examination at the hands of an experienced prosecutor.

Carle undoubtedly would have ripped Ny Nourn to

shreds, battered woman on not. Without the actions of Ny Nourn, David Stevens would be alive today. One could envision prosecutor Carle standing erect, looking at the jury while pointing at Nourn and proclaiming for all to hear, "If you would not have led David Stevens to his death, none of us would be here today! So what if Ronald Barker was going to yell at you? He wasn't going to send you to prison!" Cormicle tried the best he could to let the jury know what kind of relationship existed between Ronald Barker and Ny Nourn. John Tefft repeated to the jury what Nourn had said about Barker's control, deceit, anger, selfishness, and raging behavior. The jury knew.

So, Bruce Cormicle made a tactical decision not to have Nourn testify she was a battered woman. The key phrase is *tactical decision*. Sports team managers and coaches everywhere are second-guessed on tactics every day. "Why, for God's sake, did he have him bunt in that situation? A Little Leaguer would know better."

"Why did they punt? He only had a yard to go for a first down. You can't tell me a professional running back can't make one measly yard when he needs to."

"Why did that idiot coach have them foul that player? He's the best free-throw shooter in basketball, for crying out loud." And so it goes. It's easy to look back and see where tactics failed.

Maybe the aforementioned bunt in baseball would have set up the winning run. A football coach, charged with the success of a team, knows you can't relinquish the football in your own territory because no one is guaranteed to gain even one measly yard on fourth down against a ton of defensive lineman and three vicious linebackers, no matter who is carrying the ball. Everyone has an opinion about nearly everything. The fact that Bruce Cormicle didn't have Ny Nourn tell the jury she was a battered woman was a tactical decision. Chandra Carle didn't think it was a bad decision. She would have welcomed asking the promiscuous young woman a few select questions about how her actions resulted in the death of David Stevens.

Historically speaking, ineffectiveness of counsel has been proven when the defense attorney falls asleep during the trial, or shows up under the influence of alcohol, or exhibits signs of mental illness. But not having one's client testify in a murder trial is usually not deemed ineffective assistance of counsel.

Douglas Brown is hoping for a new trial. The wheels of justice continue to turn, albeit slowly.

EPILOGUE

For everyone except David Stevens, life went on. For Ronald Ely Barker, it was "life in prison without parole" that went on. Ny Nourn's fate will be decided soon enough.

For Team III, life also went on. Sergeant L. D. Martin retired in the summer of 2004. He spends his time teaching supervision techniques for police officers around the state. He has been sighted on a few golf courses, too. Detective Dee Warrick answered the department's need for an experienced detective on another team where she is currently working. Terry Torgersen is still with the Homicide Evidence Assessment Team unit, or HEAT. Tefft, Young, and Cristinziani are still on Team III.

Chandra Carle continues to work in the South Bay branch office as the Assistant Division Chief.

Judge Frederic Link served a stint in Civil Division. He is now back in the criminal courts and will probably preside over Ny Nourn's criminal matter.

• • •

In retrospect, the killing of David Stevens makes even less sense than almost all of the other senseless killings that happen in San Diego, or anywhere. Sometimes killings at least have a *reason*. For example, maybe one dope dealer is cheating another dope dealer and the dealer who was cheated exacts some "street justice" by killing the other. Maybe one guy beats up another guy who has a big brother with a hot temper, and a gun. For beating another, he earns death at the hands of the brother. As mind-boggling as these killings are to civilized people, at least there is a reason.

In the David Stevens killing, nothing made sense. A seemingly innocent act of consensual sex between two unencumbered adults resulted in the fiery murder of one, and the lengthy, possibly never-ending incarceration of two others. David Stevens, by all accounts, was a good guy, a good son, a good friend to have. The only wrong thing he did was to have sex with a woman who was connected to a psycho. It's crazy, yet it happened.

For the parents and siblings of David Stevens, life might go on. But it will never be the same.

TRUE CRIME FROM BERKLEY BOOKS

A BEAUTIFUL CHILD
*A True Story of Hope, Horror, and an
Enduring Human Spirit*
by Matt Birkbeck
0-425-20440-5
**The tragic, true story of the girl-next-door's
secret life.**

UNBRIDLED RAGE
*A True Story of Organized Crime, Corruption,
and Murder in Chicago*
by Gene O'Shea
0-425-20526-2
**Two cold case agents solve the mystery of the
40-year-old murder of three boys in Chicago.**

ON THE HOUSE
The Bizarre Killing of Michael Malloy
by Simon Read
0-425-20678-5
**The true story of the murder of a New York City
drunk at the hands of thugs who had taken out
an insurance policy on his life.**

HUNTING ERIC RUDOLPH
*An Insider's Account of the Five-Year Search for the
Olympic Bomber*
by Henry Schuster with Charles Stone
0-425-20857-5
**The definitive story of the hunt for the elusive
suspect in the 1996 Atlanta Olympic bombing.**

b327